Travia

The Ultimate Book of Travel Trivia

Nadine Godwin

Travia
The Ultimate Book of Travel Trivia

Published by
The Intrepid Traveler
P.O. Box 531
Branford, CT 06405
www.intrepidtraveler.com

Copyright © 2008 by Nadine Godwin and John Hawks
First revised and updated edition
Printed in the United States
Cover design by George Foster
Interior design by Tim Foster, tgfDesign
ISBN: 978-1-887140-75-1
Library of Congress Control Number: 2007943955

10 9 8 7 6 5 4 3 2 1

Alan Fredericks,
mentor and friend

Acknowledgements

Writing this book was easy, but the research was an 18-month labor (mostly of love) undertaken with the help of countless spokesmen and women representing airlines, cruise lines, hotels, tour operators, travel agents, rail and car rental companies, museums, sightseeing attractions, travel accessories, and any other business source I could think of.

Also, thanks go to tourist offices at all levels and as far flung as China and South Africa, Hungary and Malaysia, Australia and Great Britain (this list could go on and on), and to trade associations (the American Hotel & Lodging Association, Air Transport Association, Cruise Lines International Association, Travel Industry Association of America, World Tourism Organization). Countless individuals are associated with these sources, but I will single out one: Tracy Peterson (in Holland America Line's public relations department), who not only suggested ideas but did the research, too.

A number of helpful souls fall into another category. They either had no obligation to me at all, or they went way outside their job requirements to be helpful. Listed alphabetically, they are Roberto Bettoja, marketing director for Bettoja Hotels, who played newshound in Rome; Don Brown, whose books include "Ghost Towns of Ontario;" Tom D. Crouch, senior curator aeronautics for the National Air and Space Museum, Smithsonian Institution; Jim Davies, principal archivist at British Airways Museum; Greg Dillon, vice chairman and director emeritus, Hilton Hotels Corporation; Hans Disch, a vice president and general manager at Dometic Corporation, maker of minibars; H. Grant Goodell, research professor of geosciences, University of Virginia ; Paul Gromosiak, author of nine books on Niagara Falls; Paul Jarvis, director, British Airways Museum; Ted Malmgren, retired Qantas Airways employee and volunteer archivist; Julie Munro, CEO, Cosmetic Surgery Travel; Wesley Paine, museum director of the Parthenon (in Nashville, Tennessee, that is); Thom Price, owner of Squero Canaletto, gondola maker in Venice, Italy; Capt. Albert Schoonderbeek, author of "125 Years of Holland America Line;" Mary Ellen Schultz, surrogate information gatherer and translator; Angela M.H. Schuster, editor of Icon magazine, and her colleagues at the World Monuments Fund; Robert Serling, who is writing his seventh airline history, and Glenn Virchow, the journalist who led me to the first cat to fly the Atlantic nonstop.

I am particularly grateful to Patrick J. McGeehan, at the National Geographic Society, who confirmed the sad fact that geographic data such as elevations, square mileages, and geographic coordinates are not cut-and-dried matters and answered the obvious question: Which sources does the National Geographic Society rely on? (Answer: Columbia Gazetteer, Merriam Webster's Geographical Dictionary, and the CIA World Factbook, among others). I am grateful, too, to Bill Bryson because his books, aside from being good reads, are to my eyes great collections of trivia. Besides, his mother Mary was my colleague at the Des Moines Register.

This book would not have happened but for a number of friends and colleagues. For one thing, the book was the brainchild of John Hawks, a travel industry veteran and an author, too; he is my partner in this publishing endeavor.

Finally, I turn to Travel Weekly, the travel trade journal that has been my home since 1972. Besides being an obvious source of information, it has provided years of experience in the travel industry and a supportive environment for this project. I am particularly indebted to the late Alan Fredericks, who hired and mentored me through a long career; Arnie Weissmann, editor in chief, and a raft of current and former colleagues including Gerry Bourbeau, David Cogswell, Andy Compart, Laura Del Rosso, Rob Fixmer, Jim Glab, Ken Kiesnoski, Joe Kornik, Jerry Limone, Mike Milligan, Gay Nagle Myers, Margaret Myre, Barbara Sturken Peterson, Bill Poling, Joe Rosen, Dennis Schaal, Kim Scholz, and Rebecca Tobin.

No list here is exhaustive and I apologize if I have omitted any I should have included.

Nadine Godwin
New York, N.Y.

Table of Contents

Chapter 1

At Sea

Holland America Line offered its first vacation cruise in 1895, taking passengers from Rotterdam in the Netherlands to Copenhagen and back aboard the Rotterdam II; fifteen years later, its second leisure cruise took passengers from New York to the Mediterranean and the Holy Land aboard the Statendam I.

———◆———

With an eye to carrying mail to the United States and Canada, Samuel Cunard founded the British and North American Steam Packet Company (the Cunard Line today) in 1839. A year later, he launched history's first regularly scheduled transatlantic passenger operations with four ships that sailed the Atlantic in 14 days at 8.5 knots, departing weekly from Liverpool. The first of these – the 1,154-ton paddle steamer Britannia – was small enough to fit inside the Grand Lounge of the famed Queen Elizabeth 2.

———◆———

The British-based P&O Cruises was founded in 1838, making it the world's oldest cruise company.

———◆———

Cruise ships are routinely described in terms of tonnage, but that does not indicate the weight of the ship. Nor does it indicate the amount of water displaced by a ship, as some believe. Each one of these "tons" refers to 100 cubic feet of enclosed space. Hence, the Freedom of the Seas, one of the world's largest cruise ships at 160,000 tons, encompasses 16 million cubic feet of space.

———◆———

The world's largest cruise ships by tonnage are the sister ships, Freedom of the Seas and Liberty of the Seas; a third same-sized ship, Independence of the Seas, is due in 2009. Compare their volume with the Persia, the world's largest cruise ship when

Cunard rolled it out in 1856 at 390 feet long and 3,330 gross registered tons.

———◆◆◆———

If all of Carnival Cruise Lines' 22 ships were placed end to end, they would extend close to four miles in total length.

———◆◆◆———

Ships are almost always spoken of as female. The explanation focuses on the strong bond between sailors who in times past were at sea for months or years at a stretch. For them, the bond could have been compared to that of marriage or of dependence on a mother for life and sustenance. Only in France are ships masculine.

———◆◆◆———

When White Star Line's Titanic hit an iceberg while on her first Atlantic crossing in April 1912, she was carrying lifeboats to accommodate about half the number of people on board. But, at that time, ship lines had not seen the need for more, in part because of a January 1909 ship collision near Nantucket Island on the U.S. coast involving another White Star vessel, the Republic. That incident, which produced history's first wireless SOS message (Titanic's was the fourth), ended with the rescue of all on board; Republic's passengers and crew were ferried in shifts to nearby ships. However, in far different circumstances, the Titanic sank, costing the lives of 1,503 passengers and crew from among a total of 2,206 aboard.

———◆◆◆———

In wartime, cruise ships are often called to duty by their homelands, and the Cunard cruise company is so old that 11 of its ships were called into service for the Crimea War in 1854. During World War I, while carrying more than a million troops and 10 million tons of cargo, Cunard lost a lot of ships (22), but the number included small passenger vessels and cargo ships. Not all were big liners like the most famous of those lost, the Lusitania, which was torpedoed in 1915 with the loss of 1,198 lives (another 761 were saved). Another Cunard loss was the Carpathia, which had rescued Titanic survivors; it was torpedoed and sunk in 1918, with the loss of five lives. After World War II, Winston Churchill credited Cunard ships with shortening that conflagration by at least a year.

———◆———

Holland America Line lost six ships during World War I. Among them, the Statendam II had been under construction in Belfast, so the British took it over as a troop ship called Justicia, which was torpedoed and sunk in 1918. The ship line, also known as HAL, resumed operations after the Great War with only 10 vessels. During World War II, all of HAL's 25 ships were chartered by the British, Dutch and U.S. governments, and only nine vessels survived.

Early in the war, the passenger ship Westernland, berthed at Falmouth, England, served as the seat of Holland's government.

———◆———

The White Star Line's Titanic was one of three sister ships. The first, Olympic, was launched in 1910, and Britannic, under construction when the Titanic sank in 1912, was launched in 1914. The Britannic never carried a fare-paying passenger. It was commissioned by the British government as a hospital ship during World War I. In 1916, after an explosion (possibly a

torpedo), she sank; most on board escaped on lifeboats. (The
Britannic carried three times as many as the Titanic carried.)
The Olympic was requisitioned for war duty, too; she carried
troops, was outfitted with antisubmarine guns, and in 1918
sank a German submarine (the only recorded instance of a
merchant vessel sinking a warship during World War I). After
the war, the Olympic was refitted for passengers (during which
a dent was found in the hull, left by a torpedo that had not
detonated) and then retired in 1935.

Ships are usually dedicated only by women (their
"godmothers") because of a superstition holding that the first
person to touch a ship when she is coming into life should
be a female, much as in the past the first person to touch a
newborn human was a midwife (also a female). The French,
Greeks, and Japanese are the exception; they will use men as
well as women to dedicate ships.

Other shipping superstitions say it is very bad luck to change
a ship's name while it remains with the same owner, and it is
even worse luck if the bottle used to dedicate a ship does not
break the first time it whacks the vessel.

Holland America Line's first ship — one of a series of Rotterdams — was launched in 1872 and required 21 days to travel from Rotterdam in the Netherlands to New York with port stops in France and England; the Atlantic crossing itself took 15 days.

———◆———

Holland America Line, when created in the 1870s, was called the Netherlands-America Steamship Company, but it became known as the Holland America Line because it provided regular service to America. An estimated 850,000 immigrants were among the westbound passengers, mostly between the 1880s and the 1920s. However, new U.S. laws in the 1920s severely curtailed the westbound immigrant traffic, so HAL made a virtue of necessity and debuted its Caribbean cruise service aboard the Veendam II in 1926. In 1971, HAL closed out the transatlantic service it had inaugurated in 1872.

———◆———

The cost of crossing the Atlantic on the Titanic in 1912, as with passenger ships today, varied by season and type of accommodations. For its April maiden voyage (falling in the intermediate season), the cost of a Parlour Suite was $3,300 (remember, that's the 1912 dollar) for the one-way crossing for one or two passengers (plus one servant) and $50 for each additional person. This fare ($2,250 in winter and $4,350 in summer) paid for a two-bedroom suite, with sitting room, private bath, servant's room, and a private promenade. The fictional character Rose in the movie "Titanic" had a Parlour Suite. A suite without promenade dropped to $1,520 at the intermediate-season rates; an outside stateroom with wardrobe room and private bath was $775 for one and $825 for two; and first class cabins without private baths could be as low as $195.

———◆◆———

Cunard was the first line to operate a passenger ship with electric lighting (in 1881 on the Servia), and it operated the first round-the-world cruise (in 1922 aboard the Laconia).

———◆◆———

Princess Cruises got its start in 1965 with sailings from the U.S. West Coast to Acapulco, Mexico, and back aboard a chartered ship called the Princess Patricia. Because the small ship had no on-board laundry, passengers were told they could send their wash out in Acapulco and, sure enough, it came back before departure. However, all of it was packaged as if for one customer named Princess Patricia. Hundreds of passengers had to collect their clothes from the stacks laid out in the ship lobby. Never mind. The ship without a laundry gave the company its name: Princess.

———◆◆———

The Mardi Gras, the first ship operated by Carnival Cruise Lines, ran aground on a sandbar just outside the Miami port on its maiden voyage in 1972 — not an auspicious beginning.

———◆◆———

Also not auspicious: After two years in business, the fledgling Carnival Cruise Lines, owned by Boston-based American

International Travel Services (its primary shareholder: Meshulam Riklis), was close to bankruptcy. However, the entrepreneurial Ted Arison, who had been running the operation, bought it for $1 and assumed its $5 million debt. That was 1974.

Fast forward to now: Carnival operates 22 so-called Fun Ships and is only part of the considerably larger Carnival Corporation, headed by Ted's son, Micky Arison, the company's chairman and CEO. The company owns 12 cruise brands worldwide including Cunard Line, Holland America Line, P&O Cruises, Princess Cruises, Seabourn Cruise Line, and Windstar Cruises. In fiscal year 2007, ending November 30, the company earned $2.4 billion on revenues of $13 billion. Who would have guessed it? Not Riklis.

———◆◆———

It cost just over £29 million ($69.6 million based on the then-current exchange rate) to build the Queen Elizabeth 2 in 1969, but it has cost more than 15 times that over the years to refit and refurbish the ship.

———◆◆———

Royal Caribbean International, in 1971, pioneered the concept of air/sea vacations, flying passengers to Miami from across North America.

———◆◆———

The TV show "The Love Boat," which debuted in September of 1977, was based on a book of the same name written by a cruise director (Jeraldine Saunders). The series, which lasted 10 years, was filmed on various Princess Cruises ships, and it provided a huge boost for the entire cruise business. However, Princess Cruises very nearly turned the TV producers away because of the nuisance factor of on-board filming — and especially because of the cost and inconvenience of having to provide 100-plus cabins to actors and crew.

In 1978, the Song of Norway became the first cruise ship to be "stretched." It was cut in two and an 85-foot midsection was added, increasing guest capacity from 700 to slightly more than 1,000.

What is the difference between a ship and a boat? Ships are bigger, but an easier way to think of it is this: Ships carry boats

(think lifeboats) but boats cannot carry ships.

The Queen Elizabeth 2 concluded her last transatlantic sailing on arrival at Southampton, England, in the spring of 2005 — 36 years after departing that port on her maiden voyage. At that point, the ship had sailed 5.3 million nautical miles (that's 6.1 million regular miles to the landlubbers among us) — the equivalent of traveling to the moon and back more than a dozen times. Her sailings included 795 Atlantic crossings, plus 23 cruises around the world. To complete one of the transatlantic voyages, the 1,791-passenger Queen Elizabeth 2 required 2,932 tablecloths and 3,100 pillow cases.

———— ∙ ◆ ∙ ————

Passengers and crew aboard the 116,000-ton Sapphire Princess (up to 2,670 passengers) use 2,220 tons of water per day.

———— ∙ ◆ ∙ ————

Each of Carnival Cruise Lines' largest ships (accommodating up to 2,974 passengers) uses 30,000 towels and 5 million bars of soap in a year's time. Each ship requires 58,000 light bulbs in a year, too.

———— ∙ ◆ ∙ ————

Holland America Line paints the hull of its ships blue so they will stand out in a crowd (of ships, that is). That blue color, developed especially for the cruise line, adds about 10 percent to the cost of air conditioning because the blue absorbs more heat than white does.

———— ∙ ◆ ∙ ————

It is a direct result of the Titanic disaster that ships now must have lifeboat space for every person on board and passengers must attend a safety drill soon after boarding. However, as of 1999, it is no longer standard to use the Morse code to call for help because modern technology provides more efficient alternatives.

———— ∙ ◆ ∙ ————

At Sea

Cruise companies have a lot of ways of telling us how large or powerful their ships are. Consider these, in order by tonnage:

151,400 tons

The Queen Mary 2 towers 200 feet above the water line, rising to the height of a 23-story building. She is as long as 36 London double-decker buses arrayed in a single line. But if this ship were standing on her stern, she — at 1,132 feet long — would be more than three and a half times the height of the clock tower housing Big Ben in London, taller than the Eiffel Tower's 984 feet and falling only 118 feet shy of matching the Empire State Building's 1,250 feet.

142,000 tons

The Voyager of the Seas and similar ships operated by Royal Caribbean are 1,020 feet long — or as long as a 17-car freight train. Viewed a couple of other ways, the Voyager is longer than four 747 planes, or it can accommodate roughly five Goodyear blimps. It takes 100,000 gallons of paint to cover this ship.

116,000 tons

Constructing the Sapphire Princess required 21,160 tons of steel, 1,895 miles of wiring, 74,125 gallons of paint, and 51,821 square yards of carpet.

110,000 tons

Each of Carnival Cruise Lines' largest ships (the Conquest and similarly sized ships, accommodating 2,974 passengers each) generates horsepower equivalent to 298 Cadillacs — and one Toyota. Also, each contains more steel than three Eiffel Towers and generates enough electric power for a city of 60,000.

———◆◆◆———

Carnival Cruise Lines places close to 47,200 pieces of chocolates on guests' pillows each night. That translates to roughly 17.2 million chocolates a year.

———◆◆◆———

The 113,000-ton Caribbean Princess uses 4,315 pounds of ice each week for ice carvings.

———◆◆◆———

Carnival Cruise Lines calculated how much food it serves in a week on all its 22 ships combined. Here are a few sample numbers:

113,290 pounds of chicken (that's more than 56 tons!)
497,880 shrimp
121,260 hamburgers
53,610 pounds of tenderloin (or almost 27 tons)
64,275 dozen eggs

801,575 bacon slices

27,940 pounds of butter (approaching 14 tons)

310,410 potatoes

201,070 tomatoes

20,300 pounds of pasta (roughly 10 tons)

As for drinks, the stats range from 589,160 cans of beer to 566,250 gallons of soft drinks, from 84,010 bottles of wine plus 32,980 bottles of champagne and sparkling wine to 17,505 liters of Scotch.

———◆◆◆———

The ship's whistle on the Queen Mary 2 is audible for 10 miles.

———◆◆◆———

Just one gallon of fuel moves the Queen Elizabeth 2 by 49.5 feet — but in a day, the ship burns 433 tons of fuel. She is the fastest merchant ship in operation, capable of traveling at 34 knots (ordinary cruise speed is 28.5 knots). A whale travels at 24 knots. Also, the QE 2 can sail backwards (top speed headed backwards: 19 knots) faster than most cruise ships sail forward.

———◆◆◆———

The Sapphire Princess is equipped with 268 refrigerators, 68 stoves, and 67 coffee machines. To meet the needs of up to 2,670 passengers, she carries 4,998 tablecloths, 5,664 blankets, 21,216 sheets, 68,000 hangers, and 18,672 dinner plates. As to the little things, when fully stocked, the ship carries 12,000 boxes of facial tissue, 24,000 rolls of toilet tissue, 14,400 balloons, 300,000 toothpicks, and even more lace doilies (582,000 of them). In a single day, diners use 97,300 dishes and 9,100 napkins.

———◆◆◆———

The Wind Surf — a yacht-like motorized vessel — has seven computer-operated sails with 26,881 square feet of Dacron surface area. Sister ships Wind Spirit and Wind Star have six computer-operated sails with 21,500 square feet of Dacron surface area each. The Wind Surf has five masts rising 164 feet, while the smaller twin vessels have four taller masts at 204 feet high. As a result of the tall masts, none of Windstar Cruises' three ships can go through the Panama Canal; they cannot transit under the Bridge of the Americas. They also only pass under the 25 April Bridge in Lisbon, Portugal, at low tide.

———◆———

Cruise operators slice, dice, and puree their stats in various ways to make the point that they serve a whale of a lot of food and drink to crew and passengers. The following small sample makes one wonder who does all this counting:

* In a typical week, the passengers (up to 3,114) and crew on Voyager of the Seas consume 10,687 pounds — or more than five tons — of beef, lamb, and pork. That doesn't even include things that used to fly (sort of) or swim. Those numbers are 3,761 pounds of chicken and turkey, 3,575 pounds of fish, and 3,000 pieces of lobster. Diners are washing that down with 9,000 cans of soft drinks, 20,000 cans of beer, 1,000 bottles of liquor, 5,000 bottles of wine — and 21,000 pints of milk.

* The weekly rations on the Caribbean Princess (3,100 berths) include 6,060 pounds of steak plus 3,279 pounds of other beef; 10,102 pounds of potatoes plus 3,258 pounds of French fries; and a whole lot of fresh vegetables (44,592 pounds), not counting 6,304 pounds of salad and 46,397 pounds (23 tons and counting) of fresh fruit. The kitchen also prepares 5,743 dozen eggs, 10,068 pizza slices, 50,342 breakfast pastries, 10,308 canapes, and 338 gallons of ice cream.

* During a weeklong Hawaii cruise, the Pride of Aloha (up to 2,002 passengers) serves up 1,500 coconuts, 1,900 pounds of kiwis, and 7,500 pounds of pineapples.

* On the Oosterdam (up to 1,848 passengers), during a seven-day Alaska cruise, the ship's kitchen uses 206 gallons of dressings, 350 gallons of cooking oil, 4,500 pounds of flour, 1,500 pounds of sugar, and 600 pounds of coffee. The weeklong trip also requires mountains of fruits and vegetables: 22,585 pounds of fresh fruit (11 tons plus!), 13,900 pounds of fresh vegetables, and 3,630 pounds of potatoes, as well as 1,545 pounds of cheese and 2,629 yogurts.

For the tea-and-scones set, the 2,620-passenger Queen Mary 2 uses enough tea in one year to fill an Olympic-sized swimming pool and enough sugar to make 8 million scones. It also uses enough beef to supply a city the size of Southampton and almost 99 tons of pineapples (or the equivalent by weight of 50 SUVs).

Travia

Bare Necessities Tour and Travel in Austin, Texas, in February 2005, operated what it describes as the world's largest-ever nude cruise, on a Caribbean sailing at full capacity aboard the 2,124-passenger Carnival Cruise Lines ship, the Legend.

Chapter 2

Our Home, Planet Earth

There are six rivers called Avon in England and Scotland. The most famous flows in a southwesterly direction through Stratford-upon-Avon, Shakespeare's birthplace, until it joins the River Severn at the charming little village of Tewksbury near Gloucester. Another Avon is part of the scenery at Bath, one of England's prettiest cities (and once a Roman spa town), and winds its way through Bradford-on-Avon, another delightful and ancient English town. Still another travels south as it passes through the cathedral city of Salisbury. Why so many Avons? It's a Celtic name meaning simply "river."

———◆◆◆———

Detroit, Michigan, is the first city you will reach when driving north from Canada's Windsor, Ontario.

———◆◆◆———

Before the Soviet Union was broken up into 15 nations, it was the world's largest country and stretched so far around the globe it encompassed 11 time zones. Today, the part that is Russia remains the world's largest country, and it still has 11 time zones. Despite the fact that a whole raft of countries emerged from the western reaches of the Soviet Union (Belarus, Estonia, Latvia, Lithuania, Moldova, and Ukraine), Russia retained its westernmost time zone because it controls a tiny outpost, Kaliningrad, which is west of Lithuania and separated from the motherland.

———◆◆◆———

The Mississippi River is 2,348 miles long and drains an area of 1,243,700 square miles (one-eighth the size of North America). It discharges eight times as much water as Germany's Rhine and 30 times that of England's Thames. But it is dwarfed (after a fashion) by the Amazon, the world's largest river system. This South American wonder is 3,915 miles long, drains 2,722,000 square miles — or more than 50 percent of the continent — and discharges at least six million cubic feet of water per second. That is seven times as much water as the Mississippi. However, even the great Amazon can't have it all: The Nile is the world's longest river, at 4,132 miles.

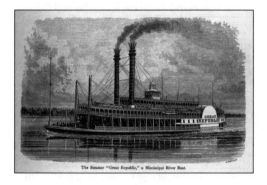

The Steamer "Great Republic," a Mississippi River Boat.

Europe's tiniest political entities (including five self-governing British dependencies marked with an *) are as follows:

Vatican City — 108.7 acres (0.44 km²)

Monaco — 484 acres (1.96 km²)

Gibraltar* — 2.5 square miles (6.5 km²)

San Marino — 23.6 square miles (61.2 km²)

Guernsey* — 30.1 square miles (78 km²)

Jersey* — 44.8 square miles (116 km²)

Akrotiri* — 47.5 square miles (123 km²)

Dhekelia* — 50.5 square miles (130.8 km²)

Liechtenstein — 61.8 square miles (160 km²)

Malta — 122 square miles (316 km²)

Andorra — 180.7 square miles (468 km²)

Liberia's capital, Monrovia, is named for U.S. President James Monroe.

Travia

Brunei, a small sultanate (2,228 square miles) surrounded by East Malaysia and sitting on the northwest coast of Borneo, is a well-known name largely because the sultan is so wealthy. But the official name is more of a mouthful — Negara Brunei Darussalam — and its capital is Bandar Seri Begawan.

The longest place name in the world is attached to a not very important hill in the Hawke's Bay region of New Zealand. There are at least three publicized versions of the name:

Taumatawhakatangihangakoauauotamateapokaiwhen-uakitanatahu (58 letters)

Taumatawhakatangihangakoauauotamateaturipukaka-pikimaungahoronukupokaiwhenuakitanatahu (85 letters)

Tetaumatawhakatangihangakoauaotamateaurehaeaturip-ukapihimaungahoronukupokaiwhenuaakitanarahu (92 letters)

The Maori in Hawke's Bay say the 85-character version is the correct one (how can one tell?). The word tells a story, and because stories vary in the telling, this word can vary in the spelling. The tale celebrates an ancestral warrior chief who is grieving for his dead brother after a battle, and it goes like this: "The hilltop, where Tamatea with big knees, conqueror of mountains, eater of land, traveler over land and sea, played his koauau [flute] to his beloved." The more practical everyday name and spelling is Taumata.

Ecuador has its name from the fact that it sits on the Equator. Before it became a separate country in 1830, the area was called Quito, named for the indigenous Quitus people. The name Quito still belongs to Ecuador's capital, which is the oldest of all of South America's capitals. The site was occupied well before 1000 A.D. The Spanish made the city their own in 1534 and planned the Old Town grid and central plaza that we see today.

The U.S. National Park Service says the 113-mile Padre Island off the coast of Texas is the world's longest remaining undeveloped barrier island in the world.

A few countries have two national capitals and one — South Africa — even has three:

* **Benin:** Cotonou (seat of government); Porto-Novo (official capital)
* **Bolivia:** La Paz (administrative capital and seat of government); Sucre (legal capital and seat of judiciary)
* **Cote d'Ivoire:** Abidjan (administrative center); Yamoussoukro (official capital)
* **Malaysia:** Kuala Lumpur (official capital); Putrajaya (administrative capital)
* **Netherlands:** Amsterdam (legal capital); The Hague (seat of government)
* **South Africa:** Bloemfontein (judicial capital); Cape Town (legislative capital); Pretoria (administrative and official capital)
* **Sri Lanka:** Colombo (official capital); Sri Jayewardenepura Kotte (legislative capital)
* **Swaziland:** Lobamba (royal and legislative capital); Mbabane (official capital)
* **Tuvalu:** Funafuti (official capital); Vaiaku Village (administrative offices)

In addition, the Taiwanese view Taipei as a provisional capital and regard Nanjing on the Chinese mainland as their real capital. Akrotiri and Dhekelia — two British territories on Cyprus — share a capital called Episkopi Cantonment, located in Akrotiri. At least three political entities have no capital — Nauru and Tokelau, in the Pacific, and Western Sahara in Africa.

———◆◆◆———

The Mississippi River forms the western boundary for Illinois with one exception. Kaskaskia, Illinois, is almost completely surrounded by the mighty river because, during a series of 19th-century flooding episodes, the river carved out a slightly altered course, stranding most of the town on an island accessible only from Missouri. What was once a thriving French settlement and the first state capital is now almost completely abandoned.

———◆◆◆———

Mount Everest's peak is the highest spot on Earth, at 29,028 feet above sea level, but the deepest known spot on Earth is deeper than that, at 36,198 feet below the water's surface. It is found in an ocean-floor "ditch" known as the Mariana Trench in the Pacific.

———◆◆◆———

The world regularly sprouts new countries, or at least gives old countries new life.
Here are several recent examples:
* **Czechoslovakia** (1992, split into Czech Republic, Slovakia): Carved out of the Austro-Hungarian Empire, Czechoslovakia was formed in 1918 as part of the peace settlement after World War I.

* **Ethiopia** (1993, Eritrea spun off): The 1993 separation occurred 31 years after Ethiopia had annexed Eritrea, triggering civil war.

* **Indonesia** (2002, East Timor spun off): This separation occurred 26 years after Indonesia forcibly took over East Timor, a move that also triggered a fight for independence.

* **Pakistan** (1971, Bangladesh, Pakistan): Previously, Pakistan (East and West together) had been a product of the partition of India in 1947.

* **U.S.S.R.** (1991, Azerbaijan, Armenia, Belarus, Estonia, Georgia, Kazakhstan, Kyrgyzstan, Latvia, Lithuania, Moldova, Russia, Tajikistan, Turkmenistan, Uzbekistan, and Ukraine): These territories had comprised the empire built by Russia's czars. It took the Soviets until 1940 to reassemble the same empire.

* **Yugoslavia** (1991, Croatia, Slovenia spun off; 1992, Bosnia & Herzegovina, Macedonia; 2006, remainder split to create Montenegro and Serbia): Yugoslavia was another post-World War I creation. After it broke up in the 1990s, Serbia and Montenegro remained a loose federation, but in 2006, Montenegro voted to go its own way. Then, in 2008, Kosovo declared its independence from Serbia.

To date, the partitioning of Israel to create a Palestinian entity remains only partial. Under an interim self-government arrangement, limited powers over the Gaza Strip and West Bank were transferred to the Palestinian Authority. Violence has undermined the emergence of a new nation.

———◆———

And then there are the countries that are "born" through unification, which often means reunification. Recent cases are Germany (1990, formerly East and West), Vietnam (1975, formerly North and South), and Yemen (1990, formerly North and South). Also, Tanzania is the product of the 1964 union of Tanganyika and Zanzibar, and Somalia was created by the 1960 union of British Somaliland and the former Italian Somaliland. Even large China has grown, with the takeover of Tibet in 1951, the recovery of Hong Kong (now a "special administrative region") in 1997, and the recovery of Macau (another "special administrative region") in 2000. It also considers Taiwan its 23rd province, but the feelings aren't mutual.

———✦———

Ushuaia, in Argentina, is the southernmost town in the world at 54 degrees 47 minutes south of the Equator.

———✦———

Lake Titicaca, which straddles the border between Bolivia and Peru in the Andean Altiplano, is the world's highest large navigable lake, at roughly 12,500 feet above sea level and measuring more than 120 miles long and 50 miles wide. It is not the world's highest navigable lake, as many have been led to believe, but it is South America's largest lake at any altitude.

———✦———

These bodies of water are the longest rivers by continent:
Africa: Nile — 4,132 miles (6,648 km)
South America: Amazon — 3,915 miles (6,299 km)
Asia: Yangtze — 3,434 miles (5,525 km)
North America: Missouri — 2,533 miles (4,076 km)
Europe: Volga — 2,292 miles (3,688 km)
Australia: Murray — 1,609 miles (2,589 km)
The Nile, Amazon, and Yangtze also are the world's three longest rivers. The Mississippi — the "Father of Waters" — drains more than twice the area of the Missouri River, but the more humble Missouri is longer. Some sources calculate the Mississippi's length by measuring from the headwaters of

the Missouri to the point where the Mississippi spills into the Gulf of Mexico. This would make the mighty Mississippi the world's third longest. However, most geographers don't take that view.

———◆———

Indonesia gives the expression "island nation" real meaning. The country, which measures about 3,200 miles the long way, roughly east to west, comprises more than 13,660 islands, of which more than 6,000 are uninhabited. Java, one of the larger islands and site of the capital Jakarta, has 61 volcanoes of which more than a dozen are active.

———◆———

The largest island in the United States is Long Island at 1,723 square miles. Two of New York City's boroughs (Brooklyn and Queens) and two of its airports (Kennedy and LaGuardia) are located on the part of the island closest to Manhattan.

———◆———

The United States counts a number of island territories and affiliates. Two are popular tourist destinations: Puerto Rico, described as a "commonwealth associated with the United States," and the U.S. Virgin Islands. A third, also in the Caribbean, is the uninhabited Navassa Island.

Travia

In the Pacific, the inventory includes these territories: American Samoa, Baker Island, Guam, Howland Island, Jarvis Island, Johnston Atoll, Kingman Reef, Midway Islands, Palmyra Atoll, and Wake Island. Also, there are the Northern Mariana Islands, described as a "commonwealth in political union with the United States," and three countries — the Republic of the Marshall Islands, the Federated States of Micronesia, and Palau — that each signed a "compact of free association with the United States." Who knew?

There have been five United States in the world: United States of America, United States of Brazil, United States of Colombia, United States of Indonesia, and United States of Venezuela. Today there is one.

Earth's surface is 70.8% water and only 29.2% land.

These mountains are the tallest in the world
(by continent):
Asia: Mount Everest in Nepal
29,028 feet (8,848 meters)
South America: Mount Aconcagua in Argentina
22,834 feet (6,960 meters)
North America: Mount McKinley in Alaska
20,320 feet (6,194 meters)
Africa: Mount Kilimanjaro in Tanzania
19,341 feet (5,895 meters)
Europe: Mount Elbrus in Russia
18,510 feet (5,642 meters)
Antarctica: Vinson Massif
16,066 feet (4,897 meters)

Australia: Mount Kosciusko in New South Wales
7,310 feet (2,228 meters)
The 67 tallest mountains in the world are in Asia, which makes
South America's not-inconsequential 22,834-foot Aconcagua
the world's 68th highest peak.

——◆◆◆——

Reykjavik, Iceland, is the world's northernmost national capital
(at 64 degrees, 4 minutes north). Wellington, New Zealand, is
the southernmost (at 41 degrees, 17 minutes south).

——◆◆◆——

London, in southern England, at 51 degrees 31 minutes north
of the Equator, lines up on the globe with southern Canada.
It is north of Winnipeg, Manitoba (49 degrees 53 minutes),
and even north of a place called Moose Jaw, Saskatchewan (50
degrees 24 minutes). Italy's capital, Rome, at 41 degrees 54
minutes latitude, is north of Denver (39 degrees 46 minutes)
and New York City (40 degrees 40 minutes), and it is an almost
perfect match with Chicago (41 degrees 50 minutes).

——◆◆◆——

New York City is the largest city in the United States, but that
statement refers only to population. The largest city in area
is Juneau, Alaska, which since 1970 has incorporated 3,108
square miles. That makes Juneau bigger than countless islands

and island groups, as well as all those tiny countries in Europe. It is not much smaller than Cyprus (3,571 square miles) or Puerto Rico (3,515 square miles) and larger than the West Bank (2,263 square miles) and Brunei (2,228 square miles). It is triple the size of Luxembourg (998 square miles), more than seven times the size of Hong Kong (422 square miles), and close to 12 times the size of Singapore (267 square miles).

———◆◆◆———

There are 1,344 pages with place names and maps in the current edition of Merriam Webster's Geographical Dictionary. Only two pages are devoted to place names beginning with the letter "X."

———◆◆◆———

Vatican City is the world's smallest political unit. With only 108.7 acres, it is smaller than the grounds of the U.S. Capitol and one-eighth the size of New York's Central Park. Vatican City also has the world's lowest birth rate: zero.

———◆◆◆———

More than 30 countries plus Hong Kong list two official languages, and those countries include such familiar places as Canada (English, French); Finland (Finnish, Swedish); Iraq (Arabic, Kurdish in Kurdish areas); Ireland (English, Irish); Kenya (English, Kiswahili); Netherlands (Dutch, Frisian); New

Zealand (English, Maori); Norway (two kinds of Norwegian);
Peru (Spanish, Quechua), and Tanzania (English, Swahili).
Hong Kong's official languages are Cantonese Chinese and
English. Two of the former Soviet republics, Kazakhstan and
Kyrgyzstan, found it practical to keep Russian as an official
language along with the local tongue, Kazakh (as the "state
language") and Kyrgyz, respectively.

Often for simplicity in lands where there are many local
languages, new nations — particularly in Africa and the Pacific
— have settled on one language, that of the former colonial
overlord, usually English, French, or Portuguese. A few former
colonies have two official languages, both European.

Others find a need for more:

* At least five list three languages: Belgium (Dutch, French,
and German); Bolivia (Spanish, Quechua, and Aymara);
Luxembourg (Luxembourgish [the "national" language] and
two "administrative" languages, French and German); Rwanda
(English, French, and Kinyarwanda), and Switzerland (French,
German, and Italian).

* Three nations settled on four official tongues: Austria
(German, plus Croatian, Hungarian, and Slovene regionally);
Singapore (Chinese, English, Malay, and Tamil), and Spain
(Spanish plus Catalan, Galician, and Basque regionally).

* For the Palau islands in the Pacific, there are six: English
nationally and, in most states, Palauan. Regionally, the official
languages are Angaur, Japanese, Sonsoralese, and Tobi.

* South Africa counts 11 official languages (Afrikaans, English,
isiNdebele, isiXhosa, isiZulu, Sepedi, Sesotho, Setswana,
siSwati, Tshivenda, and Xitsonga).

* But India takes the prize with 15, which are Assamese,
Bengali, Gujarati, Hindi, Kannada, Kashmiri, Malayalam,
Marathi, Oriya, Punjabi, Sanskrit, Sindhi, Tamil, Telugu,

and Urdu. English, which is the most important language
for national, political, and commercial purposes, carries an
"associate" status.
Some countries don't name an official language, including
the land with the most indigenous languages of all:
Papua New Guinea, with 715 tongues. The lingua franca is
Melanesian Pidgin.
Spanish is the official language of Guatemala, but 23
Amerindian languages are "officially recognized."

———◆———

Angel Falls is the world's highest waterfall at 3,212 feet.
This natural wonder is found in Venezuela's Canaima
National Park.

———◆———

Twenty-eight nations have monarchies:
Bahrain, Belgium, Bhutan, Brunei, Cambodia, Denmark,
Japan, Jordan, Kuwait, Lesotho, Liechtenstein,
Luxembourg, Malaysia, Monaco, Morocco, Nepal,
Netherlands, Norway, Oman, Qatar, Samoa, Saudi Arabia,
Spain, Swaziland, Sweden, Thailand, Tonga, and
the United Kingdom.

———◆———

Fang is the name of a language. It is spoken in at least two
countries: Equatorial Guinea and Gabon in Africa.

———◆◆◆———

For various reasons, several countries plan to or have relocated
their capitals in recent years. On the Caribbean island of
Montserrat, it was a clear necessity: Plymouth was abandoned
in 1997 due to volcanic activity, and interim government
buildings constructed at Brades Estate. Here is the story on a
few other moves:

* Cote d'Ivoire officially "moved" its capital to Yamoussoukro
in 1983, but that move to the birthplace of then-President
Felix Houphouet-Boigny seems to have created a country with
two capitals. Abidjan remains its administrative center and the
United States, like other countries, maintains its
embassy there.

* Germany wasted no time: With reunification in 1990, Berlin
was once again designated the national capital, supplanting
Bonn, which had been West Germany's government seat.

* Israel did not relocate its capital in the usual sense. It made
West Jerusalem its seat of government but proclaimed the
united city of Jerusalem its capital, waiting until it gained
control of the entire city in 1967 to make that a reality.
However, the United States, like most other countries,
maintains its embassy in Tel Aviv because of a U.N. plan to
make Jerusalem an international city.

* Kazakhstan, seven years after its 1991 independence from the
Soviet Union, relocated its capital to Astana from Almaty.

* Nigeria's capital was officially moved from Lagos to Abuja in
1991, and most government offices have now been transferred.

* Tanzania in 1974 chose Dodoma as its future capital, and
the legislative offices have now moved from Dar es Salaam.
Embassies remained in Dar.

Additional new capitals are on tap: Palau is building a new city about 12 miles from its current seat of government in Koror, and South Korea announced a controversial plan to build a new capital about 100 miles south of Seoul.

———◆◆◆———

Berlin, Germany's capital, encompasses 341 square miles, including large areas of forest and farmland. Its size is a result of an ambitious 1920 annexation plan that added to the old central city seven smaller cities, 59 villages, and 27 estates. Berlin also has around 2,000 bridges, way more than Venice. From 1993 to 1998, Berlin's Potsdamer Platz was Europe's largest single inner-city construction site, with more than 100 cranes.

———◆◆◆———

New Orleans, founded in 1718 and devastated in 2005 by Hurricane Katrina, was destroyed twice by hurricanes in its first three years of existence.

———◆◆◆———

Turkey's largest metropolis, Istanbul, is the only city in the world that sits on two continents (Asia and Europe). Known previously as Constantinople (for the Roman emperor, Constantine), it has been the capital of three empires: the Roman (in the East), Byzantine, and Ottoman.

———◆◆◆———

The Welsh have a penchant for using their lilting
Celtic language to create long place names that
mystify the rest of us. To wit: Until recently, the
longest town name in Great Britain was the 58-letter
Llanfairpwllgwyngyllgogerychwyrndrobwllllantysiliogogogoch
(LlanfairPG for short) on the Welsh island of Anglesey. It
means, roughly, "St. Mary's Church of Pwllgwyngyll close to
the wild whirlpool [and] Church of St Tysilio [near] the red
island." Before 1850, the town name was Llanfairpwllgwyngyll.
The rest of the current town moniker was fabricated to bring
attention to a small town whose railway station and a freight
yard were about to be made redundant with the completion of
a new bridge. This town's name was used as a password in the
movie "Barbarella."

The world's longest station name, with 68 letters, is
Gorsafawddacha'idraigodanheddogleddollnpenrhy-
narurdraethceredigion, in Gwynedd county, Wales, on the
Fairbourne & Barmouth Steam Railway, which has one
track extending only two miles, built merely to bring building
materials for the construction of Fairbourne village in 1895.
The train still operates thanks to tourist interest in the small
steam railway — and in a station signpost that is considerably
longer than the station's wooden shelter. The name means
"the Mawddach Station with its dragon's teeth on the
northerly Penrhyn Drive on the golden beach of Cardigan
Bay." The name was a contrivance to get into the Guinness
World Book of Records, just once, in 1985.

Now comes the latest name change, in the summer of
2004, when the village of Llanfynydd renamed itself
Llanhyfryddawelllehynafolybarcudprindanfygythiad-
trienusyrhafnauole (with 66 letters) to protest a planned wind
farm in the area. That mouthful translates as "a quiet beautiful

village, a historic place with rare kite under threat from wretched blades." The folks in Llanfynydd, etc., may wind up with a wind farm anyway, but there could be an unexpected spin-off in tourist interest and international publicity. Visitors drop by for photos and to say they have been there (and spend some money) while journalists bring free publicity as they look for amusing stories.

———◆◆◆———

Llanfairpwllgwyngyllgogerychwyrndrobwllllantysiliogogogoch. com, with 62 characters, is the longest single-word (meaning without hyphens) Internet domain name in the world. The Welsh town registered the name in 1999 as soon as it became possible to have domain names of up to 67 characters, including the four characters accounted for by the dot and "com." Before October 1999, domain names could not be longer than 26 characters including the dot-com suffix.

———◆◆◆———

This one is hard to prove, but scholars who concern themselves about such things tend to agree that Damascus, Syria's capital, is the world's oldest continuously inhabited city, covering a span of roughly 5,000 years.

———◆◆◆———

In the 1990s, there were about 1,500 national parks in the world protecting about 1.5 million square miles in more than 120 countries.

———◆◆◆———

More people speak Mandarin Chinese than any other language. The most recent statistics say it is the first language for 13.69 percent of the world's population, or approaching one in seven people on Earth. The percentages for the other most widespread languages are as follows: Spanish, 5.05 percent; English, 4.84 percent; Hindi, 2.82 percent;

Portuguese, 2.77 percent; Bengali, 2.68 percent; Russian, 2.27 percent; Japanese, 1.99 percent; Standard German, 1.49 percent, and Wu (Shanghaiese) Chinese, 1.21 percent.

———◆◆———

La Paz, Bolivia's administrative capital, is the world's highest capital, at 12,001 feet above sea level — and it sits in a valley! It sits amidst the Andes, the spine of South America, a mountain range with 49 peaks that surpass 20,000 feet.

———◆◆———

Lake Baikal in Russia's Siberia is the world's deepest lake, reaching 5,715 feet at its lowest point, and it encompasses 12,160 square miles. Baikal holds about 20 percent of the world's fresh surface water. The five Great Lakes in North America account for about another 20 percent (although Baikal's share is a little greater). The largest of the Great Lakes, Superior, holds more water than the other four combined, and, while considerably shallower than Baikal (extending a mere 1,333 feet downward), it has the largest surface of any lake on Earth, 31,800 square miles.

———◆◆———

In 1250, Portugal obtained its full current size and thus has the oldest unchanged borders in Europe.

———◆◆———

Hanoi, Vietnam, once had a name that meant "City of the Soaring Dragon," which makes the current name seem pretty mundane; it means "City in the Bend of the River." Its nickname is more alluring: Paris of the Orient.

———◆◆◆———

Alaska is the northernmost, westernmost, and easternmost state in the United States. (It is easternmost in the geographic sense because the Aleutian Island chain extends west of the 180th meridian. Hence, the easternmost point in Alaska is that piece of land, Pochnoi Point on Semisopochnoi Island, that is just across the meridian at 179 degrees, 46 minutes east.)

———◆◆◆———

Cartographers down through the centuries have differed about which country or sacred site should be placed at the center of the map and which parts of the globe belonged at the top and which at the bottom. Some have placed north at the bottom; others placed east at the top (because the rising sun represented the risen Christ) with Jerusalem at the center.

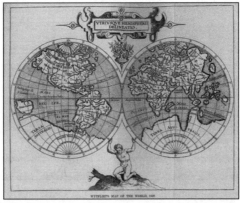

The Flemish mapmaker Gerardus Mercator (nee Gerard Kremer) put Europe roughly in the middle when in 1569 he created a new system for showing Earth's features on a flat map. The so-called Mercator projection treated each meridian (line of longitude) as a straight line parallel to all others, which had the effect of making the countries and oceans at the top and bottom of the map bigger than they really are in relation to features that are closer to the Equator.

This system helped navigators plot accurate routes, and for 400 years, it was the most common projection for navigators' maps. Mercator-style maps made it into American classrooms, too. Although he was the top European mapmaker of his time, Mercator made a few mistakes: He greatly under-calculated the size of the globe, and he treated Belgium, his birthplace, as if it were on the Equator and projected from that point north and south. Later, he produced a map collection that he called "Atlas," and that was the first time the word "atlas" was used to refer to a collection of maps.

———◆———

The U.S. record for the most rain in 12 months is held by Hawaii's Puu Kukui, a mountain on Maui, which in the 12 months between December 1981 and December 1982 set the record at 739 inches. In the world, the record is held by Cherrapunji in India, which from August 1860 to August 1861 recorded rainfalls totaling 1,042 inches. It also set the record for rainfall in a single month, at 366 inches in July of 1861.

———◆———

About 150 U.S. citizens, mostly Inupiat Eskimos, live only three miles from Russia. They live on Little Diomede Island in the Bering Strait, a small piece of Alaska that is 25 miles from the Seward Peninsula. But to the west, it is only three miles to Big Diomede Island, which is Russian and 28 miles from the Siberian landmass. The International Dateline passes between the Diomedes, as well.

———◆———

In Thailand, the local name for Bangkok is Krung Thep, which is a shortened version of the capital city's official name: Krung Thep Mahanakhon Amon Rattanakosin Mahinthara Ayutthaya Mahadilok Phop Noppharat Ratchathani Burirom Udomratchaniwet Mahasathan Amon Piman Awatan Sathit Sakkathattiya Witsanukam Prasit. That translates roughly as follows: "The city of angels, the great city, the residence of the Emerald Buddha, the impregnable city (unlike Ayutthaya) of God Indra, the grand capital of the world endowed with nine precious gems, the happy city, abounding in an enormous Royal Palace that resembles the heavenly abode where reigns the reincarnated god, a city given by Indra and built by Vishnukarn."

Ayers Rock, one of Australia's three most recognizable tourist sites — along with Sydney's Harbour Bridge and Opera House — is the largest single rock on Earth. The monolith rises 1,142 feet above the desert floor in the country's Northern Territory. It is 1.92 miles long, 1.18 miles across and 5.83 miles around its base. To climb, it is one mile from the base to the summit and requires the stamina of a highly trained athlete. It is a risky thing to do, and some climbers have died from accidents or from seizures after the climb. Australia's

— Our Home, Planet Earth —

Aborigines call the reddish sandstone monolith Uluru
and consider it to be sacred.

───◆◆◆───

Antarctica is the continent with the highest average elevation,
at about 8,000 feet.

───◆◆◆───

Here's a tourist attraction you wouldn't immediately think of:
On Valentia Island in western Ireland, there is the Tetrapod
Trackway — a trail extending about 50 feet — comprising
footprints of tetrapods, Earth's oldest four-limbed creatures.
Predating the dinosaurs, these prints were made between 350
million and 385 million years ago, making them the oldest
prints ever found in the Northern Hemisphere.
Much, much later, Valentia — as the westernmost point in
Europe and the closest to Canada — became the eastern
terminus for the first successful transatlantic telegraph cable in
1858. The cable, starting in Newfoundland on the other side,
operated for only a few weeks. A later line was more successful;
the Valentia station closed in 1966.

───◆◆◆───

The major tidewater glaciers that tourists can view during
cruises in Alaska waters are listed below, grouped by location.
Scenic ratings range from one to five, with five being
the highest:

Glacier Bay
Grand Pacific (150 feet high, 2 miles wide ***)
Margerie (250 feet high, 1 mile wide *****)
Johns Hopkins (250 feet high, 1 mile wide *****)
Gilman (250 feet high, 1/4 mile wide *****)
Lamplugh (160 feet high, 3/4 mile wide ***)
Reid (150 feet high, 3/4 mile wide **)

Yakutat Bay
Hubbard (300-400 feet high, 5 miles wide *****)
Valerie (300 feet high, 1 mile wide *****)
Tracy Arm
Sawyer (175 feet high, 1/3 mile wide ***)

The official name of the Galapagos islands, which were made famous by Charles Darwin, is Archipelago of Ecuador.

The Caribbean island of Nevis got its name in 1493 when Christopher Columbus visited. When he first saw it, the explorer named it based on the Spanish word for snow because he thought the cloud-covered mountain at the center of the island was topped by ice.

All countries in South America except Chile and Ecuador share a border with Brazil.

There are only four states east of the Mississippi River that do not have a shoreline on the Atlantic, the Gulf of Mexico, or a Great Lake. They are Kentucky, Tennessee, Vermont, and West

Virginia. Only one state, Maine, shares a border with only one other state.

❖

The longest place name in the United
States is the relatively short (45 letters)
Chargoggagoggmanchauggagoggchaubunagungamaugg, the
name of a 1,442-acre lake in Webster, Massachusetts. This
Native American name means "Englishmen at Manchaug at
the fishing place at the boundary." However, it is often better
known by a humorous translation: "You fish on your side, I
fish on my side, nobody fish in the middle," which was coined
in jest by a local editor.

❖

Russia, at 6,592,812 square miles, covers one-eighth of the
world's land surface.

❖

Chile's high-altitude Atacama Desert (up to 20,000 feet),
which extends for more than 600 miles south
from the country's border with Peru, is the driest
in the world; some parts have never experienced
a recorded rainfall. Nevertheless, more than a million
people live in the Atacama; there is underground water,
but the key source of moisture is fog which inhabitants
capture in special fog-catcher nets.
Northern Chile's top tourist destination is a desert town, San
Pedro de Atacama. Visitors come to see salt flats and their
flamingos, a salt mountain range, saltwater pools (handy for
a good float), hot springs, and geysers. The desert has yielded
countless mummies as well, and they are the ones seen in San
Pedro's Father La Paige Museum.

❖

From 1777 to 1791, the U.S. state of Vermont was an independent entity: the Republic of Vermont.

———◆◆◆———

Namibia in southwestern Africa is home to the world's highest sand dunes. The tallest of these red sand piles rises 1,066 feet from its base. The dunes are found in the Namib Naukluft Park.

———◆◆◆———

Croatia counts 1,185 islands along its meandering coastline, of which only 67 are inhabited by humans. One is Korcula, a popular holiday spot that is also known as the (disputed) birthplace of explorer Marco Polo. To this day, there are Polo families on the island who claim kinship with the famous man.

———◆◆◆———

According to the 2000 U.S. census, there are 15 municipalities with a population of zero, as follows: Chisana, Alaska; Supai, Arizona; Almanor, Caribou, and Little Grass Valley, California; Belleair Shore and Crystal Lake (Broward County), Florida; Taft, Louisiana; Frye Island, Maine; Picket Lake and Sunday Lake, Minnesota; Hoot Owl, Mule Barn, and Sportsmen Acres Community, Oklahoma; and Lewis, Vermont.

———◆◆◆———

Our Home, Planet Earth

The Dead Sea boasts a significant tourism business, attracting visitors to spas in Israel on one side and Jordan on the opposite side. The surface of this salt lake is 1,312 feet below the level of the Mediterranean, and it is the lowest point on the Earth's surface. However, the Dead Sea is escaping. It loses about three feet in depth each year. Given that the northern, deeper end reaches down around 1,200 feet, the sea may have a few hundred years left. But the movement of the shoreline is dramatic where water is shallower.

At the spa built at water's edge by the Ein Gedi kibbutz in 1985, guests are now ferried by trolley almost a mile to reach what has become brine. Israel's Ein Bokek spa development farther south is not so obviously affected because it was not built on the sea itself; it sits on the shores of the Dead Sea Saltworks' evaporation pools.

On a summer day, Niagara Falls — which straddles the U.S.- Canadian border — carries a dramatic 750,000 gallons of water over the edge every second (i.e., 45 million gallons every minute). However, that is only half of what Mother Nature provides. Under a U.S.-Canadian agreement, water is diverted

for hydroelectric power, but with an eye on tourism. At nights, when tourists aren't looking, and in the off-season (Nov. 1 to April 1) when most are not around, the amount of water cascading over those falls is halved again. Most of the water drops over the 2,500-foot-long Horseshoe Falls crest on the Canadian side, with the remainder tumbling over the 1,000-foot-long brink of American and Bridal Veil falls on the U.S. side. While reducing the water volume, diversion makes the falls look taller. The natural height of Horseshoe Falls is 155 feet, but it is 180 feet when the most water is diverted; water drops 170 feet over the American and Bridal Veil falls, but it falls 195 feet when the most water is diverted.

The world's largest living organism is a scuba diver's heaven, Australia's Great Barrier Reef. It comprises 2,900 individual reefs dating back as far as 2 million years that together occupy some 133,200 square miles — equal to half the size of Texas — and stretch for 1,240 miles along the coastline of Australia's Queensland.

For short place names, they don't get any shorter than Y, and there are two of those. Y, Alaska, had 956 residents at last count (2000 census), whereas Y, France, is one-tenth the size at 94. Apparently making up for lost letters, residents of Y in France are Ypsilonien(ne)s.

Victoria Falls, on the Zambezi River where the river forms the border between Zambia and Zimbabwe, is the world's biggest waterfall (based on the amount of falling water when the river is in full flood). Here, a great sheet of water flows over a crest that is more than a mile long (5,580 feet) and drops into a chasm that is 355 feet at its greatest depth, before continuing its journey trapped in a narrow gorge. It carries more than 130 million gallons of water over the side every minute when the waters are at their highest, usually sometime from February to April. Its local name, Mosi-oa-tunya, which means "the smoke that thunders," gives a really good idea what it is like to see the mist rise hundreds of feet and hear the water crash into the basin.

There are three instances in Russia where, when passing from one time zone to the next, the time difference is two hours because not every zone stretches all the way from the country's northern to its southern boundaries.

On the other hand, China's long northern border is south of five Russian time zones, but the entire country maintains only one.

Easily the biggest movement of wildlife on Earth is the annual Great Migration of herbivores seen in East Africa. The hordes of wildebeests, zebras, gazelles, the predators that live on them, and other animals can stretch across the landscape for 25 miles at the height of the relocation. An estimated 3 million to 3.5 million animals make the move, about half of them wildebeests heading across the 12,000-square-mile Serengeti ecosystem in search of grass. Broadly speaking, they move in a circle each year, but the big mass movement takes the animals out of Tanzania's Serengeti National Park toward Kenya's Masai Mara Game Reserve, generally in mid- and late summer. The return trip, at the end of the year, is more gradual.

———◆◆◆———

Japan is home to 10 percent of the world's active volcanoes.

———◆◆◆———

Our home, the planet Earth, is shaking all the time. There are an estimated 500,000 detectable earthquakes in the world each year, of which about 100,000 can be felt and 100 cause damage. About 10,000 of those quakes are in Southern California.

———◆◆◆———

Australia has some unique "attractions." Its box jellyfish is the most poisonous creature on Earth, and its taipan snake is the most poisonous snake on the planet. The funnel-web spider is Australia's most poisonous spider, but it is not clear if it is the world's most poisonous of its species, as well. Never mind. These dangerous critters really are tourist attractions. The taipan (and other lethal snakes) plus the funnel-web spider can be seen at the Australian Reptile Park outside Sydney.

———◆◆◆———

Everybody knows about "sinking cities." Italy's Venice is the best known but far from alone. In the last century, Venice has effectively sunk nine inches based on land sinkage and rising waters. It is expected to lose another eight inches in the coming century.

Bangkok, Thailand's capital and another city of canals, is settling faster. It was sinking about four inches a year 25 years ago, but the rate of subsidence had declined to roughly one inch as of 2004. The numbers are still more dramatic in

Mexico City, where the heaviest buildings are sinking by four to 12 inches a year. In this city, built on an old lake bed, water pipes once at ground level may protrude to the height of a low-rise building.

However, plenty of other great cities — including London, Shanghai, and Tokyo — have problems with sinking land or rising water. In the United States, Houston, Long Beach (California), and Las Vegas appear prominently on these lists, too, as does the ill-fated New Orleans.

But the most visually impressive evidence of sinkage is the Leaning Tower of Pisa in Italy. That monument began to tilt when it was under construction in the 12th century.

The builders made adjustments on the spot, which means columns at higher levels do not tilt as much as those in the bottom tier.

The United States has 3,986,826 miles of roadways, of which 2,582,368 miles are paved. Of those, 46,505 miles are expressways. The United States also counts 140,495 miles of rail lines (cargo and passenger); 149 heliports, and 14,858 airports, of which 5,119 have paved runways.

The world's largest flower is the rafflesia, which has five monster petals, is generally reddish-orange, and can be three feet or so in diameter. It also is known for its odor, which usually is bad, like rotting meat. The flower, which is a parasite on other plants, has no leaves or stems, and the bud takes months to develop, but the blossom lasts only a few days. There are several rafflesia species in a number of Southeast Asian countries, but the largest are found in Malaysia and Indonesia, often inside national parks. Because the blooms are rare and appear on an unpredictable schedule, park rangers have to help tourists find them.

Yellowstone National Park is the world's oldest national park, having been created by Congress in 1872 when Ulysses S. Grant was president. It covers 2,221,773 acres in Idaho, Montana, and Wyoming, but mostly Wyoming. It also is surrounded by national forests.

Hawaii is a sizeable group of islands, 132 to be precise. But, Hong Kong comprises double that (263), and the Greek

Islands come to a wildly larger number, more than 2,000, of which only 170 are inhabited.

———◆◆◆———

The letter "B" does not exist in the Tahitian language, so Bora Bora isn't Bora Bora. It is Pora Pora, meaning "first born," but early Western visitors could not hear the distinction.

———◆◆◆———

Roughly a third of Holland is below sea level at high tide, and another quarter is so low it would be flooded were it not for sand dunes, dikes, and another human intervention — the pumping of excess water. Holland's lowest point is just northeast of Rotterdam, at 22 feet below sea level.

———◆◆◆———

Iguazu Falls, on the Argentina-Brazil border, is the world's widest falls, stretching around a semicircle 8,100 feet long. Iguazu means "big water."

———◆◆◆———

The Chernobyl nuclear accident and subsequent evacuation of all humans from the area created Europe's largest nature sanctuary (1,800 square miles), in Belarus and Ukraine. Populations of deer, moose and wild boar are rebounding, but this is not true of the brown bear. Wild Przewalski's horses were introduced, as well, and are thriving. All the animals are radioactive.

———◆◆◆———

The world's highest border crossing is the Khunjarab Pass (about 15,500 feet), connecting China and Pakistan.

———◆◆◆———

Once in recorded times, the water stopped flowing at Niagara Falls. Because of an incredible ice jam in Niagara River, the flow over Horseshoe Falls, on the Canadian side, was reduced to a trickle, and nothing passed over the American or Bridal Veil falls on the U.S. side. This was late on March 29, 1848.

Locals frolicked on the riverbed on March 30 and said that, when the dam later broke, it sounded like thousands of cannons being fired.

In 1969, the U.S. government "turned off" the American and Bridal Veil falls to determine if it could and should clear rock debris at the base of the falls, but concluded that removing accumulated rock would cause the crest of the falls to collapse. Indeed, American and Bridal falls will collapse one day, and that could occur a thousand years from today — or tomorrow.

Chapter 3

At the Extremes

Travia

Visiting the Cathedral of St. John the Divine in New York City is the closest we 21st-century tourists can come to a trip back in time to see a medieval-style cathedral under construction the old way — very slowly. Construction started in 1892 and is about two-thirds finished. Upon completion (whenever that is), St. John the Divine will be the largest cathedral in the world, at 601 feet long (two football fields plus one foot), 146 feet wide at the nave, and 320 feet wide at the transept. The debut of the full 601-foot nave was celebrated on Nov. 30, 1941, one week before Pearl Harbor. It was 32 years before construction resumed.

———◆◆◆———

The world's largest bell, at 200 tons, is the Czar Bell, and it is on view inside Moscow's Kremlin. It has never made a sound.

———◆◆◆———

The following structures were the world's tallest when construction was completed, or they inherited that crown when something else fell. Through the 19th century, Earth's tallest buildings were churches or monuments. Starting with the Chrysler Building in the 20th century, all of the tallest buildings have been places of business. (All dates here refer to official opening dates, not top-off dates.) The list below is limited to structures that have remained standing and remained whole. Others could have been on this list, too, but tall spires are vulnerable, as explained below.

Completion Date	Structure/Height
c. 2566 B.C.	Great Pyramid of Giza* (482 feet, or 147 meters)
1439 A.D.	Strasbourg Cathedral (466 feet, or 142 meters)
1880 A.D.	Cologne Cathedral (515 feet, or 157 meters)

At the Extremes

1884 A.D.	Washington Monument
	(555 feet, or 169 meters)
1889 A.D.	Eiffel Tower
	(984 feet, or 300 meters)
1930 A.D.	Chrysler Building
	(1,046 feet, or 319 meters - 77 stories)
1931 A.D.	Empire State Building
	(1,250 feet, or 381 meters - 102 stories)
1973 A.D.	World Trade Center
	(1,368 feet, or 417 meters - 110 stories)
1974 A.D.	Sears Tower
	(1,450 feet, or 442 meters - 110 stories)
1998 A.D.	Petronas Towers
	(1,483 feet, or 452 meters - 88 stories)
2004 A.D.	Taipei 101
	(1,667 feet, or 508 meters - 101 stories)

* By the time the great medieval cathedrals started their climb skyward, the Great Pyramid had eroded to a height of not quite 450 feet (137 meters).

Travia

England's Windsor Castle, with a 13-acre footprint, is the world's largest occupied castle. It has been a royal residence and fortress for more than 900 years. After his 1066 conquest, William the Conqueror chose the site. The outer walls of today's structure are in the same position as those of William's original castle. During the 17th-century Civil War, Windsor Castle was used as a prison as well as a headquarters for Oliver Cromwell's forces. More than 100 rooms (or about one-fifth of the castle area) were damaged or destroyed in a 1992 fire; restoration was completed by 1997 at a cost of $59.2 million.

Windsor Castle.

Strasbourg Cathedral, the world's tallest building for 200-plus years, did not earn that title until catastrophe had befallen three other churches — or, at least, their steeples. Lincoln Cathedral in Lincoln, England, became the tallest structure in 1311 at 525 feet (160 meters), but its highest spire fell off in a 1548 storm. As a result, St. Olaf's Church in Tallinn, Estonia (completed around 1500 at 522 feet [159 meters]), moved to No. 1. However, it was struck by lightning, probably in 1625, and burned to the ground. Either of these could have kept the Strasbourg and Cologne cathedrals off the list above.

Meanwhile, Old St. Paul's in London always remained in the wings, never surpassing its contemporaries in Lincoln and Tallinn. Dating from 1314, it stood at 489 feet (149 meters), and without these competitors, it also surpassed Strasbourg. However, it too was struck by lightning and the spire burned in 1561. Today, Lincoln Cathedral still graces its hilltop location at the end of Steep Hill Street. St. Olaf's was struck by lightning, burned two more times, and was rebuilt three times (but not to such an outstanding height). The rest of Old St. Paul's was destroyed in London's Great Fire of 1666 and rebuilt as the shorter St. Paul's Cathedral we see today.

———◆———

Somerset Bridge, built in 1620 to link Bermuda's mainland with Somerset Island, is reputed to be the world's shortest drawbridge. The part of the bridge that can be raised and lowered measures only 13 inches, and the value of such a tiny opening is to let the masts of sailboats get through.

———◆———

At 460 feet, the widest avenue in the world is Avenida 9 de Julio in Buenos Aires, Argentina's capital city.

———◆———

The Sky Tower in Auckland, New Zealand, is the tallest tower in the Southern Hemisphere at 1,076 feet. The main observation level at 610 feet offers 360-degree views across the city and its harbors — and a startlingly good look at a citified variation on bungee jumping. Adventurers fly by in an aided plunge 630 feet down the side of the building to a landing station at ground level. This is billed as a tower jump (it is not a bungee jump, which is more like flying on a rubber band, though the tower jump looks scary enough), and about 7,000 people drop off this tower every year.

Those without jumping in their genes get their kicks by riding in glass-enclosed elevators and, at the main observation level, by walking on safety-glass floors that jut out over the streets for a dizzying look at the streets 610 feet below. Visitors may also climb, with a guide, inside the ever-narrowing tower to the highest point for viewing, aptly called Vertigo, at 889 feet.

———◆◆◆———

Maryland's State House in Annapolis has the biggest all-wood dome in the United States (about 160 tons).

———◆◆◆———

The world's tallest pyramid is the most famous of all — the Great Pyramid, the largest of a set of three in Giza near Cairo, Egypt. But it is not the world's biggest nor the oldest:
* The biggest of all is Quetzalcoatl Pyramid at Cholula, southeast of Mexico City, Mexico. It is 4.3 million cubic yards (3.3 million cubic meters).
* The world's oldest is the Djoser Step Pyramid at Saqqara, Egypt, constructed by Pharaoh Djoser's royal architect Imhotep (also a medical doctor) in the late 27th century B.C.
* As for the tallest pyramid, completed around 2566 B.C. for Pharaoh Khufu (better known by his Greek name Cheops), the Great Pyramid in Giza initially reached 482 feet (147 meters), but the wear and tear of time have worn it down to not quite 450 feet (137 meters).

———◆◆◆———

The world's largest Chinese landscape painting graces the walls of the Island Shangri-La Hotel in Hong Kong. Titled "The Great Motherland of China," it measures 167.3 feet high (or 16 stories) by 45.9 feet and was painted on 250 panels of Chinese silk.

———◆◆◆———

Washington, D.C., is home to the world's largest library (Library of Congress), the world's largest museum complex (Smithsonian Institution), and the world's most popular museum (National Air and Space Museum):

* *The Library of Congress* accommodates nearly 128 million items on about 530 miles of bookshelves. The collections include more than 29 million books and other printed materials, plus 57 million manuscripts, 12 million photographs, 4.8 million maps, and 2.7 million recordings.

* *The Smithsonian Institution*, which comprises 17 museums and galleries and the National Zoological Park, maintains more than 143.5 million objects, works of art, or specimens (including 126 million items at the National Museum of Natural History). Two of the Smithsonian's units are in New York City: the Cooper-Hewitt National Design Museum and the National Museum of the American Indian's George Gustav Heye Center.

* *The National Air and Space Museum*, which is one of the Smithsonian's units, is the most-visited museum site in the

world, with an average annual attendance of
more than nine million.

———✦———

Mexico City has nearly 90,000 taxicabs — more than any
other city in the world.

———✦———

The Pentagon, in Arlington, Virginia, is the world's largest
office building, sitting on 29 acres and surrounding a five-acre
courtyard. The gross floor area is 6,636,360 square feet, and
its corridors extend for 17.5 miles. The five-story building has
five sides (hence, the name), each of which is 921 feet long.
Its 7,754 windows require 7.1 acres of glass. There are 691
drinking fountains, 4,200 clocks, and 16,250 light fixtures
requiring 250 lamp replacements per day. Its 67 acres of
parking spaces accommodate 8,770 vehicles. To build the
Pentagon, 6 million cubic yards of earth were moved and
41,492 concrete pilings driven. For the 410,000 cubic yards of
concrete used, 680,000 tons of sand and gravel were dredged
from the Potomac River.

The Pentagon was conceived in 1941 as a temporary solution
to the then-War Department's need for more space during
World War II. Groundbreaking occurred on September 11,

1941 — 60 years to the day before a terrorist attack destroyed part of the (since-rebuilt) building, leaving 189 dead. Tours are available to groups, by reservation, and the guide walks backwards for the entire hour-long visit.

———◆———

The new Grand Mosque in Muscat, Oman, which opened in 2001, boasts the world's largest Persian carpet at 2,830 square feet. The carpet has 1.7 billion knots and weighs 21 tons; it had to be installed in pieces and then stitched together. Its main prayer hall measures 59,580 square feet. And, yes, tourists can visit this holy place, which accommodates 20,000 worshippers.

———◆———

The world's oldest (and, for centuries, the longest) man-made waterway is China's Grand Canal, which extends some 1,100 miles from Beijing in the north to Hangzhou in the south, linking five key rivers and providing China's only major north-south water route. Its first sections were dug nearly 2,500 years ago. It was extended over the centuries, with one section in the north completed under the auspices of Kublai Khan in the 13th century.

Everything about this canal is grand — even the misery associated with its construction. In the seventh century, as the Sui Dynasty oversaw the extension of the canal to its southern terminus, an estimated 5.5 million commoners were conscripted to do the work, and it is believed that about half of them died in the process. Resulting uprisings helped end the Sui Dynasty in 618.

The canal passes through or near Nanjing; Suzhou, a canal city called the Venice of the East; Wuxi; and Yangzhou, the town where Marco Polo was mayor from 1282 to 1285.

When the St. Lawrence Seaway opened in 1959 — extending from Duluth, Minnesota, to the gulf of the St. Lawrence River and linking the Great Lakes to the Atlantic — it outstripped the Grand Canal as the longest man-made waterway at 2,340 miles.

———————◆◆———————

The Forbidden City, built by China's emperors in Beijing, is the world's largest palace complex (with 9,999 rooms occupying 183 acres).

———————◆◆———————

While the following buildings are the largest religious structures in their categories, their importance as tourist attractions varies widely:

* **Largest Buddhist temple:** Borobudur, near Yogyakarta in Indonesia, which is 403 feet long on each side of a square base (3.73 acres) and 113 feet tall at its highest point (it occupies 2,118,879 cubic feet of space).

The temple of unmortared stone was constructed between 750 and 842, and after about 150 years of usage, it was ignored for hundreds of years before its rediscovery in the 19th century.

* **Largest church:** Our Lady of Peace of Yamoussoukro Basilica in Yamoussoukro, Cote d'Ivoire, covering an area of 322,917 square feet (7.4 acres) and reaching 518 feet in height. Roughly based on St. Peter's in Rome, the Roman Catholic basilica (built in record time between 1986 and 1989) was paid for by the late Cote d'Ivoire president Felix Houphouet-Boigny and is located in the city of his birth.

Our Lady of Peace is not quite as tall as the world's tallest cathedral — Germany's Ulm Cathedral, at 530 feet. In addition, the church with the world's greatest capacity is the Basilica of St. Pius X at Lourdes, France, completed in 1957 and designed to meet the needs of large numbers of pilgrims. The 660-foot-long elliptical basilica accommodates 20,000.

* **Largest Hindu temple:** Srirangam Temple at Tiruchirappalli, Tamil Nadu, India. The temple complex occupies 156 acres, which makes it larger than all of the Vatican City (108.7 acres).

* **Largest mosque:** Shah Faisal Mosque, near Islamabad, Pakistan's capital, with a complex covering 46.87 acres and the covered prayer hall measuring 1.19 acres. Dating from 1976, the mosque can accommodate 100,000 worshippers. The minarets are reminiscent of rockets, and the roof is meant to be reminiscent of a desert tent.

* **Largest synagogue:** Temple Emanu-El on Fifth Avenue in New York City, built in 1929, with an area of 37,921.2 square feet (0.87 acres). It accommodates 2,500 — more than St. Patrick's Cathedral.

* **Largest religious temple complex:** Angkor Wat. The 12th-century temple and its grounds sit on approximately 276 acres defined by a moat 570 feet by about four miles. Its outer gallery walls also boast the world's longest continuous bas-relief, which tells stories from Hindu mythology. The temple, located in northwestern Cambodia, was later turned into a Buddhist temple. Angkor Wat is part of a UNESCO World Heritage Site that includes the remains of different capitals of the Khmer Empire.

Travia

Here is an obscure claim to fame: The Woolloomooloo Bay Wharf in Sydney, Australia, is the world's largest timber pile wharf in the world. Built in 1910, it measures 1,312 feet by 230 feet and stands on 4,700 piles.

In the wake of redevelopment, the wharf now encompasses a marina, restaurants, an apartment complex and the Blue Hotel, which is owned by Taj Hotels.

———◆———

Budapest, Hungary, boasts Europe's largest parliament building, a neogothic structure with 365 towers and 691 rooms. (Romania's Palace of the Parliament in Bucharest is larger, but it is a multipurpose building with only a portion set aside as home to the Parliament.)

———◆———

This item belongs in the realm of might-have-beens: The world's lists of tallest structures might have been shorter if a huge Buddhist stupa built near Peshawar in northwest Pakistan had survived — and assuming it was correctly described.

A sixth-century Chinese pilgrim left a written description including dimensions that would translate into a height of about 700 feet, taller than the Washington Monument but not the Eiffel Tower.

———◆———

China's Great Wall is estimated to be up to 4,500 miles long (that is 18 percent of the Earth's circumference at the Equator), with a main line of roughly 2,500 miles and the rest accounted for by spurs. It was more than 2,000 years under construction, but the bulk of today's wall dates from the Ming Dynasty (1368-1644). It is 30 feet high at places, perhaps 25 feet wide at the base, and up to 20 feet wide at the top (wide enough for driving).

At the Extremes

A monstrous building project (the world's largest), it was constructed from available materials — meaning bricks, sometimes weighing 30 pounds each; stones, some estimated at 2,000 pounds each; and dirt. The soil is the stuff of many walls in China, created by adding thin layer after thin layer and pounding the dirt until it is rock solid. It can withstand the elements for centuries. It would cost about $155 billion to rebuild the entire wall.

Yonge Street in Canada, at 1,178 miles, is the world's longest street. It starts in Toronto, stretches north and then west around Lake Superior to Thunder Bay and on to a town called Rainy River on the border with Minnesota in the United States.

The Department of Irish Folklore at University College Dublin houses more than 100,000 tales, myths and legends. It is the world's largest collection of its kind.

Alaska has more active glaciers than the rest of the inhabited world. It has an estimated 100,000, which cover almost five percent of the state. The state also has 80 percent of the active volcanoes in the United States and more than 3 million lakes.

Travia

The world's largest cattle station is the Anna Creek Station in Australia. It is larger than Belgium.

———◆———

Mexico City boasts the world's largest bullring. It seats about 55,000 people.

———◆———

Kentucky's Mammoth Cave is the world's longest cave system. It extends more than 365 miles.

———◆———

Finally, we present this list of distinctions (and tourist attractions) of dubious social value:

World's largest ball of twine
Cawker City, Kansas

World's largest baseball bat
Louisville, Kentucky

World's largest cross-country skis
100 Mile House, British Columbia

World's largest frying pan
Long Beach, Washington

World's largest kaleidoscope
Mount Tremper, New York

World's largest maze
Kamehameha Highway, Hawaii

World's largest movie screen
Las Vegas, Nevada

World's largest thermometer
Baker, California

And, saved for last, the world's largest pair of concrete cowboy boots, in San Antonio, Texas. They are 40 feet tall and 35 feet wide, and we wonder: Is there a second pair of concrete cowboy boots somewhere?

Chapter 4

Winging It

The 13th-century Franciscan friar, Roger Bacon, noting that humans could not and did not know how to fly, concluded that any attempt to fly was sinful.

———◆———

Samuel Pierpont Langley, an astronomer and physicist, built and flew his first aircraft in 1896. The pilotless plane traveled 4,200 feet across the Potomac River. Based on this success, Langley obtained $50,000 in funding from the War Department (since euphemistically renamed the Department of Defense) to develop a plane that could carry a person. He designed for launches that would catapult his plane off a boat, but his project failed twice, once nearly drowning Charles Manly, his colleague, in the effort. The second failed try occurred on December 9, 1903.

The War Department then insightfully wrapped up its assessment as follows: "It would seem as if years of constant work and study by experts, together with the expenditure of thousands of dollars, would still be necessary before we can hope to produce an apparatus of practical utility on these lines." On December 17, only eight days after the Langley debacle, the Wright brothers — with Orville lying on the craft's wing — put a man-carrying machine in the air at Kitty Hawk, North Carolina. The brothers had designed and built the plane without government help.

———◆———

Winging It

Scientific American Magazine said this in 1910: "To affirm that the airplane is going to revolutionize the future is to be guilty of the wildest exaggeration." Around the same time, even Orville Wright said, "The Atlantic flight is out of the question."

———◆◆◆———

Before starting to build airplanes in 1916, William Boeing sampled existing wares by flying on an early Curtiss Aeroplane and Motor Company biplane, and "on" was the operative word: The craft required the pilot and passenger to sit on the wing. Then came World War I, and the first Boeing planes to see duty were seaplanes which could not fly from Seattle to the Navy base in Florida; they were dismantled, shipped by train, and reassembled. After the war, orders dropped to almost nothing, so the Boeing plant diversified, building dressers, counters, and furniture for a corset company and a confectioner's shop. It also built flat-bottomed boats called sea sleds.

———◆◆◆———

America's first scheduled air flight was a 21-mile, 23-minute scoot in 1914 from St. Petersburg to Tampa, Florida. The sole passenger was St. Petersburg's mayor.

———◆◆◆———

The U.S. government inaugurated airmail service in 1918. The first flight was to head north from Washington, D.C., to Philadelphia and New York City. With President Woodrow Wilson in attendance for the historic event, it was delayed because someone forgot to put fuel in the plane. Once airborne, the pilot — operating without a compass — headed south. After 25 miles, he made an emergency landing.

———◆◆◆———

By 1920, pilots were flying mail between New York and San Francisco via Chicago. In good weather, that took 78 hours with the mail in the air by day and moving by train or truck by night. When postal officials wanted to determine, in 1921, that planes could travel at night, too, farmers along the designated route participated in the trial by lighting bonfires to show the way. In the first three years of airmail service, 19 of the original 40 pilots died in crashes, one of them during the test of nighttime mail service. By 1925, 31 of the original 40 had been killed.

The airplane may have been invented in the United States, but America got off to a slow start in commercial aviation. In 1926, American companies carried barely 6,000 passengers, and private airlines didn't start hauling airmail until that same year. By then, overseas carriers were already operating regularly scheduled passenger service in 17 European countries as well as in Africa, Australia, and South America. As early as 1919, there were London-Paris services, and by 1925, those flights offered the comfort of upholstered chairs with bar service and champagne lunches delivered by jacketed stewards.

Imperial Airways (now British Airways), which launched passenger service in 1924 with a flight to Paris (in April, fittingly), was pleased to advise passengers that "practically

all British life assurance offices have removed restrictions"
regarding flying on an airplane.

The airline also provided the following information to
passengers: The cabin is entirely enclosed and windows can be
opened or closed at will so "there is no more need for special
clothing than there is on a railway journey." "Height sickness
is unknown" in an airplane. Lunch baskets will be provided if
passengers order in advance. "Air pockets do not exist," and
bumps are caused by upward and downward currents of air,
much like the waves ships deal with.

———◆◆◆———

The first concrete runway in the United States was built in
1925 by Henry Ford in Dearborn, Michigan.

———◆◆◆———

United Airlines traces its beginnings, in part, to 1926 when
one of its founding carriers, Varney Air Lines, launched an
airmail route. Varney's owner bought six planes for the service
— planes that were shipped to Boise, Idaho, as assemble-this-
yourself kits. The day before the service was to begin, two pilots
totaled one plane while on a positioning flight. As a result, it
was Varney's chief pilot, Leon Cuddeback, who made history
the next day, April 6, by piloting America's first scheduled mail-
delivery run by a private airline. He also had a tight schedule
that day, so tight he eventually used his glove as a urinal and
tossed it out the window. The day's second pilot (Franklin
Rose) was forced down in a storm, the plane got stuck in mud,
and a car came to collect the mail — after the pilot had ridden
30 miles on a horse to get help.

———◆◆◆———

American Airlines' history as a scheduled air carrier begins
with a St. Louis-Chicago airmail route operated by one of its
predecessor carriers, Robertson Aircraft Corporation. The

Travia

pilot for the first flight, April 15, 1926, was Charles Lindbergh, who missed by only nine days making the piece of history no one remembers Leon Cuddeback for — launching the first U.S. scheduled airmail service by a private airline.

———◆——

The world's first flight attendants were men, deployed intermittently by fledgling carriers in the 1920s. Also called "aerial couriers," they sometimes loaded baggage and issued airline tickets. Stout Airlines, later one of the four founding partners of United Airlines, in 1926 was first in the United States to hire aerial couriers, for flights between Detroit and Grand Rapids, Michigan.

Ellen Church became the world's first airline stewardess in 1930. It was she who suggested that Boeing Air Transport, a predecessor to United Airlines, hire women nurses to tend to passengers' needs. She said that seeing women working on the planes would help reduce fear of flying. Good argument, but she was most likely motivated by the simple desire to fly. Church as a child became enthralled by flying while watching World War I pilots train in a field near her family's Minnesota farm, then took flying lessons and wanted to be a pilot when women didn't have a prayer of being hired by commercial airlines for the cockpit.

———◆——

The College Park Airport in Maryland is the world's oldest continuously operating airport, dating from 1909. It also was the site of the U.S. Army's first Aviation Corps, where Wilbur and Orville Wright were among the instructors.

———◆——

Charles Lindbergh may have been first to fly the Atlantic solo (no small feat), but he was the 68th man to fly nonstop across that ocean. Even a cat did it first — twice.

Winging It

The first to go nonstop were two adventurers, Capt. John William Alcock and Lt. Arthur Whitten Brown, who flew from Newfoundland to Ireland, at about 120 mph, on June 14-15, 1919. The trip took 16 hours and 27 minutes. The pair of British subjects were knighted and shared a £10,000 prize offered by the London Daily Mail. Only a week later, the newly knighted Sir John was mortally wounded in a plane crash in Normandy. He died that December at age 27. Sir Arthur, born in Scotland to American parents, lived to age 62. The other 65 intervening transatlantic travelers, a stowaway cat called Wopsie, and two pigeons were aboard two dirigibles (one of them on a roundtrip journey) that crossed the Atlantic before Lindbergh's date with history. Five men died trying to be first to fly solo. Then, Lindy flew New York to Paris in May 1927; the trip took 33 and a half hours, and he collected a $25,000 prize and more notoriety than he bargained for.

Charles Lindbergh's aircraft, commissioned for the solo attempt, was built in San Diego — which meant the 25-year-old had to fly it across the United States before he could start his life-changing journey from New York's Long Island. He made that first trip in 22 hours and left for Paris eight days later.

Travia

The first irregularly scheduled transcontinental service in the United States, between New York and San Francisco, was started in 1927 on a shared basis by Boeing Air Transport (BAT) and National Air Transport, both forebears to United Airlines. Passengers donned flying coveralls, parachutes, and goggles and sat crammed into the enclosed mail pit near the roaring engine (either sitting on mail or holding it in their laps) for a 32-hour journey with 15 stops. There was space for only two passengers per trip, and there was a plane change in Chicago when they could lose their seats to mail. The fare for this? $404, in 1927 currency, that is.

————— ◆ —————

Jane Eads, a Chicago newspaper reporter, was the passenger for Boeing Air Transport's first-ever mail run on July 1, 1927. Smartly decked out in high heels, knee-length business suit, and feather boa, she traveled the 22 and a half hours between San Francisco and Chicago in a space not much bigger than a freezer.

————— ◆ —————

When Western Air Express launched Los Angeles-San Francisco passenger flights in 1928, service included on-board meals prepared by a posh Los Angeles restaurant.

————— ◆ —————

Pan Am's first headquarters and ticket office were housed in a modest-sized one-story building in Key West, Florida. At the time (1927), the building sat beside the water (Pan Am's first flights were by seaplane, and the airline carried mail between Key West and Havana; passengers came a year later). The airline's "birthplace" was later moved a bit inland and is now a restaurant, Kelly's Caribbean Bar, Grill & Brewery, owned by actress Kelly McGillis.

————— ◆ —————

Winging It

Delta got its start in 1924 as a crop duster in the U.S. South and in Mexico and Peru, based first in Macon, Georgia, and then Monroe, Louisiana; the Atlanta move did not come until 1941. The name refers to the Mississippi Delta region that the company served. The airline carried its first passengers in 1929 from Dallas, Texas, to Jackson, Mississippi, with stops in Shreveport and Monroe, Louisiana. The first westward extension on that route took passengers all the way from Dallas to Fort Worth, Texas.

Following are some female firsts in aviation:

1784: First balloon flight by a woman
(Mme. Thible, a French opera singer).

1910: First licensed woman pilot
(Baroness Raymonde de la Roche of France).

1911: First U.S. licensed woman pilot
(Harriet Quimby, a magazine writer).

1912: First cross-Channel flight by a woman
(Harriet Quimby, from Dover to Hardelot).

1921: First U.S. black woman licensed pilot
(Bessie Coleman).

1932: First solo transatlantic flight by a woman
(Amelia Earhart, from Newfoundland to Ireland
in 15 hours).

1936: First solo westbound transatlantic flight by a woman
(Beryl Markham, from England to Nova Scotia
in 19 hours).

Harriet Quimby was killed in a flying accident in mid-1912,
Bessie Coleman was killed in a 1926 flying accident, and
Amelia Earhart disappeared over the Pacific in 1937 while
attempting a round-the-world journey with a companion. Beryl
Markham, an English pilot who lived in Kenya, had a long
life and in 1942 penned her autobiography, "West With the
Night," in which she described flying blind in a storm for 19
hours on her solo flight over the Atlantic in an aircraft with an
engine that died several times. When the engine died for good,
she was over land, so she dove into mud and walked away from
the wreck.

———◆———

This story of one aviation official and three airplanes
illustrates how dangerous early air service was. Colonel
Horace Brinsmead in November 1931 boarded an airmail
flight in Melbourne, Australia, heading to London to discuss
establishing regular airmail services.

When an engine failed, the plane crashed in what is today
Malaysia, totaling the aircraft but without harming the pilot
or his only passenger. Brinsmead then opted for a KLM
flight to London from Bangkok, the Thai capital. That plane
crashed on takeoff, killing five people and leaving Brinsmead
incapacitated until his death three years later. The original
pilot, meanwhile, made it to London with the mail in a
replacement aircraft, but the day before he was to start home,
he crash landed because the airport in Croydon, England, had
failed to turn on its lights on a foggy night. After repairs, the
plane and pilot returned home safely.

———◆———

When United Airlines' predecessor carriers Boeing Air Transport and National Air Transport launched scheduled transcontinental services in 1929 with purpose-built planes accommodating 12 to 18, the passengers received comfort kits that included cotton balls for the ears (to cut out engine noise) and chewing gum to deal with air pressure. Windows could be opened, but passengers were instructed not to use them as wastebaskets. Most planes had toilet facilities, and the toilet itself was a seat over an open hole in the floor. Sometimes food was served and sometimes not, just like today.

Imperial Airways (now British Airways) inaugurated flights between London and Delhi, India, in early 1929, when service took seven days (costing £130) and, initially, the trip included a rail leg between Basel, Switzerland, and Genoa, Italy, because Italy would not allow entry from France where the Alps were less of a barrier. The carrier soon altered the routing – which in winter meant a rail leg between Skopje, Macedonia, and Thessaloniki, Greece, to compensate for bad winter flying weather in that mountainous region. Also, in the first three years, one "hotel" along the way was a specially built fort between Amman, Jordan, and Baghdad, Iraq.

One of the airlines that became part of American Airlines was the first to operate a transcontinental air/rail service as of June 14, 1929. This so-called "luxurious" service was a 67-hour journey. Westbound passengers took the train from New York to Cleveland, where they boarded the Universal Air Lines System plane to Garden City, Kansas, with stops in Chicago, St. Louis, and Kansas City. In Garden City, passengers joined another rail service to complete their trip to Los Angeles.

Speaking of 67 hours: On March 3, 2005, Steve Fossett — after 67 hours in the air — completed the world's first solo, nonstop, round-the-world flight when he touched down in Salina, Kansas. He piloted the specially built GlobalFlyer, which has 13 fuel tanks but a cockpit that is only seven feet long. The project was bankrolled by Sir Richard Branson, founder of Virgin Atlantic Airways.

———◆◆◆———

Universal Air Lines launched 67-hour transcon service in June 1929, but the fledgling Transcontinental Air Transport (TAT) bettered that almost immediately on July 7 with a 46-hour air/ rail service which it promoted as the option "for those whose time is too important to waste." Using Ford Trimotors (with the instruments oddly mounted outside the cockpit on a wing strut and a Model T steering wheel for the control yoke), TAT offered a service that was two parts air (daytime) as well as two parts rail (at night).

Westbound, passengers boarded a luxury Pullman sleeper in New York, transferred to air at the Port Columbus air/rail facility in Ohio (walking under a canopy to the plane) and flew via Indianapolis, St. Louis, Kansas City, and Wichita to the middle of nowhere in Oklahoma. They traveled by Aero Car, an upholstered trailer bus, to Waynoka. The attraction there was a train station where passengers got their dinner at TAT Harvey House and connected to Pullman service to Clovis, New Mexico. At Clovis, passengers returned to the sky for the flight to Los Angeles, interrupted by fuel stops in Albuquerque, New Mexico, and Winslow and Kingman, Arizona. Only a year later, TAT, reincarnated as Transcontinental and Western Air (T&WA), was operating an all-air coast-to-coast service that took only 36 hours (including an overnight in Kansas City, Missouri).

———◆◆◆———

Until the mid- or late 1930s, many life insurance policies carried a rider saying coverage did not apply while the insured was on an airplane. Then, the more reliable DC-3 entered service in 1936; a year later, for the first time, passengers could buy flight insurance at the airport, at 25 cents for a $5,000 policy.

Charles Lindbergh was everywhere in the early days of aviation. A consultant to several airlines, he was a technical advisor to Transcontinental Air Transport (TAT) at $10,000 a year plus stock options. When TAT launched its air/rail service in 1929, Lindbergh was the pilot for the first leg out of Los Angeles; then, he waited in Winslow, Arizona, to fly the last leg of the westbound inaugural. Lindbergh also sent the first-ever plane-to-ground commercial radio message while en route to Winslow; it was a message from a journalist asking his editor for $50. Lindbergh was accompanied by his bride of six weeks, Anne Morrow. In addition, Will Rogers was on the couple's eastbound flight. On the return to Los Angeles, the Lindberghs were joined by Amelia Earhart, another TAT consultant, called "assistant traffic manager." She was airsick in the plane.

———◆◆◆———

Northwest Airways, predecessor to today's Northwest Airlines, took off — literally — in 1926 carrying mail between Minnesota's Twin Cities and Chicago, using rented, open-cockpit biplanes. In 1938, it was the first to develop a practical aviation oxygen mask, making it possible for high-altitude flying over the Rocky Mountains.

———◆◆◆———

Western Air Express had the world's largest air system in 1930, with 40 planes and routes covering 16,000 miles. However, a merger deal with Transcontinental Air Transport (TAT) absorbed most of that business. The surviving shards of Western Air Express became Western Airlines.

———◆◆◆———

New York-Los Angeles air/rail service by Transcontinental Air Transport (TAT) in 1929 included the following airborne amenities: meals (served on lavender linen with gold flatware), flight attendants (male), lavatories, kitchens, reading lights at each of the passengers' wicker seats (five on each side of the aircraft), cigarette lighters and ashtrays at each seat — plus brown velvet curtains, but, bravely and uniquely, no parachutes. Passengers could open windows, one antidote to airsickness; lemon slices were another option and were no doubt requested often, as about three-quarters of TAT passengers became airsick during the bumpy rides. Stewards also offered cotton balls for the ears. A heater kept temperatures at 60 degrees Fahrenheit when crossing mountains at up to 8,000 feet above sea level. Staff were in uniform, and the pilot made a handsome $12,000 a year. The 46-hour air/rail trip cost $480 (about 10 times that in today's dollars), and the airline gave each of its passengers $5,000 in free life insurance and a gold fountain pen from Tiffany's.

———◆———

Now, for another trip you would rather read about than take: In 1933, Eastern Air Transport carried passengers down the East Coast from Newark, New Jersey, to Miami in 13 hours and 50 minutes. This included a 25-minute lunch in Richmond, Virginia; a 30-minute dinner in Jacksonville, Florida, and 10 intermediate stops. The one-way fare was $73.67, and transport to Newark from Manhattan was 75 cents.

———◆———

In the early 1930s, flights were canceled so often due to engine troubles or weather that U.S. pilots carried forms authorizing passengers to obtain rail tickets if needed. Indeed, in the days of TWA predecessor TAT, its pilots joked the letters meant "Take A Train."

———◆———

Except for the Ford Trimotor, dubbed the Tin Goose, early airplanes were made with wood, which could mean nicer interior features. One 18-seater in 1932 was the first ever to have reclining seats. However, with the 1933 death of Notre Dame football coach Knute Rockne in an air crash, wood lost its allure; rot had weakened his plane's wing spars. All new airliners after that were built of metal.

———◆———

Northeast Airlines (merged into Delta in 1972) got its start in 1933 as Boston and Maine Airways, a subsidiary of Boston and Maine Railroad Company. The company's first headquarters were in a hangar in a hayfield at Scarboro, Maine. The carrier's first flights were operated under contract by National Airways whose founders included Amelia Earhart.

———◆———

By 1935, it took about five and a half days to fly from London (Croydon Airport, the base for the national carrier) to Delhi, India, at a cost of £95 "inclusive of all accommodations, meals, surface transport, and tips en route." Flights aboard Imperial Airways (now British Airways) departed at midday on Tuesdays and Saturdays, arriving in the mornings India time of the following Mondays and Fridays, respectively. There were several hotel stays en route, but the service from Paris to Brindisi, Italy, was by rail. After Brindisi, there were 11 fueling stops (including the overnights) before Delhi.

In 1934, TWA had America's fastest transcontinental service. Flying DC-2s, it traveled across the U.S. eastbound in 15 hours and 20 minutes; westbound required two more hours. However, the new aircraft had a few problems, not least a leaky cockpit windshield. Pilots traveled with raincoats in case of rain.

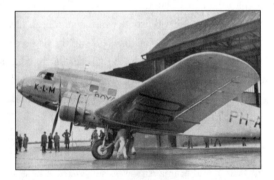

In the early 1930s, with a slow-moving and relatively obsolete fleet, American Airlines was subject to some wisecracking from its own pilots. Its advertising slogan was "From coast to coast and from Canada to Mexico." In the pilots' version, it was "From coast to coast via Canada and Mexico." No wonder then that, in late 1934, a very determined American Airlines president named C.R. Smith placed a person-to-person telephone call to Donald Douglas, Jr., in California to convince the aircraft maker to design and build a new plane. It took lots of cajoling and several promises during a call that was so long it cost $335.50 because Douglas was convinced Smith's envisioned plane was impossible to build — and, besides, his plant was already swamped with work.

What did Smith want? He wanted a plane that would not require more than three refueling stops on a transcon flight. He wanted planes for daytime service that accommodated 21, and planes that could sleep 14 during night flights. That's the story (short version) of how the DC-3 was born. More than 10,000 were built by end of production in 1946.

———◆———

To get to Durban, South Africa, from London by Empire flying boat in 1938, passengers started their journey at the Waterloo train station and overnighted in Southampton, England, the night before they first got on a plane. The flying boat stopped 19 times, including the overnight stops, before arriving in Durban. For this trip, Imperial Airways (now British Airways) charged £125 for five nights' accommodations (including one night at the Grande Bretagne in Athens), meals, ground transportation, and tips.

———◆———

London-Sydney air service in 1938 involved 35 stops en route, including nine hotel nights. Air fares included hotels, meals, and gratuities. Airline timetables also described these terms: Britain's Imperial Airways and Australia's Qantas Empire Airways advised passengers they could book seats with a 25 percent down payment, but seats would be guaranteed on full payment of the fare. Each passenger was entitled to 100 kg for personal weight and baggage. The average passenger weighing 75 kg could carry 25 kg in baggage, it said, whereas free baggage allowance decreased as personal weight increased. However, passengers weighing more than 85 kg (187 pounds) were allowed 15 kg (33 pounds) regardless of their size.

A 1939 report in the Imperial Airways Gazette chirped on about the Empire flying boat, saying it offered a degree of freedom that was "quite astonishing" due to its height of nearly 30 feet and the plane's length; a passenger could walk "in a straight line" for up to 60 feet. Further, the Empire's high-powered engines enabled the plane to leave "any marine landing ground, even in the teeth of a gale." That must have been a comfort.

Pan American launched jet service in the United States on October 26, 1958, with Boeing 707s between New York and Paris. However, BOAC (now British Airways) was first with jet flights, launching in 1952 with service between London and Johannesburg, South Africa, aboard the de Havilland Comet I, on service that took 23 hours, 38 minutes including stops. Comet I was grounded because of a poor safety record, and BOAC later launched transatlantic service on the improved Comet 4 jet, opening dramatically with two planes flying simultaneously from London and New York on October 4, 1958. Thus, the British carrier beat Pan American by three weeks as the first jet operator on the North Atlantic. (For the record: The Soviets also introduced jet service before America, in 1956, using the Tu-104, but the plane was a converted bomber and an unsuccessful venture.)

Air France and British Airways launched — and closed — the supersonic age by operating the Concorde, which flew at twice the speed of sound. The plane was created in a French-British collaboration. The countries' national carriers inaugurated supersonic service simultaneously on January 21, 1976, and retired their aircraft from regular commercial service just over 27 years later. Air France's first commercial Concorde service operated from Paris to Rio de Janeiro, Brazil, via Dakar, Senegal, and British Airways operated first from London to Bahrain on the Arabian Peninsula. The first transatlantic Concorde service was a double header, with Air France and British Airways flights from Paris and London ending with simultaneous landings at Washington's Dulles Airport on May 24, 1976. For a brief spell, from early 1979 to mid-1980, the aircraft flew domestic U.S. routes, subsonically, on Washington-Dallas service operated by Braniff. By 2003, after only one fatal crash in its history (in 2000), the Concorde was serving only New York. Air France concluded its service on May 31, 2003. And the last scheduled flight of them all touched down at London's Heathrow on October 24, 2003. Air France retired five of the needle-nosed aircraft, British Airways seven.

Aircraft are not allowed to fly over the Taj Mahal.
The no-fly path is meant to reduce pollution around this
treasure in Agra, India.

The Empire State Building in New York was hit by an airplane
in 1945. When a B-25 bomber slammed into the 79th floor,
an engine plunged down an elevator shaft, and 11 people plus
the plane's crew were killed. However, all things considered,
the damage was minor. The building was not constructed
with collisions in mind, but it was designed to function as a
lightning rod for its neighborhood, and it is struck about
100 times a year. Would fewer tourists go to the top if they
knew that?

The Commuter Club, created in 1972 by the now-defunct
Bar Harbor (Maine) Airlines, is believed to have been the
first-ever airline frequent-flyer program. Passengers were issued
a card that was punched each time they flew; after 10 flights,
they got a free flight on one of the carrier's routes in the U.S.
Northeast. Frequent-flyer programs as we know them today

originated with American's AAdvantage in 1981. The airline would have preferred to reward passengers based on how much money they spent rather than miles flown, but American did not have the technology at the time to track spending.

———◆———

Southwest Airlines is the largest carrier in the United States if you consider only domestic air service. During 2006, the airline carried 96.3 million domestic passengers.

———◆———

The Hong Kong International Airport passenger terminal, which debuted in 1998, is the world's largest airport building and the world's largest enclosed public space. It extends three-quarters of a mile from the entrance to the opposite end, and it encompasses a floor area of 5,920,127 square feet or 135.85 acres. This space includes a shopping mall of 419,791 square feet (that's 9.6 acres). Facilities include 288 check-in desks, 206 immigration counters, 98 elevators, 70 escalators, 15,000 seats, 9,900 baggage trolleys, and more than 2,000 flight display boards. The 24-hour operation employs around 45,000 people, has a capacity to handle 49 flights per hour, and ultimately expects to accommodate up to 87 million passengers a year.

———◆———

The late Najeeb Halaby, who was president and then chairman of Pan American from 1969 to 1972, has a more famous daughter. She is Queen Noor, who was married to Jordan's late King Hussein.

———◆———

Emirates, the airline based in Dubai on the Arabian Peninsula, is the fastest growing air carrier in the world. It plans to add at least one new aircraft to its inventory per month for the rest of this decade.

———◆———

Travia

Boeing's jumbo jet, the 747, was designed with a hump on top to accommodate the cockpit above the plane's fuselage and make it easier to load cargo through the craft's nose. The device also created more space for cargo. The expectation was that the 747 (first operated by Pan Am on January 22, 1970, New York to London) would eventually become a freighter after all airlines switched to supersonic craft for passenger service. In the early designs, the hump was much smaller than the trademark hump travelers recognize today; it was Pan Am founder Juan Trippe who suggested expanding the hump to house a lounge or first class seating. And the rest is history (so is supersonic transport).

When American Airlines announced in late 2004 that it would remove pillows from all of its MD80 aircraft, it said the move would save the line nearly $300,000 a year in cleaning and replacing pillows. Also, the move would save time in readying planes for their next departures. The MD80s, representing nearly half the carrier's entire fleet, are used primarily on short flights.

Winging It

The world's top 10 airports (by number of passengers) in 2006, based on preliminary figures, were as follows: Atlanta, 84.8 million; Chicago O'Hare, 76.2 million; London Heathrow, 67.5 million; Tokyo Haneda, 65.2 million; Los Angeles, 61.0 million; Dallas/Fort Worth, 60.1 million; Paris de Gaulle, 56.8 million; Frankfurt, 52.8 million; Beijing, 48.5 million; and Denver, 47.3 million.

———◆———

In 2001, El Al became the first airline in the world to launch a frequent-flyer program for pets. The program, called El Al Points for Pets, lets cats and dogs earn points redeemable by the animals for free travel.

———◆———

Airline frequent-flyer programs are considered the biggest barrier to the entry of competitive (read: low-fare) new airlines in the United States. The oldest and best-known of the current programs (AAdvantage) was the brainchild of Thomas Plaskett, who was American Airlines' senior vice president of marketing when AAdvantage was launched. It is a fine irony that in a later life, as a cofounder of the now-defunct Legend Airlines, Plaskett learned just how effective his baby had become.

———◆———

Air Canada was the first carrier to introduce a systemwide nonsmoking policy for its flights, effective December 7, 1987.

———◆———

Charles Lindbergh didn't just fly planes — he designed them, beginning with the Spirit of St. Louis, the plane he flew to Paris in 1927. On that aircraft, the fuel tanks were located in front of the cockpit for safety in case of an accident, but this meant Lindbergh could not see directly ahead except through a periscope or when he turned the plane to look out a side window. Besides personally pioneering many Pan Am and TWA routes, he supervised designs for Pan Am's transocean Clippers and influenced TWA's design for the DC-1. After World War II, he returned to his Pan Am consultancy (for only $600 a month) and worked on design specs for the 747. Then came the dawn of the supersonic era, and Lindbergh switched sides, as it were: He opposed development of SSTs for environmental reasons.

❖

Air Force One, meaning the aircraft that served U.S. presidents from Richard Nixon to Bill Clinton with one last flight for George W. Bush, is in the Air Force One Pavilion at the Ronald Reagan Presidential Library and Museum in Simi Valley, Calif. It flew its final mission, from Andrews Air Force Base in Maryland to San Bernardino, Calif., on September 8, 2001.

❖

Newfoundland and Labrador, which together constitute a single province in eastern Canada, are one and a half hours ahead of the easternmost U.S. time zone — and closer to Europe. As a result, the province hosted some 4,200 international air passengers beginning Sept. 11, 2001, after U.S. air space was closed to traffic that day.

❖

Until the current decade, the largest plane ever built was the Spruce Goose, completed in 1947 by aviation legend Howard Hughes, who at the time also owned TWA. It is a huge wooden seaplane conceived during World War II for a possible wartime role, and it flew only once, for about one minute. It measures 218 feet six inches long with a wingspan of 320 feet and height of 79 feet, four inches. It can hold 14,000 gallons of fuel.

Now comes the Airbus A380. It is longer at 239 feet six inches, and it carries a whopping 81,890 gallons of fuel. However, the Spruce Goose still has the longest wingspan; the A380's wings extend 261 feet 10 inches. As to height, the Spruce Goose is still taller, but by a mere three inches; the A380 is 79 feet one inch tall. The world's largest passenger airliner seats 555 in a three-class layout that spreads over two decks. In an all-economy configuration, it could take 840 passengers.

During 2006, Southwest Airlines served its passengers 61.5 million cans of water, juice, or soft drinks; 10.9 million alcoholic beverages; 93.8 million bags of peanuts plus a few pretzels (5 million bags); and 35.4 million other snacks. Customers downed all this while the airplanes guzzled 1.6 billion gallons of jet fuel.

During World War II, Pan American flew more than 90 million miles for the U.S. government; trained thousands of pilots, navigators, and mechanics; and built 50 airports in 15 countries.

The British and the French made a bigger splash with supersonic transport, but the Soviets were first to put an SST in the air, on December 31, 1968, two months ahead of the

Concorde. The Tupolev Tu-144, designed to fly faster than the Concorde (Mach 2.3 vs. Mach 2) and to carry more passengers (140 vs. 100), then broke the sound barrier on June 5, 1969, also ahead of the Concorde. However, the Concorde was first with passenger services (January 21, 1976, vs. November 1, 1977), and its commercial life was much longer. Having lost two Tu-144s in demonstration and test flights and lacking rich capitalists to support commercial operations, Aeroflot ceased offering SST services on June 1, 1978, after only 102 scheduled flights. Seventeen Tu-144s had been built; some went to museums, some to scrap. One sits with an Air France Concorde in the Auto & Technik Museum, Sinsheim, Germany.

In 2006, Delta handed out more than 82 million bags of snack items (chips, crackers, granola bars, peanuts, and the like) on its flights.

The U.S. Airline Deregulation Act was signed into law in 1978. In the eight years after that, from 1979 to 1987, there was a 41 percent increase in number of passengers on U.S.

carriers. Revenue passenger miles grew 54 percent in the same period. Deregulation produced an explosion in air travel, right? Think again. In the eight years before deregulation, 1969 to 1977, passenger boardings grew by a comparable 40 percent, according to the Air Transport Association, and revenue passenger miles grew at precisely the same pace: 54 percent.

———◆———

In 1936, United Airlines opened the first kitchen solely for preparation of airline food.

———◆———

Some Aeroflot rides in the 1980s and 1990s were aboard the Antonov aircraft, which were cargo planes converted for passengers. As a result, the traveler boarded at one level, left his carry-on bags on a simple shelf there, and then either walked down a few steps or up a few steps (as in a split-level house) to the seats. Aeroflot had merely installed flooring across the middle of the cargo space and inserted seats, thus creating two-story passenger seating well ahead of the huge Airbus A380. This ad-hoc approach also explains why there were no passenger-controlled reading lights.

———◆———

U.S. domestic air fares, adjusted for inflation and net of taxes, dropped 51 percent between 1980 and 2005.

———◆———

Of the 12 surviving Concorde planes, three are in the United States, one in Barbados and the rest in Europe,
as follows:
* British Airways planes are exhibited by the Museum of Flight, Seattle, Washington, and at the Intrepid Sea, Air & Space Museum, New York City.
* An Air France Concorde is on view at the Smithsonian's National Air and Space Museum Steven F. Udvar-Hazy Center

near Dulles Airport outside Washington, D.C.

* Another British Airways craft is at the Bridgetown Airport in Barbados, in a hanger purpose-built for the Concorde.

* Four additional British Concordes are located at the Bristol Aero Collection, Filton Airport, Bristol, England; Manchester Airport Visitors Park, Manchester, England; Scottish Museum of Flight in East Fortune near Edinburgh, Scotland; and London's Heathrow Airport.

* The four remaining Air France planes are at the Air and Space Museum, Le Bourget Airport, Paris; the Airbus plant in Toulouse, France; the Charles de Gaulle Airport, Paris; and the Auto & Technik Museum, Sinsheim, Germany.

———————

American Airlines operates a New York to Los Angeles flight 21, so named because, at one time, its in-flight menu mimicked the menu at New York's venerated 21 Club.

———————

The first travel agency computerized reservations system was rolled out in early 1976, and that system was American Airlines' Sabre (back when it was used as an acronym, Sabre stood for "semi-automated business research environment"). It is that system, in a later iteration, that provides the underlying technology for one of the nation's largest online agencies, Travelocity.

———————

The world's first airplane, the 1903 Wright Flyer, was built without wheels, except for the flywheel that smoothed the operation of the engine.

———————

When the British Airways Concorde (now on display at the Museum of Flight in Seattle, Washington) made its last trip, it broke a speed record for a transcontinental flight between the two U.S. coasts. It flew from New York's JFK Airport to Seattle in three hours and 55 minutes, and it was able to set the record by flying supersonic over Canada, with permission from Canadian authorities. The aircraft traveled at subsonic speeds over the United States.

The Dallas/Fort Worth Airport in 2005 launched the world's fastest (up to 35 miles per hour) and largest airport train system. Called Skylink, it has 4.81 miles in its route system and 64 trains with the capacity and expectation that it will eventually operate 114 trains.

Northwest Airlines eliminated free pretzels in coach class on all of its domestic flights in June 2005. Those little bags weighed only half an ounce and contained 18 pretzel pieces, but dropping them from the shopping list saves Northwest $2 million a year.

Japan's Kansai International Airport was built on an artificial island created from landfill — and it is sinking. Between the start of construction in 1987 and its debut in 1994, it had sunk nearly 32 feet.

In the years since then, it has sunk 9.5 feet, but the settlement rate is dropping. In 1994, it settled 19.5 inches, and by 2006, that number had fallen to roughly three and a half inches. The island was created over a very soft seabed that was 58.5 feet below the water level, so sinkage was not a surprise.

Amsterdam's Schiphol Airport is not sinking, but it is a bit more than 14.5 feet below sea level, having been built on the bottom of the former Haarlemmer-meer (Haarlemmer Lake).

———◆———

Southwest Airlines, which began testing electronic tickets in September 1994, in January 1995 became the first major U.S. airline to offer the e-ticket option on all of its flights. A lesser-known airline, Utah-based Morris Air, was first to take a stab at ticketless travel in 1993; Southwest bought the carrier later the same year.

———◆———

The United States deregulated the airlines in 1978. In the 1980s, according to retired airline-stock analyst Julius Maldutis, roughly 150 airlines were launched. Only one, America West, survived; then, in 2005, it merged with US Airways and took that line's name.

———◆———

The ski plane — meaning a plane with retractable skis — was invented by New Zealander Sir Henry Wigley. He made his first successful snow landing on the Tasman Glacier one day in 1955. Later the same day, one of his passengers was mountaineer Sir Edmund Hillary (a New Zealander, too, although much more famous).

———◆———

The U.S. Air Transport Association informally clocked 159 U.S. airline bankruptcies between the time the Airline Deregulation Act was signed in late 1978 and the end of 2004. Nearly all of those bankruptcies were, at least initially, Chapter 11 filings meant to give the carriers a chance to reorganize and survive. Not all resulted in liquidation. Although the majority of bankruptcies involved carriers spawned by deregulation, some were established carriers buffeted by it. The list includes old-timers Eastern and Pan American, which failed; TWA, which was purchased after its third Chapter 11 filing; Continental, which twice emerged from bankruptcy; and US Airways and United, which also emerged from bankruptcy. Delta and Northwest later joined this not-so-exclusive club with Chapter 11 filings and have since emerged from bankruptcy, as well.

In 1992, Air Canada became the world's first airline to offer all passengers telephones at arm's reach on all of its planes.

When Japan Airlines officials visited the Boeing plant in Seattle to look at a mock-up of the 747 which was then under development, they asked to see a movie in the plane's projection system. A technician grabbed a handy film and showed "Sands of Iwo Jima."

Some wits call this the duck-suck test, but those who do the work call it the bird-strike test. The U.S. Federal Aviation Administration requires that all aircraft engines be tested to ensure they can withstand a hit from one or more birds while in flight without endangering the aircraft itself. The FAA prescribes what that test should be for each engine, using formulas related to the engine size and its vulnerabilities.

In any case, it works like this: The manufacturer revs up the engine in a "test cell" and, using an air cannon, shoots dead fowl at 180 miles per hour at the new machine, specifically targeting the most vulnerable pieces, after which results are analyzed. For the Boeing 777, for example, Pratt & Whitney tested the machinery once with an eight-pound bird and again with four two-and-a-half-pound birds, the latter with flocks of birds in mind. Before the real-bird test, Pratt & Whitney's preliminary test involves shooting a huge gelatin ball at the engine. Aircraft makers conduct similar tests to determine that cockpit windshields can withstand encounters with birds.

———◆———

Alaska Airlines was the first airline to put a piano on a plane, on April 25, 1958. The piano and a stand-up bar were features of DC-6A service between Seattle, Washington, and Anchorage, Alaska, for about a year.

———◆———

American Airlines polishes its airplanes rather than painting them — and so saves millions on fuel each year. For example, when painted, an MD80 weighs an extra 576 pounds (equal to about four non-fare-paying passengers!). By not painting the 327 MD80s in American's fleet, the carrier is saving about $8,326,572 a year based on spring 2007 fuel prices.

———◆———

When he made his historic nonstop transatlantic flight in 1927, Charles Lindbergh took a slight detour (at 50 feet overhead) to buzz St. John's, Nova Scotia, for no reason except to announce himself. At one point toward the end of the journey, he was flying only five feet above the ocean waves, so close the water sprayed his face. For provisions, his plan was to brown-bag it — figuring if he succeeded, he would not need to feed himself in Paris, and if he didn't make it, he wouldn't need a lot of food either.

———◆———

Just imagine, there was a time when:
* Boeing and United Airlines were the same business. Both were founded by William Boeing, who, after incorporating Pacific Aero Products Company in 1916, renamed it the Boeing Airplane Company a year later. He created Boeing Air Transport in 1927 to carry airmail between San Francisco and Chicago. The combined manufacturing and airline business, which soon included other small airlines, became United Aircraft & Transport Corporation (UATC) in 1929. UATC was split up in 1934 as required by new federal antitrust laws forbidding aircraft makers from owning mail carriers. That made United Airlines a stand-alone operation.
* General Motors controlled Eastern Airlines and owned pieces of TWA and Douglas Aircraft. That came about because, by 1933, GM had bought 51 percent of North American Aviation, which in turn owned Eastern Air Transport (later Eastern Airlines) plus significant interests in Transcontinental

and Western Air, Inc. (T&WA, later TWA) and Douglas. The airlines soon passed into new hands (see below).

* American Airlines was owned by an aircraft manufacturer (there is a theme here). In 1929, the Aviation Corporation (AVCO) was formed to buy up budding aviation companies and, a year later, the airline units were incorporated into American Airways. Because AVCO owned an engine maker and aircraft manufacturer, in 1934 it had to divest itself of its airline, and that's how the airline became American Airlines.

* John Hertz, better known for putting his name on a car rental business, held controlling interest in TWA and tried to buy Eastern Airlines. GM, which had bought Hertz's car rental business in 1926, was set to sell Eastern in 1938 to a group led by Hertz for $3 million. However, Eddie Rickenbacker, who ran the airline, rounded up investors led by Laurance Rockefeller and bought the line for $3.5 million. He became CEO. In the mid-to-late 1930s, Hertz was a major shareholder of T&WA (later TWA), but his clashes with management led carrier president Jack Frye to entice a new investor. By 1940, Howard Hughes had bought the company which he owned and controlled for 25 years. (In later fun twists, Hertz Corp. also was briefly owned by an airline — United — in the 1980s and, more recently, was owned by another car company, Ford.)

———————

The new (2005) Central Japan International Airport (Centrair) is half-owned by private corporations and expects to earn at least half its revenue from non-airline activities. We knew airports were becoming shopping malls (think London Heathrow, Dubai, Hong Kong, Johannesburg, etc.), but Centrair adds to that fine dining, a wedding venue, dental clinic, health clinic, and the world's first Japanese-style onsen (natural hot springs spa) at an airport. Bathers can watch planes take off and land through an all-glass roof.

———◆———

A jet taking off on a transatlantic journey uses more fuel in the first three minutes than Charles Lindbergh burned on his entire solo trip from New York to Paris. The Spirit of St. Louis was carrying 450 gallons.

———◆———

Alaska Airlines in 2003 was the first carrier to offer in-flight entertainment on a gadget called the APS digEplayer, a portable, handheld audio/video-on-demand device about the size of a DVD player that delivers first-run movies, TV shows, and other programming.

Alaska had the inside track on this one: The device was invented by one of its own, Bill Boyer, a ramp service agent who has since left the airline to pursue his new line of work marketing the digEplayers. Boyer had previously invented a safety bumper for Alaska Air's belt loaders to protect the aircraft.

———◆———

It was typical to launch a new air service in the 1920s by breaking a bottle over the aircraft, much in the way a ship is christened today. However, in the United States, it was Prohibition, so we read of planes being inaugurated with orange soda, grape juice, ginger ale — anything to deliver a nice fizz.

Delta employees were so pleased no jobs were lost due to the 1982 air traffic controllers strike and other difficult economic circumstances that they raised $30 million through payroll deductions to buy Delta's first 767.

TWA was the first airline to configure its planes with two classes of service and charge two prices. That was in 1955, when the carrier put 12 coach seats in the front of a Lockheed Constellation; they were in the forward section because those were the worst seats in the house, opposite the propellers. First class, at the back and farther from the noise, accounted for about 50 seats. First class went to the front with the introduction of jet service in 1958 when, for U.S. domestic service, there were 56 first class and 56 coach seats in a standard Boeing 707 configuration. For international, the configuration called for only 40 first class seats but 72 for coach.

BOAC (now British Airways) had previously introduced tourist class air service between London and three North American points (Boston, Montreal, and New York), but passengers who paid the new, lower air fare traveled on different planes from those used for first class travel. BOAC proudly noted at the time (1952) that a steward and a stewardess were "in attendance" on each tourist flight.

Winging It

In 1958, at the dawn of the jet age, Pan American's Stratocruiser took 18 and a half hours to fly from London to New York, with a stop in Keflavik, Iceland. Jet service knocked about two-thirds the time off that. Then, there was the safety dividend: When jet service was introduced, one aviation observer predicted that by the turn of the century (meaning the most recent turn), we would see 10,000 air crash fatalities a year worldwide. The projection was based on the pre-jet death rate and an assumption the casualty rate would remain constant as traffic rose. Today, the odds of having a safe flight in the United States are 99.99998 percent.

By the second quarter of 2007, 72.5 percent of Southwest Airlines' passenger revenue was generated by online bookings at Southwest.com, making that site No. 1 in the aviation industry for online revenue.

Virgin Atlantic Airways is the only carrier to offer on-board massages to passengers. On flights to and from London's Heathrow Airport, passengers in Upper Class (that's first class) have the option of a hand or back massage, at the passenger seat or in a dedicated therapy area.

In late 2006, Alaska Airlines replaced its 2,500 in-flight beverage carts with units that are lighter by 20 pounds. As a result, the carrier expects to save $500,000 a year in fuel costs.

———•◆•———

There are at least 17 men, other than the Wright brothers, for whom claims have been made — and in some cases, continue to be made — that they invented a heavier-than-air machine that could be controlled by a pilot (in other words, the airplane).
The Smithsonian Institution had been so determined that Samuel Pierpont Langley, a former secretary of the institution, had built the first machine "capable" of flight that the Wrights' invention spent 20 years at the Science Museum in London.
The Smithsonian in 1942 acknowledged the Wrights as the airplane's inventors, after which Orville Wright approved returning the 1903 aircraft (the Wright Flyer) to the United States and gave it to the Smithsonian. Delayed by World War II, it did not arrive until late 1948.
As the Smithsonian Institution prepared to celebrate in 1948 its installation of the Wright brothers' plane, planners called Johnny Moore in North Carolina, who as a teenager had witnessed the famous 1903 flight at Kitty Hawk. When asked if he would like to attend the ceremony and see the plane again, he drawled, "I seen it once. The day it flew."

———•◆•———

The 1920s silent film "The Lost World" was the first movie ever shown on an airplane. The 90-minute U.S.-made movie was aired on April 7, 1925, aboard a flight from Croydon Airport (London) to Paris, operated by Imperial Airways (now British Airways) in a converted Handley Page bomber. Based on a book by Sir Arthur Canon Doyle, it was the story of presumed-extinct dinosaurs found to be alive in South America. (Sound familiar?) Transcontinental Air Transport

(TAT), which became TWA, was the next and first in the
United States to show in-flight films, turning to newsreels and
cartoons aboard a nine-hour flight from Columbus, Ohio, to
Waynoka, Oklahoma, on October 8, 1929. The Imperial and
TAT forays into in-flight entertainment were gimmicks and
seldom repeated.

In 1961, TWA became first in the world to show movies
on jets, and they were standard fare. Concerned about
propriety in the air, TWA's movie selection committee relied
on recommendations by Parents Magazine and the Catholic
Legion of Decency. The first movie selected? Alfred Hitchcock's
"The Birds," which produced its own kind of furor by scaring
the wits out of half the passengers.

———◆◆———

As of 1929, about 80 major U.S. companies allowed some
employees to put the cost of air tickets on their expense reports.

———◆◆———

Airline frequent-flyer programs have effectively converted
airline miles into a pseudo-currency. Passengers sell them
(although they are not supposed to), and the airlines sell them
to a wide range of "partners" who then dangle those miles
as part of special promotions for everything from cereal to

a mortgage. Some customers know how to "invest" in the new currency, too. Take the entrepreneurial shopper whom American Airlines executives fondly dub the Pudding Guy. When a Healthy Choice promotion offered 1,000 miles for every 10 UPC symbols, he spent $3,140 on Healthy Choice pudding cups. That earned him more than 1.25 million miles, worth $25,000 in air tickets.

———◆———

In the days of the Soviet Union, airline and rail schedules and tickets were based on Moscow time, no matter where the plane or train started or ended its journey. Tourists wouldn't have known; they did not see their tickets, but tour operators sometimes had to deal with the practice. One U.S. tour operator asked a Soviet official, "Why is everything on Moscow time?" His response: "Why not?"

Chapter 5

This 'n' That

There was a time when the words "rolling stones" really meant something, to wit:

* There are more than 2.3 million limestone blocks in the Great Pyramid in Giza outside Cairo; they average 2.5 tons each, but some blocks in the interior weigh up to nine tons. Egyptians placed these monster blocks in place between 2600 and 2500 B.C.

* The largest of several dozen sandstones at England's Stonehenge is 30 feet long and weighs nearly 50 tons. The last of the huge oblong stones was moved into place on the Salisbury Plain sometime before 1600 B.C.

* Sacsayhuaman, the remains of a humongous fortress-like temple overlooking Cuzco, Peru, was built by the Incas with outsized stones honed to fit together perfectly without mortar. The stones measure up to more than 16 feet tall and weigh an estimated 100 tons to about 138 tons. Laborers undertook the project in the 15th century without benefit of the wheel.

* The largest stones in Jerusalem's Western Wall are estimated to weigh 400 to 540 tons. The wall was part of the Second Temple, built 2,000 years ago.

This 'n' That

Here are cell phone holders with a twist. In Oman, tourists can buy woven holders, decorated with classic Bedouin designs. In South Africa, the Ndebele women — noted for their vividly colored beaded accessories (as well as wide brass bands on their necks and legs) — make beaded phone holders in their traditional colorful geometric patterns.

Auckland in New Zealand has the largest Polynesian population of any city in the world (more than 315,000) and the highest number of boats per capita (roughly, one for every 18 people).

New York City gained legislative approval in 1853 to seize land and create Central Park. The largely man-made landscape took approximately 20,000 workers 20 years to complete. The 18 original gates to this walled park have names, but only three are identified (Engineers', Inventors', and Mariners').
Now at 843 acres, the park is considerably larger than Monaco, which even after growing its space with landfill still occupies only 485 acres.

If Frederic Auguste Bartholdi, the sculptor who created the Statue of Liberty, had realized his first dream for a great lady, she would have held her torch high at the entrance to the Suez Canal. She also would have been wearing a veil. Lucky for New York City, that plan collapsed (for financial reasons).

Panama hats are made in Ecuador. The misnamed headgear was popular with workers who built the Panama Canal; when Theodore Roosevelt visited the site, he named the hats.
The fiber for the hats comes from the jungle, but the center of hat production is Cuenca, an Andean city in Ecuador at 8,468 feet above sea level. Hat styles and colors range widely, as do

the prices — from $10 to hundreds of dollars. Price is dictated by the quality of the fiber and the weaving itself. The very finest can be rolled into tubes without damage to their underlying shape. On the Web, Panama hats are offered for as much as $3,000 — some carrying a "made in Italy" label.

"Gosudarstvenny universalny magazin" means "state department store" in Russian. The Moscow store is better known to tourists as GUM (pronounced goom). No wonder.

Some of our favorite fairytales are anchored in real places, if not real events (as far as we know). Sababurg Castle in Germany's Reinhard Forest was "Sleeping Beauty's" castle, and it was from a tower at Trendelburg Castle, which overlooks Trendelburg, Germany, that "Rapunzel" let her long hair down.

Cyprus is the only country in the world with a map of itself on its flag.

———◆———

Kansas City, Missouri, travel agent Kathy Sudeikis is constantly testing the customer loyalty program at the Ritz-Carlton hotel chain. When she filled out a form that asked her to list her service preferences, she asked for rocks in her pillows. To this day, without fail, when she stays at a Ritz-Carlton, there are rocks somewhere in her pillows. For the rest of us in the West, a pillow means a cushion that provides a soft — maybe feather-filled — resting place for our heads.

Traditional "pillows" can be something else. In East Africa, souvenir shops sell local head rests that are in fact neck rests. They look like small wooden stools, and some are covered with leather and decorated with beads. In another variation available in China, the pillow is really a prettily decorated lacquered box, also with the depression to accommodate the neck. The reason for a box is to give the owner a safe place to store valuables while he sleeps. Also, in China and Southeast Asia, the pillow can be a considerably more comfortable frame made of bamboo or rattan, with a depression at the center for the neck. These are sold on the Internet, and they have appeal — the open weave keeps the head cool at night or during a day at the beach.

———◆———

There are no national holidays in the United States. Congress determines holidays for the District of Columbia and federal employees; the states do the rest.

———◆———

When the world's largest Buddhist temple, Borobudur in Indonesia, was restored after centuries of abandonment and encroachment by jungle, one large section had to be dismantled and reconstructed. This meant removing one million stone blocks, tracking each in a computer, cleaning the blocks, and then reassembling them exactly as they were found.

———◆———

Barbados is the only country outside the United States where this claim can truly be made: George Washington slept here. That's because the first president left his homeland only once, to spend a few weeks in Barbados at the age of 19 in 1751, caring for his older half-brother Lawrence Washington who had tuberculosis. The brothers rented the Bush Hill House to be their home away from home. Now it is called the George Washington House and has undergone restoration to convert it into a tourist attraction.

The Barbados climate was not enough to rout entrenched disease: Lawrence died in 1752.

———◆———

Tax avoidance is as old as taxes. In the Old Town of Riga, Latvia, visitors see an otherwise lovely 15th-century home built with numerous tiny slits for windows. That's because there was a tax on light — meaning the natural sunlight that could get into a home. In the 17th century, the builder of the next house over skipped the windows and painted them on, like trompe l'oeil. The two houses are part of a set called the Three Brothers. England imposed its version of this real estate tax based on the number of windows (rather than their size) at each residence. The law was effective from 1697 to 1851 and has left traces in the form of bricked-up windows in some older houses.

The first person to go over Niagara Falls in a barrel was a woman, Anna Edson Taylor, a former school teacher from Bay City, Michigan, who made the plunge on her 63rd birthday. That was 1901. A poor widow, she was driven by poverty (not unruly students). She survived, but she did not reap the financial windfall she sought.

Since then, another 15 have gone over the falls as a gimmick, and five died in their attempts.

The Roman theater in Jerash, Jordan, is noted for its acoustic design. By standing at the midpoint of the orchestra and facing the seats, a speaker will hear his naturally amplified voice bounce back from all directions. Take one step away from the midpoint, and that effect disappears.

It is a commonplace that one in every five miles of the Eisenhower Interstate Highway System had to be straight so those patches could be used as airstrips in case of war or emergencies. Not so, says Richard Weingroff of the Federal Highway Administration's (FHA) Office of Infrastructure. Such a rule is simply not part of the 1956 act that launched what became a 42,800-mile highway system.

The originator of this "Internet myth" might have been confused by a program operated during World War II by the Army Air Force and the FHA under which they maintained a number of flight strips meant for use by bombers and in emergencies. The strips were located for easy access to public highways, but not as part of the highways.

Teff, unique to Ethiopia and on display in its open-air markets, is one of the smallest grains in the world. Measuring only 1/32 of an inch in diameter, it takes 150 teff grains to equal a kernel of wheat. It is used to make injera, which is a grayish, rubber-textured bread. The bread is used in place of silverware to scoop up food, usually a spicy stew.

Leonardo da Vinci is so closely associated with his most famous works — "Mona Lisa," hanging in the Louvre in Paris, and "The Last Supper," painted on what was once a lunchroom wall in the Church and Dominican Convent of Santa Maria delle Grazie in Milan, Italy — that few realize he considered himself an engineer.

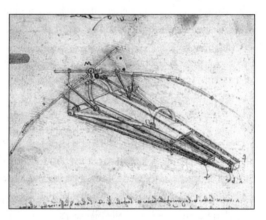

In that context, his drawings include his visions for flying machines. He focused on ornithopters, meaning devices designed to imitate the flapping wings of birds, intended to be powered by humans. Da Vinci also drew designs for helicopters and parachutes.

The original drawings are usually displayed only in special exhibits. The National Museum of Science and Technology in Milan, Italy, displays copies of relevant da Vinci drawings alongside seven machines built to reflect da Vinci's plans (that is not to say the machines would have worked). The "Flying Machine With Manoeuverable Wingtips" is among those machines. Da Vinci's flying machines did not go anywhere, but Rome's Leonardo da Vinci Airport is named for their creator.

———◆◆◆———

The name "Big Ben" does not, as is often thought, refer to the big clock tower attached to the Parliament Building in London. The name refers to the 13-ton bell inside the tower that was named after Sir Benjamin Hall, the first commissioner of works. Cast in 1858, it is nine feet in diameter and seven-and-a-half feet tall. The clock is huge, too: Its minute hand is 14 feet long, and the figures on the face are two feet high.

———◆◆◆———

In Bulgaria, it is a customary gesture of hospitality to greet guests at the door with a loaf of bread. Visitors tear off pieces and dip them in salt before eating them.

———◆◆◆———

At least since the 15th century, black has been the color of choice for Venice's ubiquitous gondolas. For one thing, in earlier times, the boats were sealed with pitch to keep them watertight. Given that the pitch was black, it was easiest to paint them black, too.

But, by the 17th century, with noble families competing vigorously to see who could create the fanciest gondolas, the city passed a law requiring that all gondolas, except a few for dignitaries, be black. The average gondola, if it remains in active use in Venice, lasts about 20 years, but the world's oldest — dating from about 1850 — is in the Mariners' Museum in Newport News, Virginia.

<hr>

The marula tree, a member of the mango family, grows wild in subequatorial Africa and produces a fruit used for jams and potent beers and wines. Tourists are frequently told the fruit, which is demonstrably popular with elephants and baboons, makes the large mammals tipsy, but level-headed observers demonstrate that this is not possible because the elephants are too big and baboons eat their fruit fresh, not fermented. For humans, it is another matter. The fruit is the base for Amarula Fruit Cream Liqueur, a South African export, and it goes down just as easily as Bailey's Irish Cream.

<hr>

Mummies lie in open coffins at St. Michan's Church in Dublin, Ireland. A likely 19th-century visitor to the crypt would have been the creator of the fictional Dracula, Bram Stoker, whose relatives were buried at St. Michan's. Local lore holds that he was transfixed by the sight of mummies in their coffins, something that may have influenced his fiction later.

Amman, Jordan's capital city, was called Philadelphia from the third century B.C. until the seventh century A.D.

———◆———

Like his predecessors, Ethiopia's Emperor Menelik II moved his capital (often better described as a royal camp) from place to place. The nomadic lifestyle was largely driven by the need for firewood. Finally, in the 1880s, when once again wood grew harder to supply to a growing capital on Entoto Mountain, the royal center was moved a short distance to a new site at Addis Ababa.

By the late 19th century, this place, too, was considered doomed, and in 1900, Menelik began construction of the next capital, called Addis Alem, about 25 miles west. However, considering so much had been invested in Addis Ababa, foreign legations and even the empress protested a move, and Menelik gave up his plan.

In reality, Addis Ababa was saved by something else: the importation of Australia's fast-growing eucalyptus tree. So many of the foreign trees were planted that the city in time was referred to as Eucalyptopolis.

———◆———

Among the Maori, the indigenous people of New Zealand, the word for tourists is "te hunga topoi." Translation: "people who go around being amazed at what they see."

———◆———

J.R.R. Tolkien visited Cheddar, England (where cheddar cheese was born), on his honeymoon in 1916. He visited the nearby Cheddar Caves, which are noted for their fantasyland interiors, and used one of the caves as his inspiration for Helm's Deep in "Lord of the Rings." The caves are open to tourists today, too.

———◆———

Travia

St. Cross Hospital in Winchester, England, is Britain's oldest charitable institution, dating from the 12th century. It is the only place in England that still provides the "wayfarer's dole," a source of sustenance intended for weary travelers. Visitors must ask for it with these words: "May I have the wayfarer's dole?" The payoff is a bit of bread and small tumbler of ale.

———◆———

The Welsh village Hay-on-Wye counts at least 38 bookstores or about one for every 38 residents. Among them, the stores stock more than a million books and give the village grounds to claim it is the secondhand book capital of the world. In the spring, Hay-on-Wye hosts a book festival called (more formally) the Guardian Hay Festival of Literature.

———◆———

Rome's popular Spanish Steps were a gift to the city from the French. Why not the French Steps? The steps are near the Spanish embassy.

———◆———

Building a town or city on or near seven hills has auspicious meaning for many — not least because that most famous city on seven hills, Rome, was the heart of one of the greatest empires in history.

A number of other cities either describe themselves or are described by their fans as cities on seven hills. Among them are Amman, Jordan; Edinburgh, Scotland; Istanbul, Turkey; Kampala, Uganda; Lisbon, Portugal; Macau, China; Prague, Czech Republic (some boosters claim the Czech city was built on nine hills); and Sheffield, England.

Smaller places claim the benefits of seven hills, including Guaranda, Ecuador (which claims the association because it is surrounded by seven hills); Veszprem, Hungary; and San Fernando, the Philippines (in the province of La Union).

In the United States, Cincinnati, Ohio, and Richmond, Virginia, by tradition have claimed to be cities on seven hills although both sit on considerably more hills (plateaus in the case of Cincinnati) and cannot identify the presumed original seven. (In fact, Richmond's earliest development was along the James River; it is worth noting, nevertheless, that Patrick Henry was standing on one of the city's hills when he urged, "Give me liberty or give me death!")

San Francisco also carries the sobriquet "city on seven hills," but points to seven principal hills, rather than striving to identify seven original hills among its 40 or so.

Smaller U.S. towns to make the claim include Rome, Georgia (it got its name because of its hills), and Lynchburg, Virginia (which can name its original seven).

Some town founders simply took the name Seven Hills, as happened in Ohio and Australia's New South Wales.

———◆———

Under the municipal law of each capital city, buildings in certain areas of Amman, Jordan, and in Jerusalem must be faced with their local stone. In Amman, the building code says the stone facades must be white. In Israel's capital, the area's cream-colored limestone is so identified with the city that it is called "Jerusalem stone." In both cases, the buildings' gentle colors mellow with age so that the cities take on a lush golden hue at sunset.

Among Native Americans, it is impolite to point with the index finger. Among the Lakota, it is OK, though not preferred, to point with the thumb or little finger, but never at a person. Instead, a polite person would indicate a direction or single out a person by pursing the lips and pointing with the eyes or by nodding in the desired direction.

Central City, Colorado, long a popular "ghost town" on the tourist circuit, is located within the so-called "richest square mile on Earth" because the ground yielded a half billion dollars' worth of gold in the town's heyday. Today's "gold rush" is fueled by gambling which became legal there in 1991.

Cafe society was born at Le Procope, a restaurant that still stands on rue de l'Ancienne-Comedie in Paris. It was Paris' first cafe in 1686, and soon after, it was popular with literary and political movers and shakers. Its patrons have included Balzac, Benjamin Franklin, Victor Hugo, Robespierre, Rousseau, Voltaire, and even Napoleon.

In the United States and many parts of the world, the handshake is a typical form of greeting. Overseas, travelers may see other traditions.
The bow that is traditional for Japanese is probably the best-known alternative greeting. In other examples, on special occasions, the Chinese may greet by putting their two hands together in a manner resembling, to Western eyes, hands held in prayer. New Zealand's Maori, in certain circumstances,

welcome guests by touching noses; by doing so, they are said to exchange the breath of life. And, among Kenya's Masai people, elders greet women and children by placing their right hand on the head of each woman or child.

———◆———

When they perform war dances, New Zealand's original inhabitants, the Maori, stick out their tongues, but that is no laughing matter. Historically, Maori were cannibals, and the tongue is meant to tell the enemy, "You would taste good."

———◆———

Babe Ruth hit his first professional home run on September 15, 1914, in a minor league game at Hanlan's Point Stadium in Canada's Toronto. These days, Hanlan's Point, which is an island in Lake Ontario near the city's harbor, has a sanctioned nude beach, but it is illegal to enter the water without wearing a swimsuit. As if that were not anomaly enough, the water is too polluted for swimming anyway.

———◆———

Tourists who have the opportunity to visit a private home while overseas may be expected to remove their shoes when entering the host's residence. Some countries where this could or will be the case are China, Czech Republic, Denmark, Greenland, India, Japan, Kenya (in some coastal areas), Malaysia, Singapore, Slovakia, South Korea, Tahiti, Taiwan, Thailand, Turkey (in the countryside), and the United States (in Hawaii). In some cases, slippers are offered. Also, shoes come off when entering mosques and the main halls of Buddhist temples.

———◆◆◆———

There is much the world does not know about Greenland:
* Greenlandic, an Inuit language, has more than 40 words for ice. Before Europeans arrived, the language had no numbers beyond 10. Kayak is an Inuit word. There are no past tense verbs in Greenlandic.
* Greenland is about 85% covered with ice, and the ice is 11,000 feet — or more than two miles — deep at its maximum. The world's largest island is, nevertheless, technically a desert.
* The Northeast Greenland National Park is the world's largest national park (375,289 square miles), and it is not accessible to the public.
* There are three stoplights in all of Greenland.

———◆◆◆———

At Boston's Faneuil Hall Marketplace, which attracts more than 15 million visitors a year, one shop — Kilvert & Forbes — was once owned by Senator and former Presidential candidate John Kerry. It still offers sweets based on recipes prepared by Kerry's mother, including the John Kerry Chocolate Fudge Cookie.

———◆◆◆———

Robert McCulloch, the founder of Lake Havasu City, Arizona, paid $2.46 million for the London Bridge in 1968 and relocated its 22 million pounds of granite in 10,276 pieces to his budding city where it was reassembled and dedicated in

1971. In the process, it was declared an antique to avoid import taxes, making it the world's largest official antique.

And it took an act of Congress before McCulloch could put the bridge where he wanted it. He planned to redirect the Colorado River to create a straighter river line, but by law the Colorado could not be redirected except for agricultural purposes. As amended, the law now allows the river to be diverted by a new and narrowly defined group: anyone who plans to put the London Bridge over it.

In the days of the Soviet Union, that vast country was dotted with so-called "antireligion" museums. Even the 19th-century St. Isaac's Cathedral in Leningrad (now St. Petersburg) and the Church of St. Casimir in Vilnius, Lithuania, were turned into anti-God museums.

However, in the last years before the Soviet Union's 1989 collapse, officials stopped showing the museums to tourists because the Soviets' heavy-handed propaganda style was not

Travia

convincing tourists of anything. Foreign visitors laughed
a lot, though.

———◆———

SeeAmerica.org, which represents the entire U.S. travel
industry to the world, suggests with tongue firmly in cheek this
Odyssey across America: Olympia, Washington; Athena and
Troy, Oregon; Iliad, Montana; Athens and Sparta, Wisconsin;
Homer, Ohio; Apollo, Pennsylvania; and Ithaca, New York.

———◆———

A lot of people want to ensure a second visit to Rome and
maybe a little romance in the Italian capital, too. Visitors toss
an average of 500 euros a day into Trevi Fountain, or 182,500
euros (roughly, $277,000) a year.
In 2002, Rome's police arrested a homeless man who (for at
least 20 years) had been scooping the bulk of the money out of
the fountain. Now, the city collects it all, and it goes to the Red
Cross. Also, these days, coin tossing is discouraged because it
damages the marble.

———◆———

Slovakians will have us understand that the inspiration for the
fictional Dracula was a woman, the infamous 17th-century
Hungarian aristocrat Elizabeth Bathory — not the 15th-century
Vlad Tepes, prince of Wallachia in Romania. They have a
point: The "blood countess" tortured some 600 Slovak peasant
women to death and sometimes bit off flesh of her victims.
Ruins of her Cachtice castle, where she was finally imprisoned
for life for her crimes, can be seen outside the Slovak village of
the same name, and there is a museum in town.

———◆———

In Jordan, it is disrespectful to show others the bottoms
of your feet.

———◆———

This 'n' That

Seeing ancient structures in their original colors could be a shock to those of us with 20th- and 21st-century sensibilities, trained to appreciate the muted, even tired, look of monochromatic ruins.

The Temple of Karnak in Luxor, Egypt, was covered with bright colors of the sort seen in the pharaohs' tombs across the Nile. Tour guides can point out fragments of original color. Mexico's Teotihuacan Pyramid was mostly a bright red; there were frescoes and wall paintings, as well. The Palace of Knossos on Crete had plenty of color inside and out, illustrated by a controversial early 20th-century reconstruction of a part of the palace. Visitors can see examples of original color here, too. Paint also adorned parts of buildings that lined Athens' Agora and Rome's Forum.

But what of that glimmering white marble complex atop the Acropolis in Athens? Like other ancient Greek buildings, these were painted with red, blue and gold. The columns were natural; the color appeared instead on statues, such as the figures on the porch of the Erechtheion. Carved figures on the Parthenon's pediments (gables) and on the friezes inside and

outside the building were not merely painted; pieces of bronze were attached to the figures to represent bridles and reins of horses. All this made it easier to see the sculptures at least 40 feet overhead.

Nashville, Tennessee, calling itself the Athens of the South, has an exact replica of the Parthenon in its Centennial Park. Recently, paint was added for greater historical accuracy, most notably on the porch ceiling. Inside is a replica of the Greeks' long-lost statue of Athena. Standing 42 feet tall, the new "Athena" is gilded and painted to look like the original, and that means garish.

———◆———

One of the best-known scenes in the history of movies has Marilyn Monroe trying to keep her skirt down as she walks over sidewalk grating when a subway car passes below. The scene, from the 1955 "The Seven-Year Itch," was shot on one of New York's less-memorable street corners (51st Street and Lexington Avenue) in front of about 1,500 onlookers.

———◆———

The Holiday magazine of June 1959 carried scads of travel ads, naturally, but one promoted trips to Hawaii by sea aboard the Matson Line's Lurline or Matsonia. The fare from California was $145 one way or $260 roundtrip.

Another ad, placed by Chicago-based Caravan Tours, promoted (at $698 to $879) a fully escorted grand tour of Europe, covering 11 countries (starting in England and ending in France). The price included passage to Europe and back, from New York or Montreal, aboard the Empress of Britain, Hanseatic, Homeric, Liberte, Maasdam, Queen Elizabeth, Queen Mary, Ryndam, Statendam, or United States ships. For that summer, the ad listed 31 departure dates, but did not say how long the tour lasted. Assuming it was at least a month (given there were two Atlantic crossings and 11 countries), daily rates would have ranged from around $23 to $29.

Women tourists to Iran cannot disembark from their arriving aircraft unless they are wearing an outer garment such as a raincoat that is dark, loose-fitting, and long enough to reach at least to the knees. Their hair must be covered with a headscarf as well, although it can be brightly colored. Skirts must come to the ankle and be worn with dark socks. These rules apply throughout a trip in Iran.

There are rules for men, too: Wear long pants at all times, shirts that come at least to the elbow, and socks with sandals.

Most Icelanders still use the old Viking patronymics rather than typical surnames. Thus, a man might be Haraldur Magnusson, for son of Magnus, and his wife Helga Jonsdottir, for daughter of Jon, whereas their son's name would end with Haraldsson and the daughter's name with Haraldsdottir or even Helgasdottir. Icelanders also are listed by their first names in their local telephone directories.

In 1900, it cost as little as £7 ($35 based on the exchange rate at the time) for a crossing from the United States to England on a Cunard Line ship, according to Baedeker's "London and Its Environs 1900," a 512-page tome on the city and surrounding areas. The book advised readers to travel with gold rather than bank notes, but urged those who chose paper to keep a list of serial numbers so the notes could be traced if stolen. It reported the availability of public baths, instituted primarily for the working classes, where a cold bath cost one penny. The Baedeker guidebook warned of the hazards of tastings in the wine vaults at the London Docks, adding women were not admitted after 1 p.m. (Reprints of this or similar historic guidebooks are sold at www.oldhousebooks.co.uk.)

———◆—◆—◆———

The first Ferris Wheel was rolled out at the 1893 World Columbian Exhibition in Chicago.

———◆—◆—◆———

Alexandre-Gustave Eiffel is best known as the designer and builder of the eponymous tower in Paris. However, as a specialist in metal construction, he built a range of things, including the iron-columned West Railway Station in Budapest, Hungary, and the interior metal framework for the Statue of Liberty. He also built kits for bridges that were distributed around the world for assembly on site. But he nearly went to prison because of his association with a scandal-ridden French effort to build a Panama canal that failed in 1889, the same year the Eiffel Tower was completed. Eiffel, whose role was to build the locks, was cleared of wrongdoing, but the episode ended Eiffel's career as a builder.

———◆—◆—◆———

Matmata is a region in Tunisia noted for its so-called invisible villages. Residences are hard to spot because they are cave dwellings that are open at the top and look like craters. The hollowed-out craters are surrounded at their below-ground patio levels by living spaces and storage rooms which residents have carved into the earth for their comfort away from the heat. The craters in this arid setting create a lunar landscape that producer Steven Spielberg used to good effect. Parts of "Star Wars" and "Raiders of the Lost Ark" were shot on this turf.

Quebec City boasts its annual Winter Carnival is the world's largest (17 days, 300-plus activities, 1 million visitors). It can also be pretty cold at the January/February event, but some revelers know how to stay toasty. They carry canes — hollow canes that are filled with a potent drink called "caribou." Here's how to make that, if you dare: Open a bottle of red wine and drink two glasses' worth. Then, top off the bottle with a high-proof vodka, four or five tablespoons of maple syrup, and a cinnamon stick. Keep refrigerated a few weeks before drinking, but shake the bottle occasionally.

———◆———

In most of the world, a nod of the head means "yes" or agreement with someone else's remarks. In Albania, Bulgaria, and Greece, the nod means "no."

———◆———

The Paris Catacombs accommodate up to six million dead in long tunnels. In the 18th and 19th centuries, remains were moved from overcrowded cemeteries. Neatly stacked leg bones form dense walls; skulls arranged in eye-catching patterns break up the monotony.

———◆———

An artist from Volterra, Italy, made a name for himself because in the 16th century he was commissioned to paint over the nudity in Michelangelo's "The Last Judgment," the painting on the altar wall of the Sistine Chapel. As a result, the younger artist was called Il Brachettone, which translates as "underwear maker," or loosely, as "underwear guy. " He was known more politely as Daniele da Volterra, for his hometown, and his real name was Daniele Ricciarelli.
However, censors overlooked a 16th century copy of "The Last Judgment," painted by Marcello Venusti. The unretouched copy is at the Capodimonte Museum in Naples.

Chapter 6

Where in the World?

Willemstad, the capital of the Caribbean island of Curacao, is noted for its very colorful colonial town center. The trademark look was created in 1817 when the Dutch Governor Piet Kasteel claimed the glare from the city's white buildings gave him headaches. He ordered up a law requiring that more soothing pastel colors be used on all buildings.

The city also is home to the oldest (1732) synagogue in continuous use in the Western Hemisphere.

The Eiffel Tower, constructed for the 1889 International Exhibition in Paris to commemorate the centenary of the French Revolution, was built to stand for only 20 years and, indeed, it was nearly torn down in 1909. It was saved by its antenna, important at the time for telegraphy. The structure is 984 feet high, with 1,652 steps to the top; it weighs 7,000 tons, and (in the two years it took to build) required 15,000 iron pieces, 2.5 million rivets, and 40 tons of paint. When completed, it inspired howls of protest from some notable Parisians who considered it a metal monstrosity and an offense to good French taste.

Where in the World?

There were at least 41 "original" copies of Magna Carta, or the Great Charter, which established that the English king's power could be limited by a written grant. King John put his seal on an initial document in June of 1215, but multiples were created so the news could be carried to points throughout the English kingdom. Four Magna Cartas survive, each differing slightly from the others in size, handwriting, and text. They can be seen at Lincoln Castle near Lincoln Cathedral; at Salisbury Cathedral, and in the British Library in London, which has two copies.

———◆◆———

The Temple Mount in Jerusalem, Israel's capital, encompasses 35 acres. Similarly, the huge royal complex of the Persian kings at Persepolis in Iran — a city largely destroyed by fire by Alexander the Great — sat on a 35-acre platform. For points of comparison, the Pentagon sits on 34 acres in Arlington, Virginia, and New York's World Trade Center occupied 16 acres. England's Windsor Castle and the Great Pyramid in Giza near Cairo, Egypt, each covers 13 acres.

———◆◆———

The original name of Rome's Colosseum was Flavian Amphitheater. With a capacity for about 50,000 spectators, it was inaugurated in the year 80 with 100 days of festivities, in which 9,000 wild animals — including lions and tigers — were killed and around 2,000 gladiators lost their lives. Animals were brought from basement cages to the arena floor via mechanical elevators. The Colosseum had a retractable canopy to protect the crowds from the glaring sun. An estimated 100 sailors were detailed to maintain the canopy and another thousand to raise and lower it. Construction required about 3.5 million cubic feet of stone, and it took an estimated 200 wagons and 400 oxen working daily for four years to bring the stone from its quarry to the building site. Blocks at the base of the pillars weigh five tons.

With the emperors long gone, stones were being hauled away to build churches and palaces until the Vatican declared the Colosseum sacred because of the Christians believed to have been martyred there. Scholars now believe Christians were martyred elsewhere, not in the Colosseum.

The Cologne Cathedral, started in 1248, took 632 years to complete — and for 282 years of that span, nothing happened. The crane on one tower was a city landmark for 500 years. The spires are 515 feet high, and those "delicate" finials at the tippy-top are 31 feet tall and 15 feet wide. Once the world's tallest building, this cathedral takes up 1,176,300 cubic yards of space and is now described as the largest cathedral in the world with two towers.

It was too late to be the world's tallest building by 1890 when Ulm Cathedral, also in Germany, outdid Cologne with spires stretching up 530 feet. By then, the Eiffel Tower in Paris (1889, 984 feet) was the tallest, but Ulm Cathedral remains the world's tallest cathedral.

Where in the World?

Some things you will want to know about Morocco:

* The so-called "blue men" of the Sahara really are blue. Their skin takes on the color from the dye in their robes.
* Goats graze in trees — at least where they can find the argan tree. They are after the fruit.
* And a signpost in Zagora, which is called the gateway to the Sahara, says Timbuktu in Mali is 52 days away. That's by camel.

———◆◆◆———

The Baha'i Gardens, which brighten a narrow strip on the side of a steep hillside, constitute the most beautiful attraction in Haifa, Israel's third-largest city. The gardens, with formal displays at 19 different terrace levels, lead to and surround a burial site and shrine, built in 1953, to honor the prophet of the Baha'i religion, a 19th-century Iranian known as the Bab. The gardens cost $253 million to build over a 13-year period. Entry is free to tourists (the Baha'is take contributions only from coreligionists). Tourists must visit in groups and typically start at the top, walking 700 steps down through the gardens to reach the shrine, which is about at the half-way point on the hillside. A hundred gardeners tend these lawns and flowerbeds daily, all of them Baha'i volunteers. There are 6 million Baha'is worldwide; 800 are in Israel as volunteers staying for about a year each.

They are not allowed to settle permanently; the fear is they might flock to be near holy sites in such numbers as to endanger the nature of Israel as a Jewish state. The volunteers who care for their holy sites (including another location in Acre) also agree not to proselytize or translate their writings into Hebrew. The Baha'is themselves limit pilgrimage numbers in order to keep the holy sites from being overrun.

———◆◆◆———

Albany, New York's state capital, boasts a 19th-century capitol building that is reminiscent of the Hotel de Ville (city hall) in Paris, and it is one of only nine U.S. state capitols without a dome. When it was built (between 1867 and 1899), the stonemasons left behind sculptures of one another tucked discreetly among the ornate columns.

———◆———

Notre-Dame Cathedral in Paris was used as a warehouse for forage and food during the French Revolution. Some years later, during the Commune of 1871, it was nearly burned by the Communards. It is not a certainty, but some accounts say a mound of chairs was set afire in the cathedral's interior.

———◆———

Nelson's Dockyard in English Harbour on Antigua is the only surviving Georgian dockyard in the world. It is named for Admiral Horatio Nelson, who was commander of the British Royal Navy at English Harbour for three years beginning in 1784. The admiral, better known to us now as Lord Nelson, referred to English Harbour as an "infernal hole," saying it had no shade, too much drink, and too many women. On the other hand, he did encourage music, dancing, and "cuddling with women" to relieve boredom for his men during hurricane season.

When he left the Caribbean in 1787, he was so ill he had a barrel of rum hauled aboard ship to preserve his body in case he died en route home to England. But he died more famously while winning a major victory over Napoleon in 1805 at the Battle of Trafalgar.

———◆◆◆———

The Walt Disney World Resort in Orlando, Florida, encompasses 27,500 acres (roughly 43 square miles), making it nearly twice the size of New York's Manhattan Island (22 square miles).

———◆◆◆———

You could build a day's sightseeing in Vienna around the burial sites of Austria's emperors. The bodies of three centuries' worth of Hapsburgs rest at the Capuchin's Crypt. However, they left their hearts in the crypt of St. Augustine Church, and — there's more — their other internal organs sit in the catacombs of St. Stephen's Cathedral.
It was at St. Augustine Church, by the way, that Napoleon Bonaparte married one of the Hapsburgs, Marie-Louise. However, he did not show up, sending a stand-in for a marriage by proxy. The pair did have a son, Napoleon II, presumably not by proxy. (There also were two more marriage ceremonies in Paris that both attended.)

———◆◆◆———

Ancient Greek architects tricked the eye when building Athens' Parthenon nearly 2,500 years ago. They utilized curves that

counteract the severe and lifeless look of countless long straight lines and perfectly square corners while giving the impression all was straight and square. The marble columns bulge slightly, with the largest diameter about one-third of the way up from the bottom. The horizontal lines — stair steps, beams, and roof line — are curved in a slight dome shape. In addition, the columns incline inward slightly. Therefore, if the columns along the length of the building were extended upwards indefinitely, they would meet when they were 7,218 feet long, or about a mile and a third away from their base. The columns on the building's ends would meet at 16,240 feet, three miles into the sky.

The covered bridges of Madison County in Iowa were already the focus of an annual Covered Bridges Festival before they became a serious tourist attraction after the appearance of the popular 1992 book and 1995 movie, "The Bridges of Madison County." There are six bridges. The Cedar Covered Bridge, which appeared on the cover of Robert James Waller's book, was destroyed by an arsonist in 2002. It had been built in 1883 and restored at a cost of $128,000 in 1998. Madison County rebuilt it in 2004 from the original plans and using authentic materials and methods. The reconstruction cost a little more than $575,000. (Coincidentally, the county seat Winterset is John Wayne's birthplace; the house is a museum.)

Turkey made a lot of history in ancient times and created quite a few tourist attractions in the bargain.

Troy — as in the Troy of the Brad Pitt movie — is identified with a site also called Hissarlik. Gordium, the Phrygian capital, gave us the tale of the Gordian Knot (that Alexander the Great supposedly cut with his sword), and was home to King Midas — as in the fabled "Midas touch." Likewise, Sardis was the capital of Lydia, and Croesus — as in "rich as Croesus" — was its last king. Two of the Seven Wonders of the Ancient World were in Turkey: the Temple of Artemis (built by Croesus) in Ephesus (home of the Ephesians addressed in the Bible) and the Mausoleum at Halicarnassus (now Bodrum).

Turkey was also the birthplace for a wildly varied cast of characters. Aside from Midas and Croesus, there were the poet Homer (who purportedly gave us the "Iliad" and the "Odyssey," assuming he existed), the historian Herodotus (he called Halicarnassus home), St. Paul the Apostle, and St. Nicholas (who became Father Christmas).

A chunk of Turkey's southwestern shore was a wedding gift from Mark Antony to Cleopatra. Today, travelers can visit ruins at Troy (Hissarlik), Gordium, Sardis, and Ephesus, plus the ancient mausoleum in Bodrum, or what was left after it was pilfered to build a crusader castle. But, as a time saver, not to mention a protection for some heritage, many of the best finds from these sites are at the Archaeological Museum in Ankara.

———— •◆• ————

Karlovy Vary (Carlsbad), set prettily in a deep valley in western Czech Republic, preserves dignified classical structures dating from the turn of another century, when the wealthy and

aristocratic made this and nearby spa towns their playground. Karl Marx (no plebe, he) hobnobbed here, too, on three occasions.

———◆———

India's Taj Mahal may look like a palace, but that delicate and rather small (for a palace) white marble structure was commissioned by a brokenhearted Moghul emperor, Shah Jahan, to entomb his beloved queen, Mumtaz Mahal, who died in 1631 giving birth to their 14th child. The emperor later was buried beside his much-mourned queen. In the 1830s, Lord Bentinck, the British governor general, considered dismantling the Taj Mahal and selling the pieces in England.

———◆———

Gabrovo, a small city in Bulgaria, is the laughing stock of the country. The reasons for this, and the corny humor itself, may be a little hard for outsiders to fathom, but it is connected to the alleged miserliness of its citizens. For example, it is said the statue honoring the founder of the city was erected in the local river "to save space." Also, it is said, Gabrovites stop their clocks at night and carry their shoes to save on wear and tear. One joke has a local asking another where his wedding ring is, and the reply: "My wife's wearing it this week." For tourists, guides instruct motorcoach drivers to make several circuits on a roundabout, describing this as "sightseeing the Gabrovo way." But, Gabrovo may have the last laugh: In 1972, it opened a House of Humor and Satire, where exhibits are labeled in English as well as Bulgarian (though they don't always find the English-speaker's funny bone) and the shop sells gag gifts. Also, an International Festival of Humor helps bring visitors to an industrial city that does not appear on tourists' must-see lists.

———◆———

The most fascinating church at Wieliczka, in Poland near Krakow, is 331 feet underground in a salt mine. Chapels and statues of saints and heroes (plus the teardrops on the chandeliers) were all carved out of salt by miners in the 17th century. Soon after, the Polish Crown, which owned the mine, began tourism of a sort. It entertained guests here, mostly royals, with dining and dancing. Today it is open to all of us, and there is a museum of salt mining two levels below the chapel. The Durrnberg salt mine near Austria's Salzburg (which means "salt town") also has a history of entertaining sightseers as early as the 17th century. Initially, the visitors were the elite guests of the archbishop of Salzburg. Today, like guests of old, visitors take a ride across a subterranean salt lake. They also descend into the mine by riding down giant wooden slides, just the way 17th-century miners got to work.

The 17th-century palace of Versailles was built to house the French royal family, 1,000 noblemen, and 4,000 attendants. At its debut, it had no plumbing for toilets or bathing although it opened with a regal collection of gushing outdoor water fountains. Today, it is in the early stages (counting from 2003)

of a top-to-bottom restoration project that is expected to last 17 years and cost 390 million euros (about $592 million). It is a huge undertaking, given there are 700 rooms, 67 staircases, 2,153 windows, and 27 acres of roofing. With its related buildings, gardens, and other grounds, Versailles occupies 2,100 acres.

———————————

Mohenjo Daro, now an archaeological site about 140 miles northeast of Karachi, Pakistan, is deemed by some to be, effectively, the world's first planned city because of the antiquity of a still-obvious orderly town layout as revealed by surviving walls, towers, streets, and drainage systems, all constructed of bricks — thousands of them. Mohenjo Daro, which offers to tourist and scientist alike the most impressive remains of the prehistoric Indus Valley Civilization, thrived from about 2500 B.C. to 1600 B.C.

———————————

Rome's Pantheon, a circular temple built between 120 and 125, is among the best-preserved of ancient Rome's monuments. The building's diameter and height are exactly the same, at 141 feet, nine inches. That is the same as the distance between the Statue of Liberty's sandals and her torch. At its base, the Pantheon's dome is 23 feet thick, but around the 27-foot-wide hole in the center at top, it is two feet thick. The dome required 5,000 tons of concrete. Until the Duomo in Florence, Italy, (143 feet in diameter) was built in the 15th century, the Pantheon also had the largest cupola ever constructed. Its impressive proportions influenced architects through the centuries, including the builders of the U.S. Capitol in Washington (where the dome is smaller at 96 feet in diameter).

———————————

Herewith, a few facts about curious animals that lure us to distant places for a look:

* Australia's best-known marsupials, the kangaroos. The fastest recorded speed for a kangaroo is 40 miles per hour. (But, rest assured, they don't always run like that! They would die of it.)

*The tortoises that gave the Galapagos islands their name ("Galapagos" means saddle, and that is what the tortoises' huge shells resemble). They can live 150 years or more. The largest of these, now deceased, was four feet, 5.5 inches long; three feet, 3.6 inches wide, and two feet, three inches tall; he weighed 920 pounds. There once were 14 tortoise subspecies but now there are 11, including one group with only one survivor.

*China's pandas. They are called "living fossils" because of an evolutionary history extending back more than 2 million years. Bamboo-type plants account for 99 percent of their food, but they are carnivorous, too. They are classified with bears but do not hibernate.

*"Killer whales" (more correctly, the orca). Found along Argentina's Atlantic coast and North America's Pacific coast (among other places), these creatures are carnivorous but they are not whales. They are the world's largest dolphins.

———◆———

Kingston, New York state's first capital, harbors 21 pre-Revolutionary, Dutch-style stone houses. One, built in 1676 and now a museum, was the first meeting site of the New York Senate. Four stone houses sit at the intersection of John and Crown streets, said to be the only place in America where there is an 18th-century stone house on each of four corners. At nearby New Paltz, Huguenot Street is described as the "oldest street in America with its original houses." These survivors, now house-museums, date from 1705 to 1894 and comprise five stone houses, a Federal period house, and a late Victorian house, plus the French Church and graveyard, a carriage museum, and other attractions highlighted in walking tours.

———◆◆———

Some of the world's finest Old Town walls, generally dating from medieval times (sometimes earlier), may be found in Acre and Jerusalem, Israel; Dubrovnik, Croatia; Lucca, Italy, and York, England. In addition, there is Carcassonne, France, a jewel that has a unique system of double fortifications. In all of these cities, visitors can walk on the ramparts.

———◆◆———

The largest ancient structure in sub-Saharan Africa is the Great Enclosure, located in Zimbabwe at the site of the capital of a people who prospered in the 13th to 15th centuries. Elliptical in shape, the stone structure measures close to 328 feet across and 837 feet the long way.

———◆◆———

Where in the World?

Tbilisi, the capital of Georgia (the country) and founded in 458, has been destroyed 29 times. Among those to do the dirty deed, in alphabetical order, were the Arabs, Byzantines, Mongols, North Caucasian tribes, Ottoman Turks, Persians, and Seljuk Turks. No wonder one finds such a diverse collection of Tbilisi buildings: churches dating from as early as the sixth century; a 12th-century monastery; a 19th-century Persian caravanserai, with Russian domes; Turkish baths; a Shiite mosque; the Art Nouveau residence of the former Russian patriarchate, plus a few other palaces; and a Persian fortress that Tbilisi's founder, King Vakhtang, occupied.

———◆◆◆———

Rome's Colosseum, an ellipse measuring 620 feet long and 513 feet wide, was the largest amphitheater in the Roman Empire but far from the only one. Examples can be found as far afield as Amman and Jerash, Jordan; Aspendos, Turkey; Bosra, Syria; Caesarea, Israel; Chester, England; Durres, Albania; El Jem (or El Djem), Tunisia; Lyon and Nimes, France; Plovdiv, Bulgaria; Tarragona, Spain; and Verona, Italy (the setting for "Romeo and Juliet").

Some arenas were free standing, like Rome's, but many were built with an arc-shaped seating area backed up against a hillside. Chester's Roman theater, the largest unearthed in Britain, is only partially excavated. Others are well enough preserved, or restored, to be the settings for theater or other events in modern times. Among the best-preserved and still used today, the Aspendos theater was built to accommodate 15,000. The smaller Caesarea theater hosts an annual opera festival, and the Jerash theater hosts festivals, too. Even Rome's arena reopened as a place of entertainment in 2000 after a 1,500-year break. Plovdiv's theater, built into the side of a hill, was rediscovered in 1972 after a landslide exposed the stones;

it has since hosted theater and opera. The free-standing Verona arena is one of the largest and best-preserved, and as many an opera-lover knows, those old stone seats did not soften over the centuries.

———◆◆———

The first thing and the last thing tourists see in Albania is concrete bunkers. That's because Enver Hoxha, the severely paranoid Stalinist dictator for more than 40 years, ordered the installation of thousands all over the small country on the grounds that the Yugoslavians, then the Greeks, then the British, then the Soviets were about to invade. They required three times as much concrete as France's equally useless pre-World War II Maginot Line. How many are there? Estimates vary from 600,000 to nearly 900,000, and any big number is believable because they are everywhere — at the Tirana Airport, in the fields, lining the roads, in the gardens, in cemeteries, and on the beaches. They are going to be there awhile, too. The bunkers were built to withstand a head-on assault by a tank.

———◆◆———

There is Venice, Italy, and then there are the places that like to be compared to that most popular of all canal cities. To wit:
* Amsterdam, The Netherlands; Bruges (or Brugge), Belgium, and St. Petersburg, Russia — all dubbed Venice of the North.
* Bangkok, Thailand, and Suzhou, China, both called Venice of the East, although the characterization is waning in the case of Bangkok where many canals have been filled in.
* Colmar, France (birthplace of Frederic Auguste Bartholdi, the creator of the Statue of Liberty), called Petite Venice.
* Little Venice, a bucolic area in the middle of London where pieces of the English canal system converge.
* Mopti, Mali, called the Venice of Mali.

* Mykonos, Greece, where a section of the island's capital
is called Little Venice.

Some communities simply adopt the name, as in Venice,
California, and Venice, Louisiana. Much earlier, not long after
the arrival of Europeans in the Western Hemisphere, explorers
found houses sitting over water supported by poles and so
named the area Venezuela, meaning Little Venice.

———◆◆———

Ponte Vecchio was first constructed around 50 B.C. but
appears today as the version completed in 1345. The covered
bridge is the oldest bridge in Florence, Italy, and the only one
to survive World War II bombings.

———◆◆———

Hadrian's Wall, named for the Roman emperor who built it in
122-123, extends for 73.5 miles end to end across the north of
England and was meant to protect Roman Britain from unruly
tribes farther north. At about eight feet thick and 15 feet high,
it linked 16 major forts plus a series of turrets, called mileposts,
as each was a Roman mile (4,860 feet) from the next. It
required 9,500 men to man the wall. The best surviving part of
the wall is in the Northumberland National Park, and the most
recommended site there is the Housesteads Fort. The park's

information center is in a town called Once Brewed (which is not too far from Twice Brewed).

---◆---

White Cliffs in Australia's New South Wales was a mining town, with opals the quarry. Miners dug an estimated 50,000 holes in the sandstone which gives the area a distinctly lunar look. As early as 1894, residents began converting played-out or useless mine shafts into homes because building materials were scarce and miners could escape summer's oppressive heat. There are approximately 140 dugouts, or underground dwellings, inhabited by many of the town's 210 residents. In 2005, one three-bedroom dugout was listed for sale on the Internet at Australian $595,000 (about U.S.$560,000).

Tourists — about 25,000 each year — can choose an underground motel (with conference facilities!) or an underground bed and breakfast. Underground attractions include Jock's Place, a dugout home, museum, and old mine with an opal seam in the wall; Wellington's Underground Art Gallery; and Top Level Opal which has gem displays. Things are a little odd topside, too: Joe's Stubby Opal Shop is a house built of 50,000 beer bottles. Also, a solar power station erected a string of solar dishes here, making the landscape just that much more otherworldly.

---◆---

Stonehenge is a generic name for a somewhat mysterious assemblage of gargantuan mostly upright stones on England's Salisbury Plain. Constructed in stages between c. 3100 B.C. and 1600 B.C., it consists of a few dozen sandstones, the largest of which stands 22 feet high and weighs nearly 50 tons. The lintels are nearly eight tons each.

Heights reflect only the parts that are above ground; for the largest stone, there are another eight feet in the ground.

Educated estimates suggest it took 30 million man-hours to build the site, presumably for religious ceremonies and perhaps as a kind of calendar. The central axis aligns with the sun on midsummer day. This famous Stonehenge, which attracts about 800,000 visitors a year, originally was one of several stonehenges (meaning circles of stone) in Britain and Ireland; stonehenges were preceded by others made of wood — called woodhenges, naturally.

In Budapest, Hungary's capital, nearly 100 thermal springs feed 12 spa baths and several spa hotels with 19 million gallons of thermal water daily.

It is not unusual for a megalomaniac's outrageous monuments to himself to become tourist attractions in a later era. The Palace of the Parliament in Bucharest, Romania, is remarkable for the speed with which it moved from one category to the other. Named, incongruously, the House of the People by the communists, the mondo structure was intended to house government offices, organs of the party, and apartments, but Romania's communist dictator Nicolae Ceausescu was ousted and executed in December 1989 when not much of the building's interior had been completed. Now it is home to the Parliament and the setting for international conferences and exhibitions. This still-unfinished behemoth is plenty big for both, with 3,552,076 square feet of space, in a square building measuring 886 feet on each side and 282 feet tall; in addition, there are seven levels below ground, of which only four are accessible to the public. There are roughly 1,100 rooms, some truly gargantuan. The builders worked with mountains of marble as well as cherry and walnut paneling, not to mention gold, plus (literally) tons of crystal. There are 4,500 chandeliers — falling short of the 11,000 in the original plans. The building has two bunkers outfitted for nuclear warfare deep in its bowels plus eight escape tunnels. Above ground, the ornate (think extravagant, as in 17th-century baroque) Union Hall measures 23,680 square feet and 52.5 feet high. Its floor wears a 14-ton, 10,764-square-foot custom carpet. And the roof can accommodate helicopter landings. The communists destroyed 40,000 homes, churches, and other buildings to construct this monster.

Tourists are offered daily escorted tours, and Union Hall is on the itinerary, but the bunkers remain part of the national defense system and are off limits.

Where in the World?

Some sources say the Galleria Vittorio Emanuele (or, simply, the Galleria) in Milan, Italy, is the world's oldest shopping mall, having been completed in 1877. That case is hard to make because of the older, enclosed bazaars in places like Istanbul, Turkey. Nevertheless, the Galleria is arguably the loveliest of the world's shopping centers. It is laid out in a cruciform plan like a cathedral. The shopping arcade is topped by a 96-foot-high barrel-vaulted roof of glass, with a domed octagon at the center. Named for Italy's first king, this splendid structure is neoclassical in style, with leanings toward the more ornate baroque. Giuseppe Mengoni, the mall's architect, fell from the roof to his death a few days before the Galleria's debut.

Near Puno, Peru, about 2,000 members of the Uros indigenous people live on a group of small islands created from the totora reeds that are native to Lake Titicaca. Dense roots support the island tops, but the tops rot and must be improved regularly with the addition of more reeds. Strolling on these islands is akin to walking on a waterbed. The Uros also build reed houses and reed boats.

Church builders have always incorporated contemporary elements with Biblical themes. These four major modern projects, three coincidentally launched in the 1890s and one a decade later, are no different.

* The Cathedral of St. John the Divine in New York City, a combination Romanesque-Byzantine and Gothic church in the works since 1892, depicts a TV on a stained-glass window in tribute to the media's support for the construction project.

*The Gothic National Basilica in Quito, Ecuador, was built between 1893 and 1993. In the niches where a medieval builder would have placed gargoyles, the basilica features stone replicas of caimans, turtles, boobies, anteaters, and other animals that live in Ecuador's Galapagos islands.

* The Sagrada Familia, under construction since 1895 in Barcelona, Spain, offers not only avant garde renditions of the Holy Family but figures that look like spacemen. The full name of this church is Expiatory Temple of the Holy Family, and the original (in every sense) architect was Antoni Gaudi.

* Washington National Cathedral in the U.S. capital, a Gothic structure first envisioned by George Washington and built between 1907 and 1990, has a stained-glass window that depicts manned space flight and incorporates a 7.18-gram basalt lunar rock brought back by the Apollo 11 crew. Also, on the exterior, one of the carved grotesques is Darth Vader, the result of a competition that elicited designs for cathedral sculptures from children.

Rome's Trevi Fountain is fed by spring water brought to the city on the Agua Virgo, a Roman aqueduct built in 19 B.C.

Where in the World?

The fragrant and aptly named Valley of Roses in Bulgaria each June hosts a Rose Festival where visitors can witness the harvest and see scores of men and women of all ages, in bright costumes, dance and sing to celebrate this season. Bulgaria produces about 30 percent to 40 percent of the world's attar of rose, which is the distilled rose oil used in perfumes. (Turkey produces another 40 percent to 50 percent of the total.) The 50-mile-long Valley of Roses produced an estimated 3,300 pounds of oil in 2006. It takes between 190 and 220 pounds of rose petals to get just one ounce, so the season's production would have required at least 10 million pounds of petals! Bulgaria could sell the oil (usually to top perfume makers) for roughly 130 euros per ounce (nearly $200). Besides producing attar of rose for export, local factories produce rose water, rose liqueur, rose brandy, rose jam, rose shampoo, plus a kind of Turkish Delight, with, of course, the rose scent.

———◆———

It's time to bone up on some really weird tourist attractions:
* The walls of the Capela dos Ossos (Chapel of Bones), inside the 15th-century Igreja de Sao Francisco in Alentejo, Portugal, are lined with the bones and skulls of 5,000 monks, laid out in a variety of intricate patterns.
* The 17th-century church of Santa Maria della Concezione in Rome has five chambers in its crypt that are rather artfully decorated with the bones of some 4,000 Capuchin monks. Some full skeletons are seen in monks' habits, as well.
* The Sedlec Ossuary, a church near Kutna Hora, Czech Republic, was decorated — one might even say furnished — in the late 19th century with the bones of more than 40,000 bodies buried in its graveyard from the 13th century onward. Even crucifixes and chandeliers are made from bones.

———◆———

In France's Loire Valley, noted for its chateaux, the largest of these is Chambord with 365 chimneys and a staircase that is sometimes attributed to Leonardo da Vinci. In the last years of his life (1516-1519), da Vinci was painter, engineer, and architect to King Francis I, who installed him in the Manoir du Clos-Luce (now a museum) near another of the chateaux, Amboise. When da Vinci came to France, he brought a few of his favorite paintings, including the "Mona Lisa." A chapel on the grounds of Amboise is said to contain da Vinci's tomb. Chambord, meanwhile, was the site of the world's first sound and light show in 1952.

Potala Palace in Lhasa, Tibet, is one of the world's largest buildings covering 4,399,560 square feet (101 acres) and encompassing, according to cautious estimates, more than 1,000 rooms; that estimate may be way too low. The structure was built as a sacred place, an administrative center, and a home to the Dalai Lama and his staff. Started in the 7th century and mostly dating from the 17th century, it is made entirely of stone and wood — but there are no nails. The 13-story palace is 383 feet tall, and walls average 10 feet thick. The whole complex sits 12,139 feet above sea level, overlooking the valley (at 11,830 feet) where Lhasa itself is situated.

San Francisco's Lombard Street is called the world's crookedest street. In one very steep block, cars (traveling downhill only) make eight U turns. The sidewalk for pedestrians is steps, 250 of them.

———◆———

One of the finest of Roman aqueducts, in Segovia, Spain, was built in the late first century atop two tiers of arches to bring water from about 10 miles outside of town. It marches close to half a mile through the old section of Segovia — and it still delivers water. Constructed of 20,400 huge granite stones (but without mortar or clamps), it reaches just over 92 feet tall in the Plaza del Azoguejo where the ground is lowest, and its arches are high and wide enough for roadways to pass underneath.

———◆———

Ethiopia has a long and mythic history. It claims the fabled Queen of Sheba who is said to have had a son by the Hebrew King Solomon, and it claims, to this day, to house the

Israelites' Ark of the Covenant in the ancient capital, Axum (the treasure is off limits to all but one priest). But high (at 8,629 feet) in Ethiopia's mountains, Lalibela is where legends come to life, in the form of churches dating from the 12th

century that were carved entirely out of rock and
entirely below ground.

In the small city itself, an Ethiopian capital from the 10th to
mid-13th centuries, there are 13 rock churches, including the
world's largest. That is Bet Medhane Alem, which is close to
38 feet high and covers approximately 8,600 square feet. The
best-known of them, Bet Giorgis, stands around 49 feet tall (or,
more accurately, 49 feet down) and is carved in the shape of a
symmetrical cruciform tower. Among the rock churches and
monasteries outside Lalibela, the Asheton Maryam monastery
is more than 13,000 feet above sea level. The out-of-town
sites are accessible by mule and on foot. It is said that one
of Lalibela's rock churches was built in a single night with
help from angels, a tradition that is almost as believable as
imagining the labor of thousands carving these monumental
structures out of rock.

Venice, Italy's city of canals (177 of them), comprises 118
islands and has almost 400 bridges. Built on millions of
wooden pilings, this pearl on the Adriatic Sea counts about
450 palaces and old houses of note. Its three most famous
sons are composer Antonio Vivaldi, who left the priesthood
for music; ne'er-do-well Casanova, who was slated for the
priesthood, too, but shenanigans got him expelled from the
seminary (until his last years, he moved, was expelled from,
or had to flee from one city to the next across Europe), and
adventurer Marco Polo, who left Venice at age 17 for his well-
known excursion to Asia and didn't come home for nearly 25
years. (He can be claimed as Venetian although it is not clear if
he was born here or in Korcula, Croatia.)

The piece of confection on Moscow's Red Square known as the Cathedral of St. Basil is really nine churches incorporated into one. They are identifiable from the nine picture-perfect onion domes painted using every bright color on an artist's palette.
Stalin nearly had St. Basil's knocked down.

The Statue of Liberty was a gift from France in observance of America's 1876 Centennial (dedicated in 1886). It cost the French 450,000 francs to build the statue, and the Americans collected $323,000 to build the base. The 1986 restoration cost close to $70 million. Its sculptor was Frederic Auguste Bartholdi, whose birthplace in Colmar, France, is now a museum. Pictures of the statue appear here and there in Colmar, but there are two small replicas of the statue in Paris — one next to the Pont de Grenelle and the other, tucked away among the trees in the northwest corner of the Luxembourg Gardens.

The Grand Mosque in West Africa's Djenne, Mali, is built entirely of mud; walls of close to 40 feet high vary from 16 to 24 inches thick and support three massive towers. The sun-dried bricks are held together with a mud mortar and smoothed over with a fermented mud-and-chaff plaster. The mosque begins to dissolve when the annual rains come, but citizenry re-plaster it each year. Palm wood spikes stick out at various points all over each side. These take stress off the bricks and form a scaffolding for workers' use during the repair season. The earthen architecture, which can survive for centuries if maintained, is typical all through Mali. Rounding out the Djenne Old Town are approximately 2,000 traditional mud houses that, like the better-known mosque, survive regular rainy-season meltdowns and repairs. Non-Muslims are no longer allowed inside the mosque because of a 1996 French fashion photo shoot involving scantily clad models in suggestive poses. Ubiquitous claims that the mosque is the world's largest mud brick building don't stand up to challenge.

———◦◦◦———

The Guggenheim Museum in Bilbao, Spain, has the world's largest single gallery space, extending to a length of 450 feet.

———◦◦◦———

Even the Montana Historical Society does not claim to have an exhaustive list of the state's ghost towns, but the best-estimate number — more than three dozen abandoned places — gives the Big Sky state more ghost towns than any other in the United States. While some are abandoned in every sense, those most popular with tourists are Bannack, Elkhorn, Garnet, Nevada City, and Virginia City.

Although Ontario's ghost towns are less accessible — there is a lot of "up north" up north, some of it without roads — there are lots more of them. Don Brown, who wrote the book(s) on this subject, estimates there are about 250 partially or totally abandoned towns. A few (Balaclava, Ballycroy, Creighton, Depot Harbour, and Millbridge Station, for example) are beginning to appear in tourist literature.

❖

Diocletian's Palace, in the city of Split in Croatia, was built in the late third century for the Roman Emperor Diocletian. Parts of the palace and its walls still stand, and the grounds (around 7.4 acres) are home to about 3,000 of Split's 300,000 population. To build the palace, stone and marble were taken from quarries on the Croatian island of Brac; builders of the White House in Washington, D.C., drew from the same source. Diocletian's fourth-century mausoleum was on the grounds, too, but ironically, the burial site of this persecutor of Christians was converted into a church (St. Doimus) in the fifth century.
It is still there.

❖

In Turkey's Cappadocia region, eons-old lava rock made it possible for inhabitants over the last 3,000 to 4,000 years to carve housing and other building interiors into the stone.

At least 1,000 ancient chapels and houses were created that way. In addition, as a survival tactic when Roman armies and then, after the sixth century, Arabs threatened residents, local farmers created underground hideaways that, with stored supplies, were good for several months.

More than 200 underground communities extended at least two levels below the surface.

The best-known are Kaymakli, extending four levels down and able to accommodate 15,000, and Derinkuyu, with eight levels open to tourists (although it is thought to be deeper).

These cities, often accessible by tunnel openings right on villagers' property, had communal kitchens, deep wells, extensive ventilation systems, stables for horses, chapels with confessionals, and even wineries. The more recently discovered Ozkonak (1972) extends an impressive 10 stories into the ground and could accommodate 60,000 for three months; only four levels are open to visitors.

Some rock establishments are still in use, including at least a dozen cave hotels. The 18-room Gamirasu Cave Hotel in Ayvali was created from a former Byzantine monastery.

Where in the World?

Mitchell, South Dakota, has made something of a name for itself by maintaining "the world's only corn palace." The "a-maize-ing" building, serving as a multipurpose community center for stage shows, sports events, and the like, is covered with artwork created with grain.

And the work is redone each year. Murals, designed by a local artist, are framed with 3,000 bushels of milo rye, oatheads, and sourdock (natural grains found in South Dakota). The murals themselves are made with 275,000 ears of corn, which are sawed in half lengthwise and nailed to the building's exterior. About 20 locals are employed to assemble the murals and frames each summer.

———◆◆◆———

The U.S.S. Constitution (Old Ironsides) in the Charlestown (Massachusetts) Navy Yard is the oldest commissioned warship afloat (1797). The ship was never defeated in 42 battles.

———◆◆◆———

All distances from Paris in France are measured from a point in the square at the front of Notre-Dame Cathedral. A bronze plaque — called Le Kilometre 0 — marks the starting point.

———◆◆◆———

Travia

York, England, is the spookiest city on Earth. That is according to the Ghost Research Foundation International, a nonprofit that researches psychic phenomena. York earned its curious distinction with a total of 504 recorded ghost sightings, if sightings is the right word. And those are only the reported incidents, involving around 140 different ghosts, it is believed. The most famous York ghosts, and the oldest, are a group of Roman Legionnaires who walk across the basement of the Treasurer's House. The building, constructed in 1648, sits atop a patch of Roman roadway. Ghosts also have been seen in York Cathedral, Holy Trinity Church, the Theatre Royale (in the dress circle, if you please), and in historic public establishments like the Black Swan pub, Cock & Bottle pub, Old Starre Inn, and York Arms.

Chapter 7

Travail, et al

Travia

The oldest root of the word "travel" was a Latin word that meant a kind of rack — as in a rack used for torture — which says a lot about the hardships of taking a journey in medieval Europe (the period during which the word "travel" emerged). Travel shares with "travail" this etymology: The first Latin source word was "tripalium" (meaning a kind of rack) which led to "tripaliare" (also Latin, meaning to torture on the rack). From these sources evolved the Old French word "travaillier," which originally meant to torture, torment, or trouble and then meant to suffer, be troubled, or become tired or worn out. From those origins, it also came to mean to tire out by taking a journey, and then, to journey. It was in English that travaillier spawned two words: "Travail," which still refers to suffering, came first in the 13th century and was followed in the 14th century by its variant, "travel," which these days also sometimes refers to torment.

———◆———

The word "tour" came from the Old French word "tourn," understood to mean a lathe, circuit, or turn. It seems fitting that "tour," which joined the English language in the 14th century, should have roots referring to moving in a circle. Today's tour often returns to the trip's starting point, producing a circle of sorts.

———◆———

"Vacation," new to English in the 14th century, came to us as the Middle English "vacacioun" from the Latin "vacatio," meaning freedom or exemption, and ultimately from the verb form "vacatus." "Vacate" also derived from vacatus. In other words, when we say we want a vacation, we are saying, "We're going to vacate" or "We're outta here."

———◆———

"Kremlin," as used in the West, refers to both the Russian central government and the place where it is located. The word "kremlin" means "citadel," and Russia's government buildings sit inside Moscow's ancient Kremlin along with a must-see museum (the Armory), centuries-old palaces, and medieval Orthodox churches. Other historic Russian towns and cities — such as Novgorod, Rostov, Suzdal, and Nizhny Novgorod (Nizhny for short and Gorky under the Soviets) — have kremlins or the remains of old kremlins, too. The large square on one side of Moscow's Kremlin got its current name, Red (Krasnaya) Square, in the 17th century, but in those days, "krasnaya" meant "beautiful" and "red." Eventually, it came to mean only red.

———◆———

As William Shakespeare was the first to use the word "luggage," he is credited with coining the word. It described something that is lugged and that is inconveniently heavy. We all have had suitcases like that, but, in the word's early usage, in "Henry IV, Part I," the thing being lugged, or the luggage, was a cadaver. (Falstaff was carrying the late Hotspur.) The bard used the word six times in his plays. Shakespeare also gave

us "jet," obviously not referring to aircraft. The playwright used it as a verb meaning to intrude or encroach. Thus, for example, characters or events "jetted upon" the rights of others. The word evolved from the French "jeter," which means "to throw," and after Shakespeare, it came to mean "to spurt or stream." In that way, the word found new lives as an adjective and a noun, as in jet propulsion, jet engine, and jet airplane, and then, simply, as the jet that we fly on.

———— •◆• ————

As to the game's name, it has been said that the letters G-O-L-F are an acronym for "gentlemen only, ladies forbidden," but that is just too cute to be true. The name has a history believed to be tied to the words for the Dutch ice-based game, "kolven," and the club, called "kolf." The terminology is thought to have passed to the Scots, where the game became "golve," "gowl," or "gouf" — and by the 16th century, it was "golf."

———— •◆• ————

"Posh" is another four-letter word with an apocryphal origin story. As the supposed acronym for "port outward, starboard homeward," the word was said to indicate the way the well-to-do traveled from Britain to India and back in the 19th century — by ship and on the shady side for each journey. The Oxford

English Dictionary, however, links the word to 19th-century slang, when "posh" could be used to mean "money" or "a dandy."

———◆———

"Dollar" has its roots in a 16th-century silver mining town, Jachymov, at the western edge of the Czech Republic. The coins minted there were called Joachimstalergulden or Joachimstalergroschen — words longer than most tongues. Shortened to "taler" or "thaler," the name traveled the world with the 12 million or so coins minted in a 100 years' time in Jachymov. Taler eventually came to signify any large silver coin, and the best-known — the Austrian Maria Theresa taler — became so popular that succeeding governments minted an additional 800 million between 1870, the year of the empress' death, and 1975 — all dated 1870. Meanwhile, "taler" passed into English in the 16th century when the Scots called a 30-shilling piece a "dollar," and they brought the name to America. Today, Jachymov is most noted as a small spa town. Uranium is a byproduct of silver production, and the springs are radioactive.

———◆———

"Holiday" comes from the Middle English "halidai" meaning holy day.

———◆———

The word "hotel" has a colorful linguistic history that links it to "hostage" and maybe "hostile." Most of these and related words entered the English language in the 13th or 14th centuries, but "hotel" was a late-comer in the 18th. To explain, the word "host" (meaning an innkeeper or entertainer of guests) is part of a word batch including "hospice," "hospital," "hostage," "hostel," and "hotel" that derived from the Latin "hospes," meaning either a guest or person who entertains a guest. The appearance of "hostage" with words relating to guests refers to a time when individuals offered, or were forced, to live in an enemy's court to guarantee that a promise would be kept. They were guests of a special kind. As for the word "hostile," it is related to "host," but only when "host" is defined as an army or a multitude. The source word for "hostile" and this kind of "host" was the Latin "hostis," which meant foreigner, stranger, or enemy.

The tulips that draw so many people to Holland each spring came to Europe from Turkey. The word "tulip" originates from the Turkish word "tulbent," meaning turban.

The word "cruise" has its roots in the Latin noun "crux," which was an instrument of torture such as a cross or stake, and by extension might mean trouble or misery. The word moved into Middle Dutch as "crucen," meaning to make a cross, and then "kruisen," meaning to sail "crossing to and fro," before it became an English loan word in the 17th century. The Latin "crux" is also the root for "crucial," "crucifix," "crucifixion," "cruciform," "crucify," "crusade," and "excruciating," making all of them cousins to "cruise." It doesn't sound very auspicious, does it?

———◆———

The following are samples of expressions in the English language that have come down to us from the days of Shakespeare. Tourists can come away with a raft of these when taking the hop-on, hop-off bus tour in Stratford-upon-Avon, England.

About food:

Square meal. Meals were square because the wooden trenchers that served as plates were square.

Cold shoulder. This was a cold piece of meat (usually the shoulder of a carcass) that was served to an unwelcome guest.

Lick the platter clean. Diners literally licked their plates clean for reuse because the dishes were never washed.

By hook or by crook. People could have any food from public lands that they could extract from the ground with a hook or from trees with a crook.

Chairman of the board. This comes from the fact that the head of the household was the only person to have his own chair (making him the "chair man") — and, because he was sitting at the table (or "board"), he was chairman of the board.

About bedtime:

Sleep tight. Several mattresses were stacked on the bed and supported by ropes strung from a wooden frame. One tied the ropes tight to keep from falling through to the floor.

On the shelf. Children slept on a broad shelf and, because they slept there until marriage, unwed daughters were on the shelf.

Bed and board. Tabletops were simply boards laid on top of wooden supports, and so — as the place where food was laid out — the word board came to mean food, too. In addition, the boards were moved to the floor to serve as beds for guests. Hence, guests were offered bed and board.

About nonsense:

Rule of thumb. A husband was encouraged to beat his wife, but he was discouraged from using a stick any wider than his thumb.

———◆◆◆———

The word "junket" has negative connotations when it refers to a free trip taken by someone else, especially when that someone else is a politician. The word first appeared in English in the 15th century, and it referred to any sweet dish (and a bit later, the word's application broadened to include a feast or a banquet). This evolved by about 200 years ago to mean a large picnic or outing where there would be plenty of eating and drinking. Eventually, the word came to mean any trip taken for pleasure, and from that, it was a short leap to today's commonly understood reference to a trip that is a freebie. By the way, Webster's first definition still encompasses a dessert ("of sweetened flavored milk set with rennet"), and the second is "a festive social affair."

———◆◆◆———

"Safari" is a Swahili word for journey. The first journeys to carry that name were early Arab caravans trekking inland from the East African coast. Then, safaris were hunting expeditions, with guns, before they became hunting expeditions, with cameras.

———◆◆◆———

The word "taxicab" has its roots in two words. The first part to see light in the English language was "cab," a shortened version of "cabriolet," referring to a light, two-wheeled one-horse carriage brought to England from the continent in the early

1800s. It was a carriage for hire and had a tall partition (called the "dashboard") in front of the passengers to protect them from dirt and splashing mud. By the end of the 19th century (especially when cabs became horseless things), a mechanical device came into use for measuring the distance traveled and hence the amount owed for the cab ride. It was the "taxameter" (German), "taximetre" (French), and "taximeter" (English), with the "taxa" or "taxi" from Latin for tax or charge and "meter" from Greek for a measuring device. The horseless carriage for hire then became a taximeter cab, then eventually taxicab or taxi or cab again.

Sauna is the only Finnish word to have become part of the world vocabulary.

The British often use French words for food or food-related items. And that is just one reason Americans may need a little cribsheet to get by at an English restaurant. In the French/English category, the British say aubergine (for eggplant); courgette (zucchini); gateau (cake); haricots (green beans); serviette (napkin), and mange tout (which means "eats all" and descriptively refers to peas in a pod). The rest of these are Britishisms: Beetroot means beets (OK, that was easy), and pudding means any type of dessert. Swede, pretty much impossible to decipher, refers to the yellow turnip, aka rutabaga. To really tangle the matter, the Scots call white turnips swedes, and yellow turnips are, simply, turnips. For typical pub fare, we have bangers and mash (sausages and mashed potatoes) and bubble and squeak (a patty made from cabbage and potatoes).

The following items are all desserts, and they taste better than they sound:

Banoffi pie: a specialty with a cookie base and topped with bananas, caramel, and coffee cream.

Bread and butter pudding: a dessert made with bread and butter, naturally, but cooked with sugar and egg custard.

Orange treacle (pronounced tree-kle with a long "e"): a sweet made with oranges, golden syrup, cookie crumbs, and butter on a pastry base (Treacle means syrup in British.).

Raspberry syllabub: a dessert consisting of the berries, cream, white wine, and sugar, but resembling a mousse.

Spotted dick: a steamed pudding, made with flour, suet, and currants (It is called spotted because of the little bits of fruit throughout, and the other part of the name comes from, well, the pudding's shape.)

Chapter 8

Pastimes

Shop till you drop: The largest gold market in the world is the gold souk in Dubai, where 400 storefronts lure and dismay tourists. Not one, but two, Dubai developers claim they will build the world's largest shopping mall. Like Dubai needs them: There are 40 shopping malls already. Then, there is the annual Dubai Shopping Festival just to keep everyone in the right frame of mind.

Colorado's capital Denver hosts the Great American Beer Festival, the nation's largest beer-themed bash based on number of beers (1,600) and number of breweries (380) represented at the event.

Also, Colorado is home to the Coors Brewery in Golden, which has the capacity to produce more beer at a single site than any brewery on Earth: 23 million barrels a year, or 713 million gallons.

Meanwhile, Portland, Ore., boasts more breweries than any city in the world: 32 in the city, 38 in the larger metro area. It also claims America's largest beer fest based on attendance. Its annual Oregon Brewers Festival draws more than 50,000 people.

Pastimes

Le Mars in Iowa — dubbed Ice Cream Capital of the World — has trademarked its moniker. The town's ice cream maker, Wells' Dairy, makes more ice cream per year (more than 120 million gallons of the Blue Bunny brand) than any other single plant in the world. That hook helps the small town (population: 9,500) lure about 16,000 tourists annually for "udderly delightful" visits to the Wells' Dairy facilities and related attractions, not the least of which is an old-fashioned ice cream parlor.

———◆———

The Brits win the competition for dreaming up the wackiest contests. Get a load of this set, arbitrarily organized alphabetically:

* *Cooper's Hill Cheese Rolling* (a 200-yard race chasing a seven-pound Double Gloucester cheese down a near-vertical slope, winner take all — all of the cheese, that is).

* *Cotswold Olympicks* (where the shin-kicking event gets our attention — it's about wrestling and beating the devil out of the opponent's support system).

* *UK Mobile Phone Throwing Championships* (as distinct from the older Finnish phone toss competitions).

* *World Black Pudding Throwing Championship* (a delectable opportunity to toss around allegedly edible animal innards).

* *World Bog Snorkeling Championships* (the world's dirtiest competition, in which entrants snorkel 360 feet in a peat bog through mud and who knows what squirmy animal life).

* *World Conker Championships* (a nutty game, in which one contestant slaps his nut against his opponent's nut to see which breaks first — these are chestnuts, by the way).

* *World Haggis Hurling Championships*, (in which contestants, from atop whisky barrels, toss animal innards — sometimes considered lunch — great distances).

* *World Mountain Bike Bog Snorkeling Championships* (same idea as the above bog event, but on specially outfitted bikes — as well as snorkels to keep riders alive).
* *World Pea Shooting Championships* (just what the name says).
* *World's Biggest Liar Competition* (just what the name says).
* World Toe Wrestling Championships (ditto).
People fly across oceans for these events.

———◆———

Duffers (roughly one percent of the world's population) can play golf just about anywhere:
* There are approximately 31,850 golf courses in the world.
* Florida has more golf courses than any state in the United States, with nearly 1,400. Florida's Palm Beach County has more than 10 percent of those (160).
* The Mount Massive Golf Course near Leadville, Colo., is the highest-altitude golf course in North America at 10,430 feet. But, then, the highest in the world is the La Paz Golf Club, Bolivia (12,001 feet), and the lowest is in California at Furnace Creek Resort (minus 214 feet) inside Death Valley National Park.
* The southernmost course is at Ushuaia Golf Club, Argentina (54 degrees 47 minutes south), and the northernmost is North Cape Golf Club, Norway (71 degrees 10 minutes north).

———◆———

Portugal's Douro River Valley, noted for wines of all types, but especially port, is the world's oldest designated wine region. In 1756, the Marquis of Pombal created the demarcated region with rules to regulate production and trade.

———◆———

Lucy — the 3.2 million-year-old remains of an Australopithecus Afarensis woman unearthed in Ethiopia in 1974 — is probably the world's most famous individual hominid fossil. She is highlighted in a most unpretentious setting, in a display case found in the basement of the National Museum in Addis Ababa, Ethiopia's capital. For years, visitors to this East African nation have seen a plaster cast of the original, but the real Lucy, starting in 2007, began a six-year tour to several U.S. museums where millions of Americans will see her.

———◆◆◆———

Boudin Bakery — the creator of the Original San Francisco Sourdough French Bread — is that city's oldest ongoing business, dating from 1849. Its founders were a family of French bakers who aimed to bake traditional French bread in the New World. However, they had to use wild yeast gathered locally. Et voila! They had created a distinctive new bread. The bread is still baked daily using a portion of the bakery's original 1849 "mother dough." Now a popular and edible souvenir, the sourdough bread is the centerpiece of Boudin at the Wharf, a tourist destination that opened in spring 2005. Visitors can see bread-making demonstrations, eat at Boudin Cafe and Bistro Boudin, shop in Bakers Hall, and opt for the Boudin Museum & Bakery Tour.

Toronto in Canada's Ontario province claims the world's largest underground shopping complex. The 6.8-mile PATH underground walkway in downtown Toronto links 48 office towers, six hotels, 1,100 shops and restaurants, plus lots of transportation: the intercity bus terminal, five subway stations, and Union Station.

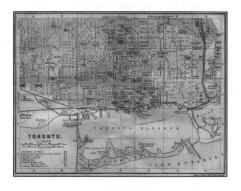

The International Pancake Race has two simultaneous venues: Liberal, Kansas, and Olney, England. It is the centerpiece of a three-day celebration in Liberal that also encompasses a pancake feed plus eating and flipping contests. The Brits pack it all into one day. Both pull in tourists and international media. About the race: It is said to have originated with a 15th-century Olney wife who ran so quickly to Shrove Tuesday Mass that she carried her skillet, with pancake, to services. That sprint morphed into an international race pitting Liberal women against Olney women — and all against the clock. Wearing traditional housewifely clothes, they run with a pan, flipping their pancake at the start and again at the finish. After the 2007 race, Liberal was ahead with 32 winners to 25 for Olney. Stay tuned.

Pastimes

The list of imaginative North American festivals is irresistible beginning with the Coondog Graveyard Celebration, for a chance to picnic in the world's only graveyard for coondogs (the hunting man's best friend). All of this takes place in Helen Keller's hometown of Tuscumbia, Alabama. The short list of these festivals is so long, in fact, that it appears as the Appendix to this book.

———◆———

The 41st staging of the Oberammergau Passion Play in Oberammergau, Germany, is set for 2010. When first presented in 1634, the stage was built in the local cemetery above the fresh graves of Black Plague victims.

———◆———

Things you might try (to eat, drink or chew) but don't want to bring home:

* *Betel nut* (a seed from the betel palm). The "nut" is native to Malaysia but dispersed widely in Asia. It is wrapped in the leaf of the betel pepper (a different plant) with lime and possibly some spices, all of this for a chew. The taste is bitter, but for those who can chew long enough, it produces blood-red saliva and leaves chewers with red teeth.

* *Durian* (a large oblong fruit). Because it is covered with hard spikes, it is said the durian can kill if thrown at someone's head. It is tasty — from sweet to "bittersweet nutty"— but goes straight from ripe to rotten. It smells so bad, people are generally not allowed to carry it into public buildings or hotel rooms. Indonesia is the home of the classic durian, but others are found across Southeast Asia, and a mild variety is exported to the West from Thailand.

* *Haggis* (a Scottish meat dish). Traditional haggis is minced sheep's heart, liver, and lungs mixed with suet, oatmeal, onions, and spices and stuffed into a sheep's stomach for

boiling. The pungent results are served with mashed potatoes and mashed turnips. It stands to reason anyone who can eat sausage can eat this, right?

* *Kumyss* (fermented mare's milk). Offered to tourists in Outer Mongolia and parts of the former Soviet Union, it tastes like very sour yogurt. In Uzbekistan, a version based on camel's milk is called shubat and may be offered in a screw-cap bottle.

* *Mopane* (an edible caterpillar). A staple in southern Africa, the caterpillars are gutted and fried for immediate consumption or cooked in salty water, then set out to dry for later use. They also may be stored in ashes, which makes them black. They may be eaten as a dry snack food or rehydrated and used in stews. The snack is chewy and salty. For those who are impatient for a sample, they are for sale on the Internet.

* *Qat* (a mild drug). Its users in places like Yemen chew qat leaves, often as an afternoon social activity. The euphoria is short-lived.

* *Rotten shark* (an Icelandic specialty cured by burying). Smelling just the way it sounds, it is washed down with the desensitizing Black Death schnapps. Alternative specialties are boiled sheep's head or ram's testicles pickled in whey, and these are delicacies.

* *Thousand-year-old egg* (a duck's egg that is about three months old). Preserved in a casing made by mixing wood ash, lime, salt, and strong tea, the egg's white goes off toward purple-black, the yolk toward green — and the odor toward sulfur. Hungry yet?

It takes 1.5 million hyacinths plus thousands of narcissus and other flowers to create the floats for the Bollenstreek Flower Parade each April in Holland. The procession, which winds its way from Noordwijk to Haarlem, is the largest of the flower processions seen in Holland from April through September. In some flower parades, only dahlias are used to decorate floats. Clearly, Holland is not all about tulips.

———◆———

Maryland made jousting its official sport in 1962. There is a long tradition of jousting tournaments in the state, dating from colonial times, and, since 1950, enthusiasts have capped their season with an annual Maryland State Jousting Championship. The sport also is a top attraction at the Maryland Renaissance Festival in Crownsville. Less surprisingly, in the home of the Iditarod dog sled race, Alaska's state sport is dog mushing. And, for South Dakota, the rodeo fills that role.

———◆———

Golfers in the annual Arctic Open in Akureyri, Iceland, tee off each year at midnight of midsummer night.

———◆———

The world is flush with museums devoted to the lowly, and sometimes not-so-lowly, loo. For an idea of the range, we offer these:

* *American Sanitary Plumbing Museum*, Worcester, Massachusetts
* "Flush With Pride" exhibit in the *Gladstone Pottery Museum*, Stoke-on-Trent, England.

* *Goyang Exhibition Hall for Sanitation*, Goyang,
South Korea.
* *Kiln Plaza Museum*, Tokoname, Japan.
* *Kohler Design Center, Museum Gallery*, Kohler, Wisconsin
(featuring Kohler products, naturally).
* *Sulabh International Museum of Toilets*, New Delhi, India.
* *Chamber Pot Museum* and the *Bourdalou Museum*, two
subsections of the larger ZAM museum in Munich, Germany.
For those who never had a need to know, the Bourdalou was a
luxury version of the chamber pot, made for fashionable 18th-
and 19th-century women who could use this device in secret
under wide dresses. It was named for a long-winded preacher
who made such receptacles necessary. Among the last people to
see the Bourdalou poised for action were tourists. As recently
as 1980, the German railroad placed the devices in a corner
cabinet of its sleeping car compartments.

For the Ski and Snowboard Camp outside Red Lodge,
Montana, the only ski season is in summer conditions, roughly
Memorial Day to Independence Day. There are literally tons
of snow earlier in the year, but the access road, the Beartooth
Highway, is closed until late May.

Each year, an estimated 24,000 bulls are killed in Spain's
bullrings in front of audiences totaling 30 million people. A
"running of the bulls," which can precede bullfights, refers
to the transfer of animals from a holding pen to the bullring.
Pamplona stages its world-famous event daily for the eight
days of the San Fermin Festival each July. Seventeen bulls
travel the half-mile route, led by eight tame bulls, followed
by the six doomed to meet the matadors and another three
tame animals. The average run lasts almost four minutes, with

thousands of people running in front of the huge horned creatures. As far as is known, no one died in the runs until the 20th century, but since 1910, 15 have been fatally injured. Pamplona's Running of the Bulls in 2002 spawned the annual Running of the Nudes, also in Pamplona, a counter event in which participants streak to protest the cruelty of bullfights.

The world's oddest traditions include some large-scale food fights:

* *Batalla del Vino*, in Haro, Spain, where on a June day participants waste thousands of gallons of Rioja wine by battling one another with it.

* *Feast of Sao Joao* (Saint John), in Porto, Portugal, where on a June night revelers take to the streets to do battle until sunrise with lemon balm and leeks or, more likely these days, plastic hammers.

* *Ivrea Carnival*, Ivrea, Italy, where carnival season winds up with three afternoons of orange-tossing battles.

* *La Tomatina*, in Buñol, Spain, a weeklong event in August that closes with a huge tomato fight, turning more than 120 tons of the fruit into paste and producing rivers of tomato juice as much as a foot deep.

There is always water as a weapon, too. Revelers use H^2O to wash away evil and sorrow — and drench each other — at Thailand's Songkran New Year celebrations and during the springtime festivities in China's Xishuangbanna region. There are a couple of wet ones in Spain, too: the Villagarcia de Arosa Water Festival and Requena Grape Harvest and Water Festival. At least, the second one promises some wine tasting, too.

The Cedar Point amusement park in Sandusky, Ohio, has 17 roller coasters — more than any other park in the world — with a total of 51,803 feet of coaster track. It also has more rides (68) than any other park. Cedar Point opened in 1870, and its first ride, in the early 1880s, was a water trapeze that hurled customers into Lake Erie. Way to go.

Shopping is a major reason for discretionary travel, and the Mall of America in Bloomington, Minnesota, is proof big time. The largest enclosed mall in the United States (total area: 4.2 million square feet), it has attracted an average of 33 million visitors each year since its 1992 debut, and tourism accounts

for four out of every 10 of those visitors. The complex boasts
more than 520 shops, 60 restaurants, an indoor theme park, a
walk-through aquarium, and a 14-screen movie theater, among
other attractions. Tour operators in Great Britain offer Shop
Til You Drop packages built around the mall, and more than
35 local hotels offer free shuttle services to the place. But it
is not even necessary to stay overnight to have a meaningful
shopping experience. The mall is less than two miles from the
Minneapolis/St. Paul International Airport, and, since the
launch of a light-rail service in December 2004, the airport and
mall are only 11 minutes apart.

———◆———

In an eye-popping mix of paganism and Catholicism, Las
Nieves in Spain annually stages the Fiesta of the Near-Death
Experience. Participants who nearly met their Maker in
the previous year pay their respects to the patron saint of
resurrection, Santa Marta de Ribarteme, by carrying or riding
in a coffin to church for Mass. Then, the procession of coffins
moves to the nearby cemetery and back to circle the church.

———◆———

Food festivities celebrate everything from garlic to chocolate
— and testicles. The latter events draw thousands who hunger
for tender morsels of boneless protein to festivals across North
America, from Calgary, Alberta, in Canada, to Oklahoma,
from California (the Oakdale Cowboy Museum) across to
Nebraska and Ohio. Usually, the delicacies are beef or pork,
but Illinois is the home of turkey testicle festivals. And,
Montana is home to at least four festivals, including the world's
largest with crowds of more than 15,000 for a five-day event.
The location is Clinton (jokes about the name of the town
would be in poor taste, of course), and the revelers, many
arriving by bike, chow down about 2.5 tons of nuts. Between

meals, the adults-only event charms with cowpie Bingo, plus cowpie-toss, wet-T-shirt, and hairy-chest contests.

The Whistler Blackcomb Ski Resort at Whistler, British Columbia, is the only resort in North America offering options to ski and snowboard on a glacier. The site is Blackcomb Mountain and the season runs early June through July.

Hissing and jeering were the order of the day when Englishmen went to the theater in the time of Shakespeare. Playgoers can do the same today at the reconstructed Globe Theatre in London. The original was built in 1599 on the south side of London's Thames River; the bard was a part owner. The circular Globe was also in a bad neighborhood, an area peopled by the licentious and sleazy. Pastimes included bear baiting (loved by Queen Elizabeth — the First, that is), games of chance, and drinking lots of ale. Actors and playwrights were not considered too reputable either. In the late 1990s, the Globe was reborn as a replica — and as another theater in a city full of them and a tourist attraction in its own right — located only 600 feet from the original. Weather dictates a roughly May-through-September season for the open-

air facility. Actors, in works by Shakespeare and others, play to an audience of up to 500 standees in an open pit strewn with straw, surrounded by another 1,000 who are rather snugly arrayed on wooden benches (it's a bring-your-own-cushion setup). However, that maximum of 1,500 playgoers is half the 3,000 raucous, smelly patrons who would crowd the same space in the early 17th century.

———◦◦◦———

The Grand Bazaar in Istanbul, Turkey, is a covered shopping mall close to 550 years old. It has 80 streets, 4,000 shops, and 22 entrances.

———◦◦◦———

There are 562 federally recognized Native American tribal governments in the United States alone. Across the United States and Canada, there are an estimated 1,000 pow wows a year. The largest of the pow wows is the Gathering of the Nations in Albuquerque, New Mexico, an intertribal event that brings together more than 3,000 Native American dancers and singers from more than 500 U.S. and Canadian tribes each April. It attracts 150,000 spectators.

———◦◦◦———

The world's largest comedy festival is staged each July in Montreal, Quebec, in Canada. Called the Just for Laughs/Juste Pour Rire Festival, it attracted an audience of more than 2 million in 2007 to laugh at 1,682 performers at 1,733 shows. The Web address is good for laughs, too: www.hahaha.com.

———◦◦◦———

Six Flags Great Adventure in Jackson, New Jersey, in 2005 launched Kingda Ka, the world's tallest (456 feet) and fastest (128 miles per hour) roller coaster.

———◦◦◦———

George Eastman, a founder of the Eastman Kodak Company in 1881 (originally the Eastman Dry Plate Company) and inventor of all sorts of technologies that brought photography to the masses, also dreamed up the name Kodak for his first camera in 1888. He said the letter "K" was a favorite with him, "a strong, incisive sort of letter," so he tried various combinations to come up with a word that started and ended with K. He also selected the yellow color identified worldwide with Kodak film. Eastman's entire enterprise was triggered when he was planning a vacation to Santo Domingo in 1878. To record his trip, he bought a camera and the associated paraphernalia (to develop film on the spot). He became engrossed in improving the technology of photography and did not take the trip. This very successful inventor was a high school dropout who had been judged "not especially gifted."

Camel, crocodile, and ostrich meat are on the menu at the world-renowned Carnivore restaurant in Nairobi, Kenya. They are charcoal grilled.

India is home to the world's oldest continuing festivals, events that are believed to go back at least 5,000 years. They are the

Hindu festival Ganesh Chaturthi and Holi (the latter also called Festival of Color). Observed in northern, central, and western India, Holi is celebrated to welcome spring and is meant to be lots of fun. To that end, celebrants exuberantly toss colored water on one another — and any tourists in the line of fire.

———◆———

Tourists may one day enter Sing Sing, a working prison in Ossining, N.Y., to visit an on-site museum. Advocates propose converting the prison's old power plant plus the abandoned original cell block (constructed of prisoner-quarried marble in 1825) into a tourist attraction to compete with the very popular Alcatraz, the prison on a rock in San Francisco Bay which is now part of the U.S. National Park Service. For the time being, Ossining's in-town historical museum includes a couple of cells and a replica of the electric chair for which Sing Sing is famous. The infamous prison is not the stated reason the community of Sing Sing changed its name to Ossining in 1901, but it would be a good one. (Sing Sing and Ossining are both based on Sint Sinck, the name of a local Native American tribe.)

———◆———

On the same theme but more ghoulish: The Museum of Colorado Prisons, a former Women's Correctional Facility, in Canon City, Colorado, displays a gas chamber and hangman's noose (both used) and offers a tour of 32 cells, whereas the Clink Prison Museum, on Clink Street in London, displays a torture chair, foot crusher, and whipping post, plus items tourists can try on. This museum was built on the site of the real Clink Prison that dated from the 12th century and gave us the word "clink" (believed to reflect the sound of chains) as slang for jail.

———◆———

Munich's Oktoberfest, held mostly in September, is the world's largest beer festival. It was born in 1810 when, at the conclusion of a royal wedding, the couple invited locals to celebrate in the fields around town.Fast forward to the 21st century, and each fall, six breweries open 14 beer tents that can seat 100,000 drinkers. The festival draws more than 6 million visitors, but they don't all imbibe in a big way: They consume roughly one liter (or a little more than a quart) per person.

———◆———

Bungee jumping, based on a practice in Vanuatu of jumping from high towers with only vines tied around the legs to break the fall, was created in New Zealand by A.J. Hackett. The first site opened in 1988 at Kawarau Bridge near Queenstown on the South Island. It continues to offer jumpers the chance to plunge 141 feet into the abyss. The world's highest commercial bungee jump, measuring a whopping 709 feet, is at Bloukrans Bridge in the Eastern Cape Province of South Africa.

———◆———

With a permit from the Hawaii Department of Health, tourists can visit the former leper colony of Kalaupapa on the island of Molokai. The town is still inhabited by survivors of the leper colony although they are no longer confined to the town.

Victims of the much-feared disease (formally, Hansen's disease) were isolated first in Katawao and then Kalaupapa between 1866 and 1969. Both sites are encompassed by the Kalaupapa National Historical Park, established in 1980.

Golf may be the national sport in Scotland, but it was not invented there. Some histories say Holland is its birthplace because of a medieval game called "kolven" played on frozen lakes and canals using clubs and grapefruit-sized balls weighing around two pounds each. Another origin theory centers on a Chinese game, first mentioned in the 10th century, called "chiuwan." It involved clubs with hardwood heads, wooden balls, tees, and holes in the ground. In any case, the game had landed on British shores by the 14th century, where it is depicted in a stained-glass window at Gloucester Cathedral. By the 15th century, the Scottish Parliament passed a law trying to stamp out the game because it interfered with archery practice (an activity deemed more important for national defense). By a century later, in 1552, a local charter affirmed golfers' rights to play on links that later became part of the famous St. Andrews golf club.

Attendees at England's Royal Ascot races, held annually in June, consume the following during a typical four-day event: 120,000 bottles of champagne, 75,000 bottles of wine, 12,000 bottles of Pimms (an oh-so-English alcohol-based drink), 5,940 pounds of beef, 6,380 pounds of fresh salmon, 5,280 pounds of smoked salmon, 6,000 lobsters, 9,900 pounds of strawberries, 550 gallons of cream, and 1,761 kegs of beer. The event requires 440,000 pounds (220 tons) of ice.

Travia

The Cannabis Cup is a five-day celebration of marijuana staged annually in Amsterdam. Experts come to test the smokes in the way of wine connoisseurs, but all sorts of fashion items and foods are on offer, too. (Sampling is not limited to festival days: So-called "space cakes" are sold in Amsterdam bars.) To round out a high-flying experience, Amsterdam also is home to the Hash Marijuana Hemp Museum. Its gift shop includes things like T-shirts made from hemp — and seeds for a little private planting.

— ◆ —

The Japanese can teach the West a thing or two about festivals. For a few samples:

* *Hadaka Matsuri (Naked Festival)*, in several cities. Participants are really a mob of men in loin cloths; they compete vigorously in order to touch a naked man whose role is to absorb bad luck and to catch or snatch sacred sticks or charms.

* *Hari Kuyo*, in many cities (including Tokyo). These are memorial services for used needles and pins, reflecting a time when such were among a woman's most important possessions.

* *Hamamatsu Matsuri (Kite Fighting Competition)*, in Shizuoka prefecture. Giant and beautiful kites are flown into battle to cut the strings of other teams' kites.

* *Honen Matsuri*, in Komaki City. An eight-foot, 1,000-pound wooden phallus is hauled around town on a shrine, and there is candy designed to match.

* *Kanamara Matsuri*, in Kawasaki. A giant phallus is paraded through the streets, participants sport huge penises, male and female revelers of all ages hug a phallic statue (photo op!), and, again, candy in the relevant shape is sold.

* *Shiritsumi (Rump-Bumping Festival or Rear End Sumo*

Competition), in Ito Onsen. Rivals use their bums to push one another off a wooden tub.

* * *

The first swimsuits, dating from the mid-1800s, were outfits for covering oneself when bathing in lakes, rivers, or oceans. And they were deadly dangerous, especially for women. Bathers wore full-body costumes — skirts and all — of flannel, alpaca, or wool plus the usual bloomers, stockings, and shoes. When wet, the outfits could weigh as much as the wearers. No wonder waterlogged bathers often drowned. Fast forward to the second decade of the 20th century when clinging one-piece swimwear emerged, thanks in large part to Danish-American Carl Jantzen, who was a partner in Oregon's Portland Knitting Mills. Responding to a friend's request, the company used its sweater-cuff rib-knit stitch to create a clingy, wool outfit for rowers. It was adopted by swimmers who called it a "Jantzen."

* * *

When those extra pounds help: At the Witches Weighhouse in Oudewater, Holland, tourists can weigh in on scales that date from 1482. The purpose? To prove they are not witches.

The scales were set up as a way to determine who was and who was not a witch, in the belief that witches weighed next to nothing. How else could they fly around on brooms? In 1545, Charles V (the Hapsburg emperor) granted Oudewater rights to issue documents certifying that the weighee was not a witch, and the town did a brisk business with people in need of the certificates. Tourists can qualify for the certificates, too, and tour what is now a museum highlighting the history of witch hunting.

For more shudders and not a few nervous titters, read on:
* Houston's aptly named *National Museum of Funeral History* includes a re-created casket factory of a century ago.
* Vienna, Austria's capital, has its *Undertaker's Museum* which tourists can visit by prior arrangement.
* Vienna is also home to the *Crime Museum*, which documents the most sensational Austrian crimes from the Middle Ages to now, plus various methods of capital punishment.

* Headhunters (actually, their quarry) are showcased in a private collection in Penampang, East Malaysia (in other words, on the island of Borneo).
* The *Glore Psychiatric Museum* in St. Joseph, Missouri (once the 19th-century State Lunatic Asylum #2) tells a story of mental illness and its treatment over the centuries.
* Mummies are the central feature of the *Mummy Museum*

in Guanajuato, Mexico, but they can also be found on view elsewhere around the globe, such as in the *Egyptian Museum* in Cairo, the *Father Le Paige Museum* in San Pedro de Atacama, Chile, and the *Capuchin Monastery* in Brno, Czech Republic.

* A section of the *National Museum* in Lusaka, Zambia, is devoted to witchcraft and helpfully annotated by the curator.

* The *Emigrant Trail Museum* sits inside the Donner Memorial State Park in Truckee, California, near the infamous campsite where the stranded Donner Party was driven to cannibalism in the winter of 1846-47. The Donner story is part of the museum's broader focus on emigration to California.

* The *Museum of Questionable Medical Devices* (part of the Science Museum of Minnesota in St. Paul) is described as the world's largest collection of goodies ever hawked by a quack. Displayed items you wouldn't want touching you include a "vibratory chair" (said to cure constipation and improve respiration through violent shaking) and the "orgone energy accumulator" (a box large enough to sit in that was said to collect energy that would cure everything from the common cold to sexual dysfunction).

* Philadelphia's *Mutter Museum* in 2005 opened the Gretchen Worden room featuring a collection of grotesque anatomical specimens ranging from diseased body parts and skeletons of giants and dwarfs to the corpse of a two-headed baby.

* The *Devil Museum* in Kaunas, Lithuania, houses hundreds of devil figures, representing the devil as the rather foolish misbehaving character depicted in Lithuanian folk tales.

* Rudesheim, Germany, a sweet village of winemakers on the Rhine; the picture-perfect hill town San Gimignano, Italy; and Ceske Krumlov, Czech Republic, another dramatically situated

hilltop town, are all charmers — and home to torture museums. Such eerie places also are found in nice cities like Amsterdam and Vienna.

———◆———

The West Edmonton Mall in Canada is the No. 1 tourist attraction in Alberta. It features more than 800 stores and more than 110 eateries in 5.3 million square feet (121 acres) of space, making it the largest shopping mall in North America. Expressed differently, the facility (including parking) sits on the equivalent of 48 city blocks, enough space to accommodate 40 Boeing 747s. The mall attracts 22 million visitors a year, and 10 percent of those come from outside Canada (and the majority of those from the United States). The owners of the West Edmonton Mall (the Triple Five Group) are part owners of the Mall of America in Bloomington, Minn., as well. West Edmonton also has been the biggest mall in the world, but that claim is under challenge with developers in China asserting their malls are or will be larger. West Edmonton, nonetheless, is confident it remains the largest mall under one roof.

———◆———

The Roadkill Cook-Off is just what the name suggests. An annual event which attracts up to 8,000 avid meat-eaters to Marlinton, West Virginia, it requires contestants to prepare a dish featuring any animal commonly found dead on the road, such as deer, groundhog, possum, rabbit, snake, and squirrel as well as domesticated farm animals. Rules and terms include the following:

1. Skin, gut, and clean the animal at home, although "special allowance can be made for fresh roadkill occurring en route to the cook-off."

2. Judges will deduct points for any chipped tooth resulting from gravel not extracted from real roadkill.

3. Judges have been tested for cast-iron stomachs and sworn to be free of vegetarian tendencies.

4. Judges reserve the right to not taste anything that looks suspiciously unfit to eat.

5. Not to put a dampener on things, but most judges prefer that the featured creatures were not really picked up off a road. Attendees are welcome to taste the roadkill culinary creations, too. Why else go to the cook-off?

⬥

Mud walking is called an "exciting and adventurous" way to experience Holland's Wadden Sea during low tide. It's also the hard way to visit one of the Wadden Sea's islands: Waders slog through thigh-deep mud and waist-high water to reach their destination.

⬥

As must be clear by now, local eats often are entertainment, not lunch. The annual Hokitika Wildwoods Festival in New Zealand serves up mysteries and near-mysteries like horopito, mako shark, Maori potato, mutton bird, octopus, paua, punga fern, seagull eggs, and whitebait. Still more challenging (for most, anyway) are these delicacies: possum pie, wasp larvae, worm sushi, and turbot fish bathed with sandfly dressing.

As far as can be determined, the granddaddy of Europe's Christmas markets was the so-called "winter market" in Dresden in 1434. Today, every German town has a Christmas market, and the larger cities have multiples. These events, lasting about a month during the run-up to Christmas, attract more than 160 million visitors a year and sales of 4.85 billion euros (close to $7.4 billion).

——◆——

Some festivals can be a pain. Better to watch than participate in these:

* *Anastenaria Fire-Walking Ritual* in Ayia Eleni, Langada, and other Greek villages. Adherents in a trance and carrying church icons walk on hot coals. Despite a Christian veneer, the ritual is considered a survival of practices of the Dionysian cult in ancient Greece. Events include animal sacrifices.

* *Broomstick Beating Festival (Pukul Sapu)*, Mamala and Morella villages, Indonesia. Men beat one another's bare backs with brooms, then treat wounds with a coconut oil believed to have supernatural powers.

* *Festival of Burning Barrels*, Ottery St. Mary, England. This is one of several events in Britain where participants carry flaming tar-soaked barrels through town to drive out evil or to commemorate old martyrdoms. In Stonehaven, Scotland, participants swing fireballs.

* *Thaipusam* events, the largest of which is near Kuala Lumpur, Malaysia. Up to a million watch as hundreds of entranced Hindu devotees do penance by running metal hooks and spikes into their flesh and skewering cheeks and tongues. Thaipusam is observed in other Asian countries, too.

* *Vegetarian Festival*, Phuket and Trang, Thailand. Sacred rituals, of Chinese origin, meant to drive out evil and bring good luck include masochistic displays by devotees in a trance,

such as walking barefooted over hot coals and ascending ladders made with bladed rungs.

Finally, there is the tradition of a stone-throwing festival (Sati Pradha Mela) in a northern India village. Meant to commemorate the death of a 19th-century queen, it is now banned.

——◆——

The first sunglasses were smoke-tinted to hide a judge's eyes (and hence his expressions) from others during a trial. That was in China before 1430. In their modern form, the U.S. Army Air Corps got the ball rolling, asking Bausch & Lomb to devise something to protect pilots from high-altitude glare. Those first shades came to the public in 1937, a year after they were developed, as Ray-Ban aviator sunglasses.

——◆——

Tourism is built on the back of the darnedest events. To wit:
* *The Boulia Camel Races* in Boulia, Australia, one of a dozen or more fests Down Under where camels become sprinters. Revelers also compete here in a camel-undecorating contest. (Camel racing is not to be confused with the equally odd camel wrestling staged yearly in Izmir and other parts of Turkey.)
* *The Festival of the Betrayed Spouse* (Festa del Cornuto) in Rocca Canterano, Italy, which celebrates the victims of spousal dallying with a parade, food, and gentle ribbing of the betrayed. The event officially honors St. Martin, protector of betrayed husbands.
* *The Festival of the Pig* in Trie-sur-Baise, France, featuring piglet

races, sausage-eating contest, piggy-costume contest, and the national pig-imitation competition for which, surely, ear plugs were invented.

* *The International Bathtub Regatta* in Dinant, Belgium, one of the world's several races involving numerous goofy-looking, but mostly seaworthy, inventions with bathtubs as their centerpiece. The Belgian version was dreamed up with at least one eye on bringing tourists to the charming little Dinant on the River Meuse.

* *The International Festival of Ghosts and Spirits* in Bojnice Castle, Slovakia, at which the honored spirits are among the guests because they, too, are on holiday. The fun starts when ghosts arrive without reservations.

* *The Mount Tsukuba Toad Festival* in Japan, an event at the eponymous mountain honoring the toads killed to make toad grease, which is used to treat cuts. Bearers parade with a 1,760-pound toad-shaped shrine.

* *The Prune-Pit Spitters World Championship* in Sainte-Livrade-sur-Lot, France, which is exactly what the name says, with prune pastries on the side.

* *The Sauna World Championships* in Heinola, Finland, honoring the one who can sit the longest while the heat is turned up.

* *The Wife Carrying World Championship* in Sonkajarvi, Finland, a race in which each runner carries an adult woman, not necessarily his own wife (after all, this has roots in a wife-stealing past). This is a global event, honest.

The forerunner to tennis dates at least as far back as 12th-century France, when the ball was hit with the palm of the hand. The game was called "paume" (meaning palm) and later "jeu de paume" (game of the palm). Players next discovered the protection of gloves and eventually wore gloves with strings stretched across them.

In Nunavut, Canada's newest territory in the far north, golfers routinely play their game on the world's most unusual "turf":

* *The July Midnight Sun Golf Tournament* in Kugaaruk is played on a course where rugs from local homes are the "greens." The all-night event also takes advantage of the midnight sun, as the name would have us understand.

* It may be August, but the *Summer Sun Golf Classic* at Gjoa Haven is played on frozen tundra.

* *The Peter Gzowski Invitational* tournament, which moves between cities in the Northwest Territories and Nunavut, is played on ice using colored tennis balls.

* Most exotic of all, the *Toonik Tyme Festival* golf competition, held at Nunavut's capital Iqaluit, is played, in April, on the frozen ice that has not yet melted off Frobisher Bay. Players brave below-zero temperatures to swing at florescent golf balls.

The Chinese were the first known to have used playing cards for entertainment, and this was in the 10th century. After the cards turned up in medieval Europe, the French created the names and shapes (clubs, diamonds, hearts, and spades) of the four suits seen on gaming tables today. The king of clubs was Alexander the Great, the king of diamonds Julius Caesar, the king of hearts Charlemagne, and the king of spades King David. Americans invented the joker around 1870.

Museums don't get much weirder than this batch found in the United States:

* *Cockroach Hall of Fame*, Plano, Texas, a collection of about two dozen dead roaches dressed up as well-known personalities, giving us the likes of Roach Perot and Liberoache.

* *Devil's Rope Museum*, McLean, Texas, and the *Kansas Barbed Wire Museum* in LaCrosse. Who knew there was enough to show and tell about prickly wires to fill even one museum? The Kansas site exhibits more than 2,000 barbed wire varieties, it says here.

* *Insectarium*, Philadelphia, billed as "the largest insect museum in the nation," housing scads of live bugs as well as (dead) mounted bugs and plenty of interactive displays, such as the

man-made spider web. It's a kid's world, in other words.
* *Julia C. Bullette Red Light Museum*, Virginia City, Nevada,
telling the story of one Ms. Bullette and her brothel, with what
one may call fitting displays. Not a kid's world.
* *Leila's Hair Museum*, Independence, Mo., a collection of
wreaths and more than 2,000 pieces of jewelry containing or
concocted of hair, all made before 1900.
* *Museum of Bad Art*, Dedham, Massachusetts, an assemblage
of art "too bad to be ignored" hung in a theater basement but
"conveniently located just outside the men's room."

———————◆◆◆———————

The military needed sunscreen lotions to protect GIs stationed
in the Pacific during World War II. Benjamin Green, a
pharmacist who assisted the military in developing suitable
lotions, used the knowledge he had gained to, in 1944, invent a
suntan cream for the general public. He called it Coppertone.

———————◆◆◆———————

We humans will collect anything. Herewith a global tour that
proves the point:
* *British Lawnmower Museum*, Southport, England, celebrating
the grass cutter — of course — with 200 examples of mowers
and other machinery from as far back as 1830.
* *Dutch Museum of Ironing Implements*, province of Groningen,
Holland, displaying about a thousand irons spanning recent
centuries, meant as a prism through which visitors look at the
history of Western culture. Quite ambitious.
* *Gas Station Museum*, Milan, Italy, housing 7,500 pieces that
include 150 gas pumps alone, 2,000 oil tanks, and countless
other items that tell the story of filling stations.
* *Giant Earthworm Museum*, Bass, Victoria, Australia, featuring
live specimens of Megascoloides Australis which can be as long

as three meters (that's almost 10 feet, mates). It is described as "possibly" the world's largest species of earthworm. Possibly?

* *Hokonui Moonshine Museum*, Gore, New Zealand, revealing "time-honored secrets" of the days when an illicit whiskey called hokonui was made in nearby hills.

* *International Spy Museum*, Washington, D.C., the world's only museum devoted exclusively to espionage that does not limit its interpretation of the subject by geography or specific time frames. It boasts the world's largest collection of espionage artifacts and invites visitors to test their skills as spies.

* *Knowing and Playing With Waste Museum*, Turin, Italy, focusing on the environment and how garbage is collected, disposed of or even used as art.

* *Pawnshop Museum*, Macau, China, commemorating a 3,000-year-old Chinese practice. It is located in a restored century-old pawnshop which is why it has the earmarks of a small fortress, but with elegant trimmings.

* *Perambulator Museum*, province of Groningen, Holland, where creative museums must be a specialty. This one claims 350 prams, cradles, and other gadgets associated with snoozing babies.

* *Tinkers' Craft Exhibition*, part of the Povazie Museum, Zilina, Slovakia, described as the only museum in the world to document the life and times of itinerant tinkers.

Timberline Lodge Ski Area boasts the only essentially year-round ski season in North America; it is closed for only two weeks in late September. Timberline is one of five ski areas on Mount Hood in Oregon. Mount Hood is a so-called "sleeping" volcano, with steam constantly rising from fumarole areas. Its most recent eruption (a minor one) occurred in 1907, but

Pastimes

experts believe it could have a significant eruption
within 75 years.

———◆———

Touring Hong Kong's markets doesn't always mean finding
tote-across-an-ocean goodies. Foodstuff includes eel's stomach
and fish's stomach (well, it's protein), plus deer's penis and
other animals' private parts meant for use as Viagra — but our
favorite is frogs' ovaries which are considered dessert when
served with syrup.

———◆———

The Gold Mountain Ski Area, near Graeagle, California, is the
Western Hemisphere's oldest reported sport-skiing area.

———◆———

Cabbages & Condoms is a restaurant in Bangkok. Founded as
part of a campaign to promote birth control, it distributes free
condoms to diners and has become a popular attraction. Its
profits support family planning and anti-AIDS projects
in Thailand.

———◆———

The Underground Salt Museum in Hutchinson, Kansas,
is the only salt museum in a working mine in the Western
Hemisphere. It produces 500,000 tons of rock salt a year.

———◆———

Canada is creating an 18,000-kilometer (11,160 miles)
recreational corridor, called the Trans Canada Trail, which
will reach into every province and territory and link some 800
communities. When complete, it will be the world's longest
recreational trail.

———◆———

The Venetian Macao resort, opened in 2007 on the island
of Macau, boasts the world's largest casino floor, at 550,000

square feet. It has 870 table games and more than 3,400 slot machines.

———◆———

Consider museums devoted to things that don't exist (well, maybe they don't):
* A Bigfoot exhibit as part of the *Willow Creek-China Flat Museum* in Willow Creek, California, highlighting the numerous reported local sightings of a huge man-beast dating from as far back as 1886.

* *UFO Museum & Research Center* in Roswell, New Mexico, centered on the purported 1947 crash landing in New Mexico of a vehicle from outer space.
* *Official Loch Ness 2000 Exhibition Centre* and *Original Loch Ness Monster Exhibition Centre*, both in Drumnadrochit, Scotland, built around reported sightings of "Nessie," a supposed prehistoric monster.
* *Ghost Centre* in Stokkseyri, Iceland, to listen to local ghost stories and walk through a "ghost maze." (This is in the country where roads are rerouted and building plans altered or dropped rather than disturb rocks where elves live.)

Chapter 9

On Track

Travia

Moscow has the world's largest subway system by ridership, with about 3.2 billion passengers a year. However, London's Underground is the world's longest subway system with 257 miles, followed by New York with 230 miles and Moscow with 211 miles. On the other hand, New York's 24-hour operation has the world's largest fleet of passenger cars, about 6,200. As for longevity among the world's largest systems, London (with 1.1 billion riders a year) has the oldest system, dating from 1863, followed by the Paris Metro (2.3 billion passengers a year) which opened in 1900, and New York's subway (more than 1.6 billion riders a year), 1904.

―――――◆―――――

The first public railroad in the world began carrying passengers in 1823, in England.

―――――◆―――――

Istanbul, Turkey, boasts the Tunel, the world's shortest subway. Traveling only 1,880 feet and built in 1875, it takes passengers up and down a hill, and it makes the one-and-a-half-minute trip every few minutes. The city has a modern subway system, too, launched in 2000.

―――――◆―――――

The world's fastest train, based on average speeds during normal operations, is the Japanese bullet service between Hiroshima and Kokura. The average is 162.3 miles per hour which means passengers travel the 119-mile route in 44 minutes.

―――――◆―――――

The world's longest rail journey is, of course, aboard the Trans-Siberian Railway which connects Moscow with Vladivostok, a port on Russia's Golden Horn Bay in the Sea of Japan. The journey covers seven days, eight time zones, and nearly 5,760 miles. There are other rail routes from Moscow into Siberia and beyond. Among tourists, the most popular alternatives are the Trans-Mongolian and the Trans-Manchurian spurs, both of which wind up in China's capital, Beijing. The former travels via Mongolia's capital, Ulan Bator, and the second via Harbin. The distances between Moscow and Beijing on these train routes are 4,878 miles and 5,581 miles, respectively.

Jungfraujoch in Switzerland, at 11,333 feet above sea level, is the highest train station in Europe. It is accessed aboard the Mount Pilatus Cog Railway.

George Pullman is best known for developing the Pullman sleeper, which came out in 1865. It was a finer version of earlier sleeper railcars, including his first experiments with the concept. He introduced the Pullman dining car in 1868. Pullman leased the cars to the railroads and got a share of the surcharge passengers paid to use the cars. There were 700 of his sleepers in operation by 1875. Before he turned to the railways, Pullman was a building mover (his father's business). In the 1850s, Chicago established a new sewer system, but to make that work, it elevated the pipes and raised streets by as much as 10 feet. With partners, Pullman moved buildings vertically onto shored-up versions of their original foundations.

———◆———

Switzerland has a wide choice of scenic Alpine train and motorcoach routes, and some have the most appealing names: Heidi Express, Mont Blanc Express, St. Bernard Express, William Tell Express, and (tastiest of all) the Swiss Chocolate Train. The Chocolate Train, seasonal with a June-to-October schedule, is a circle trip starting and ending in Montreux with luxurious travel aboard vintage Belle Epoque 1915 Pullman cars or modern panoramic cars. Passengers visit the Nestle chocolate factory in Broc, but the itinerary also includes Gruyeres to tour the castle and cheese factory there. This could so easily have been the Swiss Cheese Train.

———◆———

Railroad companies created time zones in North America. They and their passengers were constantly hampered by the fact that every city and little burg across the country set its own time. The railroad operators divided the United States and Canada into time zones, with each zone to be one hour different from the next. On November 18, 1883, all railway clocks and watches were set to the new standard, and eventually businesses, municipalities, and states fell into line. Only in 1918, 35 years later, did the U.S. Congress pass the Standard Time Act.

The first successful commercial electric streetcar system was inaugurated in Richmond, Virginia, in 1888.

The first firm to build and operate a railroad in the United States was the Granite Railway Company in Massachusetts, in 1826. The first company to carry passengers as well as freight by rail was the Baltimore & Ohio, beginning in 1830. Both companies used horses for power. It was only months later, in December 1830, that the South Carolina Canal and Rail Road Company in Charleston began the first scheduled service with a steam locomotive; it operated on six miles of wood and metal rails. A journalist, describing the inaugural trip, said the passengers "flew on the wings of wind at the speed of 15 to 25 miles per hour, annihilating time and space . . . leaving all the world behind."

The first underground railway (i.e., subway) in continental Europe opened in Budapest, Hungary, in 1896. Original cars and other equipment are on display in the city's Underground Railway Museum, located (fittingly) under ground.

In 1916, Harris Saunders and a brother, who owned a real estate business in Omaha, Nebraska, ran an ad offering a

Ford for rent with a car-and-driver arrangement or on a self-drive basis. Charges were based on miles driven as "the only reasonable arrangement," the ad said. Those fees were 10 cents a mile, three miles minimum. That was the first small step in the car rental business. Soon after (1918), 22-year-old Walter Jacobs opened a car rental business in Chicago with a dozen Model Ts that he repaired and repainted himself. It was a million-dollar business when in 1923 he sold it to John Hertz, president of Yellow Cab and Yellow Truck and Coach Manufacturing Company and the man who gave the business a new name — his.

———◆———

In most parts of the world, hitchhikers use their thumbs to indicate they want a lift. However, in Kenya and Tanzania, hitchhikers extend an arm out straight, with the palm flat and facing down, and wave the arm up and down.

———◆———

Enterprise Rent-a-Car, North America's largest car rental firm, had nearly 800,000 cars in early 2007; a merger with Alamo and National car firms brought that to more than 1.2 million.

———◆———

On Track

The 25-mile Semmering Railway in Austria — built over high mountains between 1848 and 1852 as part of the link between Vienna and Graz — is on the UNESCO list of protected sites because it is "one of the greatest feats of civil engineering from this pioneering phase of railway building."

This short stretch counts 15 tunnels, 16 viaducts, and 129 bridges, creating one of Europe's top scenic rides. Sixty-five million bricks and 80,000 flagstones were used in construction. Its main tunnel, at 4,692 feet, required 4,000 men and 4 million man days' work to construct.

———◆·◆·◆———

The Sultan of Johore built Malaysia's first railway in 1869, but the rails were made of wood and were soon eaten by ants.

———◆·◆·◆———

The 288-mile rail line between Guayaquil and Quito, Ecuador, was considered "the most difficult railway in the world" to build when it was constructed between 1899 and 1908. It is most difficult to maintain, too. Heavy rains, landslides, and earthquakes have kept parts of it unusable for years. So, the rail line is a tourist attraction. Most of the tracks are more than 8,000 feet up in the Andes and, of necessity, create a twisting trail through tunnels and across river gorges and ravines. Numerous volcanoes abutting the route surpass 15,000 feet, and one is the world's tallest, Chimborazo at 20,702 feet. On this route, the Devil's Nose is a 1,000-foot vertical rock cliff; the train ascends and descends on a switchback that was cut into the mountainside.

Passengers peer straight down to a river far below. Visitors can travel the Devil's Nose and other parts of the line aboard an autoferro, a one-coach train that resembles a bus on rails and includes open-air seating on top.

———◆·◆·◆———

Travia

The Eastern & Orient Express launched its luxurious Asian service between Singapore and Bangkok via Kuala Lumpur in 1993. The train covers the 1,262 miles in roughly 52 hours, including time for land tours. The service staff changes uniforms each day to match the country the train is passing through.

━━━◆━━━

San Francisco's cable cars were invented in 1873 by Andrew Hallidie who had witnessed a dreadful accident in which five horses were dragged to their deaths while trying to pull a streetcar up a wet and steep cobblestone street. The cable system by around 1900 numbered more than 600 cars rolling on 110 miles of track, the highest track mileage of any U.S. city (although Chicago had the most cars and riders). Much of the rail line was destroyed in San Francisco's 1906 earthquake, and not all was restored. Today, 40 cable cars are a tourist attraction operating on three short routes totaling 8.8 miles, and in 1964, they became a National Historic Landmark — the first

"moving" landmark to be designated by the U.S. National Park Service.

———◆———

The Pikes Peak Railway in Colorado is the highest cog railway in the world. It travels 8.9 miles from 6,571 feet above sea level to the summit at 14,110 feet.

———◆———

A French train, a research model of the nation's high-speed equipment, holds the record for the highest speed ever recorded on rail, 357 miles per hour, set in April 2007. The Maglev has traveled faster, but that train does not touch the rail.

———◆———

JR Central Towers, in Nagoya, Japan, is the world's largest rail station building, with 4,413,185 square feet of floor space and a height of 803 feet 10 inches. A complex encompassing offices, a store, and hotel, it also houses the Nagoya Station.

———◆———

Under communism, hitchhiking was encouraged as one way to meet the public's transportation needs in Poland. For a nominal fee, prospective hitchhikers bought books of coupons from the government which they waved to flag down drivers. Riders paid for their transportation with the coupons, which drivers redeemed for money from the government.

———◆———

For a period of time beginning in 1964, National Car Rental paid travel agents with Green Stamps when the agencies booked cars for business travelers.

———◆———

We call them bullet trains, but in Japan, the high-speed train service is called Shinkansen, which means "new trunk lines." The fast trains, operated by six private rail companies, have among them 26,000 departures a day. Since Shinkansen was introduced in 1964, the trains have carried several billion passengers, and only one customer has died in an accident.

After a 1954 typhoon sank five ferry boats in Japan's Tsugaru Strait (killing 1,430 people), the Japanese took on the monumental task of building a tunnel to link the main island of Honshu with the northern island of Hokkaido. Called the Seikan Tunnel, it is the world's longest railway tunnel stretching for 33.4 miles, with 14.3 miles of that lying below the strait. The rail track, at 787 feet below the sea, also is the world's deepest railway line. There are two underground stations, meant for emergency use, but visitors can visit on guided tours.

Avis Rent A Car, founded in 1946 by Warren Avis, was envisioned as an on-airport business which explains the company's original name: Avis Airlines Rent A Car System. The first two sites were the Detroit and Miami airports. Avis' initial investment in the company was $85,000. He sold the business in 1954 for $8 million. When Cendant Corporation bought Avis in 2001, the price tag was $937 million.

In the heyday of train travel, regular rail service brought countless escapees from summer heat to Bretton Woods and its grand hotels in and around New Hampshire's Mount Washington. Rail service to the region maxed out at 57 trains a day. To ascend Mount Washington itself, the world's first cog railway, which climbs 3,600 feet to the summit, debuted in 1869 (becoming one of America's first tourist attractions). It is still operational, but with modern iterations or upgraded versions of old equipment. For these journeys, the engine and passenger car are not coupled. The engine pushes the passenger car up, then the passenger coach coasts down against the engine.

The 15.2-mile Laerdal Tunnel, on the road linking Oslo and Bergen in Norway, is the longest highway tunnel in the world.

The steepest funicular in the world travels at a 45-degree angle. The Peak Tram takes passengers to the top of Victoria Peak, which at 1,805 feet is the highest point in Hong Kong and, on a clear day, offers stunning views of a world-famous harbor and nearby islands. Actually a railway, it opened in 1888, sparking the development of Victoria Peak.

The Japanese, on December 2, 2003, set a world's record of 361 miles per hour for a manned test run of a superconducting magnetically levitated train (in other words, a Maglev). The Japanese have been testing the train's technology for reliability and durability on an 11.4-mile track.

Travia

The Channel Tunnel, which for the first time since the Ice Age provides a ground link between Britain and the rest of Europe, is really three connected tubes — one for travel in each direction and a third which is described as the service tunnel. The third tube also is the escape tunnel, and it was used for that purpose one year after its 1994 debut when 31 people trapped by a fire on a London-bound Eurostar train were able to evacuate via that service tunnel.

Also called the Chunnel or the Euro Tunnel, this rail link was a major engineering feat. To create the parallel tunnels, each of which is 31 miles long (of which 23 miles are under water at an average depth of 150 feet below the seabed), workers removed rubble in a volume that was triple the volume of Egypt's Great Pyramid. Some tunnel-boring machines were as long as two football fields and could bore 250 feet a day. It took the machines three years to chew their way to a meeting point hundreds of feet below the Channel. As a project side effect, the size of Britain increased by 90 acres; the new land is a park. Eurostar trains can carry 770 passengers (the equivalent of two jumbo jets) and travel at a maximum commercial speed of 186 miles per hour. The London-Paris trip is two hours, 35 minutes; Eurostar also serves Lille, France, and Brussels. Only 20 minutes of each Eurostar trip is spent in the tunnel.

The longest straight stretch of rail track (271 miles) runs from Nurina in Western Australia to a point near Watson in South Australia.

The Avis car rental company says cell phones, wallets, and eyeglasses are the three things most often left behind in its cars. In other words, all the things it takes to get through the day.

The Sydney Harbour Bridge, an icon of Australia's largest city, is the widest long-span bridge in the world at 161 feet across. It accommodates eight vehicle lanes and two train lines, plus one path each for walkers and cyclists. Its dramatic arch rises 440 feet above the water. Paul Hogan once worked at the top of the arch, but that was before he became actor Paul Hogan, best known for "Crocodile Dundee." More than 1.5 million people have climbed to the top since the BridgeClimb option became available in 1998.

SYDNEY HARBOUR BRIDGE.   BRIDGE UNDER SEARCHLIGHT AND SERVICE ILLUMINATION.

The highest railroad in the world operates between Golmud in China's Qinghai province and Lhasa in Tibet. Often traveling at altitudes above 13,000 feet, its highest point is at Tanggula Pass where the rails sit 16,640 feet above sea level. Light aircraft don't fly that high. Oxygen is pumped into the train cars to protect occupants when they ride on the roof of the world. The train crosses permafrost for 340 miles of the 700-mile route. In an attempt to keep the frozen earth from melting under the weight and heat of trains, Chinese engineers took several steps: They elevated the tracks and installed pipes to circulate nitrogen and cold air beneath the rails. They added metal sunshades on south-facing locations to deflect the sun's heat. The Golmud-Lhasa rail line, opened in 2006, cost $4.2 billion to build.

Chapter 10

Sleep on It

Travia

The Mayfair Hotel in St. Louis, Missouri, is credited with being the first property to place chocolates on guest pillows at night. When Cary Grant stayed at the property, circa 1950, he laid a trail of chocolates from the parlor of his suite into the bedroom, culminating at the pillow with a chocolate and note to his woman companion. This story, told by the housekeeper, inspired the manager to place chocolates and goodnight wishes on guest pillows. The property is now the Roberts Mayfair, a part of the Wyndham historic hotels group.

The Windsor Court in New Orleans traditionally places its own handmade pralines on guest pillows at night; that adds up to nearly 50,000 a year.

Dubai is slated to have the world's first underwater luxury resort hotel (date to be determined). Currently dubbed the Hydropolis Hotel (referring to its location under water, of course), it will be built down to 66 feet under the sea. It will have a land station for check-in and administrative offices, a connecting double-track tunnel which guests traverse by special cars, and 200-plus suites under water.

There are 1,500-plus Holiday Inn locales and 1,400-plus Holiday Inn Express locations but, until May 2006, you wouldn't have known it at www.holidayinn.com, which spotlighted only one hotel. It's a long story, but here's the short version: The Holiday Inn Motel & Restaurant opened in Niagara Falls, Ontario, in the 1940s before the Holiday Inn Hotels and Resorts brand was founded in the United States in 1952. Owners of the Canadian business, who had eventually opened Holiday Inn by the Falls and closed the first property, beat the big guys to the HolidayInn.com domain name. Owners of the Holiday Inn registered trademark tried negotiations to obtain the domain name. When that failed, in 2001 they sued the Canadian operator, charging trademark infringement. Five years on, the parties settled, the Niagara Falls hotel joined the franchise group, and www.holidayinn. com became the chain's new Internet home (replacing the hyphenated www.holiday-inn.com).

The Dracula Hotel near Bistrita, Romania, was built to look like the fictional Dracula Castle conjured in Bram Stoker's novel "Dracula." Fittingly, it has a dungeon in the basement. Another hotel in the town, the Golden Crown, is named for the fictional hotel where Stoker's character Jonathan Harker overnighted. It serves food based on Harker's meal there.

Chicago's Palmer House Hilton, built in the 1920s, had predecessors. Potter Palmer built Palmer House in 1871. It debuted on September 26 and burned to the ground 13 days later in the Great Chicago Fire. But the wealthy Palmer persevered, rebuilding and reopening in July 1873 with a property that was the first to put electricity in every guest room and that boasted it was the "only thoroughly fireproof hotel in the United States." Also, the floor in the barber shop was tiled with silver dollars. In 1879, the Palmer House claimed another first: It installed a telephone in every room, only three years after Alexander Graham Bell invented the gadget.

———◆◆◆———

The Victorian house in Fall River, Massachusetts, where Andrew and Abby Borden were axed to death in 1892 (possibly by his daughter Lizzie) is now the Lizzie Borden Bed and Breakfast. Furnishings are replicas, but the handful of family bedrooms available for rent includes the room where Abby was murdered. (Andrew was killed in the living room.) Breakfasts are described as "reminiscent" of the last breakfast the elder Bordens ever ate, and online gift shop novelty items include a bobble head Lizzie Borden doll and a hatchet key chain, but the really gory stuff is at the Fall River Historical Society's museum.

———◆◆◆———

The Olde Angel Inn in Niagara-on-the-Lake, Ontario, which dates from 1789, claims to be the oldest continuously operating inn in North America.

———◆◆◆———

Sleep on It

The Royalist Hotel in Stow on the Wold, dating from 947, claims to be England's oldest inn. The stone structure offers eight bedrooms, a restaurant called 947 A.D. and a pub called Eagle and Child (once the name of the inn, too). The Saxon Duke Aethelmar founded the Royalist as a hospice to shelter lepers — and there is still a leper's hole, through which food could safely be passed to the afflicted, in the oldest part of the cellar. Other signs of the inn's past include a tunnel leading from the bar to the church across the street, witches' marks (to fend off witches) in the rooms, and evidence of a bear pit.

———◆◆———

In 1900, Boston's Lenox Hotel (now the Lenox Hotel & Suites/Village Lodge) promised "fireproof lodging, unexcelled cuisine, a shower bath, roof garden, and American/European lodging plans," starting at $2.

———◆◆———

There is nothing plain-vanilla about these housing arrangements:
* Guests of the Hotel Lindenwirt in Rudesheim, Germany, located in wine country along the Rhine, can opt for a "barrel room." These are tiny cottages fashioned from barrels that were once used in winemaking. De Vrouwe van Stavoren in the Dutch harbor town of Stavoren (a former Hanseatic League city) also offers, besides regular rooms, four rooms fashioned from Swiss wine barrels, each of which once held 15,000 liters (3,937.5 gallons) of wine.
* "Bedrooms" at AYH Ranch Hostel on Washington state's Vashon Island include covered wagons and teepees. Space is tight for two in tiny wagons, but teepees come in several sizes, even dorm sizes.
* Certain expeditions in the Bolivian Andes operated by Viajes Explora (based in Santiago, Chile) utilize renovated cargo

containers. However, travelers sleep in tents; the containers accommodate the kitchen and bathrooms.

* Jules' Undersea Lodge was built as La Chalupa mobile undersea laboratory, but the 20-by-50-foot facility 30 feet under water at the bottom of Emerald Lagoon in Key Largo (Florida) Undersea Park has been converted for visitors. Guests scuba to their hotel and watch passing marine life through 42-inch round windows.

In 1929, when the Grosvenor House debuted in London, room rates ranged from one to 10 guineas per night (in today's decimal system, £1.05 to £10.50), and servants were accommodated at 18 shillings per day (90 pence). The new hotel, as the city's first with bathrooms in all rooms and Europe's first with ice water in bathrooms, was built with Americans very much in mind. But not all Brits liked it: Letters to the Times of London called it "an insult to ... good taste and aesthetic judgment," while nicknames included Sing Sing and Westminster Workhouse.

Hilton Hotels placed 37,763,520 bars of soap in hotel rooms during 2004. Broken down, that was 6,371,700 bars in Doubletree's 40,922 room; 5,560,800 in Embassy Suites' 42,715 rooms; 3,946,620 in Hampton Inn's 130,398 rooms; 16,989,900 in Hilton's 89,256 rooms; 3,197,700 in Hilton Garden Inn's 29,841 rooms, and 1,696,800 in Homewood Suites' 16,054 rooms.

In 1983, VingCard invented the optical electronic key card used by many hotels worldwide.

Sleep on It

The Langham Hotel in London (now the Langham London), when it opened with 300-plus rooms in 1865, was the first in the world with "rising rooms" (elevators). It also promised its "precautions against fire are all that human forethought can devise." It had firemen on duty around the clock — two during the day and two at night — plus "a patent electric fire alarm" to allow guests or servants to call the firemen in case of an "accident." The hotel had a secret, too: the Cockpit in the basement that was the venue for illegal cockfights.

———— ◆ ————

The sail-shaped Burj al Arab, or Arabian Tower, in Dubai is the world's tallest hotel at 1,053 feet, which makes it taller than the Eiffel Tower (984 feet high) and not far behind the Empire State Building (1,250 feet).

———— ◆ ————

The 555-room Grand Hyatt Shanghai is the world's highest hotel: It is located on the 53rd to 87th floors of the Jin Mao Tower, which is 1,380 feet high and quite a bit taller than Dubai's Burj al Arab.

———— ◆ ————

Travia

The Chateau Frontenac in Quebec City, Quebec, has a rooftop herb garden that the chef can access only one way, through a window.

———◆———

The Westin New York at Times Square offers guests a special room rate if they participate in an annual autumn charity drive. "Housewarming" gifts, celebrating the property's debut in October of 2002, totaled about 500 pounds of nonperishable foods which went to the Coalition for the Homeless. In succeeding years, the hotel solicited books and new or "gently used" sheets or clothing.

———◆———

This is a sniff test: The W Hotel in Seoul, South Korea, labels some of its rooms Scent Rooms, where guests have a choice of aromatherapy, meaning they decide how their rooms should smell. It's the same, more or less, in the 13 Spa-Inspired Rooms at the Westin New York at Times Square, which releases choices of "soothing fragrances" into rooms.

———◆———

The coolest hotels on Earth are made of ice. There are several, and four are listed here. In order of size, they are found in Sweden, Canada (Quebec), Norway, and the United States (Alaska). The sleeping rooms, with inside temperatures from the high teens to 28 degrees Fahrenheit, and a few public rooms are of ice; bathrooms are not. Snow also is a component in most ice construction. The first three properties are rebuilt each year, so they vary in size and appearance from season to season.

* *The Icehotel* in Jukkasjarvi, Sweden, debuted in the 1990-91 season and, in its latest iteration, had 85 rooms requiring about 3,000 tons of ice. It opens at mid-December and closes when the roof starts dripping (toward the end of April). The two

restaurants are in warm spaces, but one offers ice plates. The Absolut Icebar, ice chapel, and ice art exhibition hall are, of course, icy.

* *Ice Hotel Quebec-Canada*, launched in 2001 just west of Quebec City, operates from early January to early April. In its most recent incarnation, it had 32 rooms and suites, a chapel, art gallery, two exhibit rooms, the Absolut Icebar, and the N'ice Club, all of ice.

* *The Alta Igloo Hotel* near Alta, Norway, first constructed in 2000, most recently counted 24 rooms and suites, ice bar, ice chapel, ice gallery, and several lounges. Even the glasses in the bar are made of ice. The season is typically mid-January to mid-April.

* Alaska's ice accommodation is an adjunct to the *Chena Hot Springs Resort*. It opened in the 2003-04 season and, by blowing really cold air on metal walls, keeps its ice and operates on a year-round basis. There are only four sleeping rooms, plus these icy add-ons: Stoli Ice Bar, igloo, ceremony stage, turret, and ice-art studio.

Travia

And, there is the 33-room *Mammut SnowHotel*, which is one part of SnowCastle in Kemi, Finland. SnowCastle also includes a chapel, restaurant, and art gallery, all made of snow. Only ice sculptures, tables, and a few other details are of ice. Its most recent hotel season was December 31 to early April.

More about that Alaska ice "hotel": It opened New Year's Eve 2003, later than planned, because Alaska's fire marshal thought the ice structure might be a fire hazard. Therefore, its owner, the Chena Hot Springs Resort, had to install smoke detectors and fire extinguishers in the ice rooms. That took time because the smoke detectors had to be protected in waterproof casings. In addition, government regulations stipulate the operation cannot be called a hotel so, focusing on its ice sculptures, it is the Aurora Ice Museum. Guests can rent and sleep in the "galleries," each with uniquely carved beds. One bed is a polar bear, on its back, with the paws serving as the four posters.

Many Italian cities and towns have a type of hotel where you cannot spend the night. It is a day hotel, but it's not what you think. At the "albergo diurno," visitors can get a haircut or pedicure, have clothes cleaned and shoes polished, or simply take a bath and grab a nap. Day hotels are usually found in central-city sites near railway stations. They typically are open from 6 a.m. to midnight.

Every guest at the Mount Kenya Safari Club in Nanyuki, Kenya, crosses the Equator to get from the entrance of the main building to the restaurants. The building was constructed so the Earth's natural divide falls right down the middle of the club's main U-shaped building and its central lawn. To prove this really is the Equator, the club invites guests to a daily demonstration. On one side of the line (the north), they watch water flow clockwise through a hole, and on the south side, they watch water flow counterclockwise. The water is neutral when right over the Equator and flows without circling. Vines growing around a pole or tree, circle in different directions, too, depending in which side of the Equator they are on.

The New Yorker Magazine was born in a hotel — after a fashion. It was at the Algonquin Hotel in New York where the magazine's founder Harold Ross won enough money in a poker game to fund the project.

The 10 largest hotels in the United States, by room count, are all located in Las Vegas, with the MGM Grand Hotel and Casino (5,034 rooms) topping that list. Among the top 20 U.S. properties, 17 are in Las Vegas. The MGM Grand also has been described as the world's largest hotel, but the company does not make that claim.

Major hotels in Japan equip guest rooms with computerized toilets that include wash, dry, and bidet elements plus a heated seat. An instruction sheet provided at the Four Seasons at

Chinzan-so, Tokyo, assists guests in setting the temperatures for spraying water, drying functions, and the toilet seat itself, as well as adjusting water pressure. The instructions caution guests not to try operating the toilet "without first being seated" (to avoid a shower from the wrong device). With all that, the toilet can only be flushed manually. Providing a pre-trip sampler, Japan Airlines installed the computerized equipment in its business class lounge at JFK Airport in New York.

An amenity for its time: The Cornell Quarterly, in 1960, reported that the Jack Tar Hotel in San Francisco had an air raid warning alert tied to the televisions in guest rooms.

Traditional housing converted to accommodations for tourists takes some unusual twists:

* *Gypsy caravan.* The Hotel Herberg de Emauspoort in Delft, Holland, a canal house-hotel, has two wooden Gypsy caravans furnished as guest rooms.

* *Lavvos.* These are traditional tents for Sami (aka Lapp) reindeer herders. Tent camps are built in winter. At Alta Friluftspark in northern Norway, tourists can overnight at a camp, eat reindeer meat, and go ice fishing.

* *Longhouses.* Borneo's Dyaks, headhunters of yore, have historically built a single stilted longhouse for the entire village. An open public space (some of it roofed) extends the entire length on one side, and private quarters are carved out of the other half and added onto as families grow. In the Malaysian part of Borneo (Sabah and Sarawak), communities build longhouses for tourists.

* *Marae.* New Zealand's Maori communities near Gisbourne invite tourists to overnight in their traditional stockaded communities, sleeping in the open room of the marae, which

is the traditional meeting house.

* *Riad.* Tame by comparison with the above, the riad (meaning "big house") is the Moroccan version of a large private home converted into a guest house. Riads, found in old medinas and promising traditional Arabic architectural features, can be luxury establishments.

* *Yurts or gers.* Sleeping in a Mongolian felt tent (modeled on tents and furnishings used by the country's nomadic herders) is a typical way to experience the Gobi Desert. These can come in deluxe versions, too.

———◆———

Club Med, founded in 1950 by Belgian Olympic water polo champion Gerard Blitz, was the first to offer the all-inclusive resort concept.

———◆———

The world's largest single-brand hotel chain is U.S.-based Best Western International with more than 4,200 independently owned hotels offering more than 315,000 guest rooms.

———◆———

Holiday Inns loses an estimated 590,000 towels a year to theft.

———◆———

Travia

The world's first motel (meaning the modern iteration of the ancient roadside inn) was the Milestone Mo-Tel, opened in 1925 and sited in San Luis Obispo, California, as a convenient stopping point for those on a car journey between Los Angeles and San Francisco. When developer Arthur Heineman used "mo-tel" in the name, he was signaling the combination of "motor" and "hotel." Early on, he helped get the message across with a neon sign that alternately flashed "hotel" and "mo-tel." His new word caught on as effectively as the concept itself of roadside way stations for the 20th century.

———◆◆◆———

Conrad Hilton bought his first hotel, the Mobley, in Cisco, Texas, in 1919.

———◆◆◆———

A few hotels are former prisons.
At the high end is the Four Seasons Hotel Istanbul, in Turkey, where the prisoners' exercise courtyard is now an open-air restaurant, but this is above all a five-star hotel so all those cells are gone.
In addition, the four-star Liberty Hotel in Boston was the Charles Street Jail. The 1851 granite jailhouse, which is listed on the National Register of Historic Places, was preserved.
Vestiges of authentic cells are part of the lobby bar.
For something quite different, at Old Lock-Up Guest House in Wirksworth, Derbyshire, in England, one cell is the bar, and another is preserved for viewing. The four bedrooms formerly accommodated the resident magistrate, visiting lawyers, the coachman, and a hayloft. (This establishment's fifth room is a tiny former chapel that sits in a graveyard.)
But Canada's Trois-Rivieres Prison in Mauricie, Quebec (operational from 1822 to 1986), does not call itself a hotel and for good reason. It is, in fact, the Quebec Museum of

Folk Culture's "Go to Jail" exhibit. For up to 40 persons per night, the cost of admission covers a night in the cells, which guests share with one to seven fellow "inmates." Aside from having a tour led by ex-cons, guests are "booked" by a warden, photographed, fingerprinted, and provided with prison shirts. Before their release the next morning, "inmates" clean their cells and breakfast on porridge and toast. Clearly, this interactive museum is not for everyone.

———◆◆◆———

The revolving door at the entrance to the Excelsior hotel in Hong Kong was installed in 1978 especially for scenes in the late Peter Sellers' "Revenge of the Pink Panther."

———◆◆◆———

The Four Seasons Hotel Hampshire is located outside of London in Dogmersfeld Park, a 1,000-year-old, 500-acre estate that was the site of the first meeting between England's future King Henry VIII and Catherine of Aragon, who would become his wife (well, the first of six, we mean to say).

———◆◆◆———

There are 3,350 hotel rooms on Tahiti and the other 117 islands in French Polynesia. Compare that with the MGM Grand in Las Vegas, which has 5,034 rooms.

<hr />

Kemmons Wilson founded Holiday Inn in 1952, having hatched the idea for a chain of standardized, clean, and reasonably priced accommodations after his family's 1951 driving vacation. He had found most properties second-rate, and he was particularly annoyed at paying an extra $2 per child; he had five. The first Holiday Inn in Memphis, Tennessee,

posted these prices: $4, single, $6, double (nothing extra for the kids). He took the name for the chain from "Holiday Inn," the movie in which Bing Crosby introduced the song, "White Christmas." Wilson aimed to open 400 properties across the United States, but oversaw the creation of a much larger hotel group that spans the globe. And all of this was brought to us by the same man who managed, not once, but twice, to build his own family residence on the wrong town lot.

<hr />

Gideons International placed its first Bible in the Superior Hotel in Superior, Montana. That was in 1908.

<hr />

The world's three oldest operating Otis elevators can be found in the Hotel del Coronado in San Diego, California.

They have been running since the hotel
debuted in 1888.

———◆———

The InterContinental Hong Kong is the only hotel to be built
entirely over water. It sits on stilts over Victoria Harbour.

———◆———

James and Nicole Frankel, the original owners of La Samanna,
built in 1973 on St. Martin in the French West Indies, named
the property after their children. They combined letters from
these names — Samantha, Anouk, and Nathalie — and added
the French prefix "La." Et voila! A new name.

———◆———

In 1925, a young entrepreneur took over a corner drugstore in
Wollaston, Massachusetts. To capitalize on his popular soda
fountain, he created a better ice cream with a secret recipe
(based on his mother's with natural ingredients and twice the
normal amount of butterfat). By 1928, he had rolled out 28
flavors and was selling $240,000 in ice cream cones. That let
him borrow money to open his first restaurant in Quincy,
Massachusetts. When this ambitious wunderkind could not
grow fast enough, he created franchising — and a nationwide
chain. The franchisee kept most of the money but had to
run his restaurant based on detailed instructions written by
the master himself. So, when the time was right, in 1954, it
was natural that Howard Dearing Johnson would apply his
principles to a new franchise business, the Howard Johnson
Motor Lodge.

———◆———

Westin Hotels & Resorts, noted for its so-called Heavenly
Beds, has installed 77,408 of them in 121 hotels globally, and
topped them with 309,632 pillows. If the beds were lined
up end to end, they would extend 90.9 miles. Assembled

differently, they would cover slightly more than 60 pro football fields.

———◆———

In 1900, the standard first class hotel offered steam heat, gas burners, electric call bells, baths, closets on all floors (as even closets were shared down the hall), billiard rooms, barber shops, liveries (precursor to the on-site garage), and sample rooms for the convenience of traveling salesmen who needed a place to show their wares. Then, in 1908, Ellsworth Statler launched the Statler hotel chain in Buffalo, with a raft of innovations, installing private baths, closets, running ice water, full-length mirrors, and a writing desk with hotel stationery in every guest room. Also, there were lamps over each bed and light switches near the door. Telephones in every room were standard for the fledgling chain, too. This was the slogan (and the offer): "A room and a bath for a dollar and a half."

———◆———

Statler introduced a number of amenities in one fell swoop, in 1908. Here are some other firsts for the hotel industry, introduced after that date in one or more locations of the named chain:

1925: Radios in all guests rooms,
Statler Hotels (Boston).

1934: Air conditioning in all public rooms,
Statler Hotels (Detroit).

1951: TV sets in all guest rooms,
Hilton Hotels.

1952: Free ice machines in hotel corridors,
Holiday Inn.

1957: Direct-dial telephones in rooms,
Hilton Hotels.

1969: 24-hour room service,
Westin Hotels.

Sleep on It

1984: Nonsmoking rooms,
Quality Suites (Flagstaff, Arizona).
1991: In-room voice mail,
Westin Hotels.
2003: Free high-speed Internet access in all rooms,
Kimpton Hotels.

The first Super 8 motel opened in Aberdeen, South Dakota, in 1974; it charged $8.88 per night.

InterContinental Hotels & Resorts (initially named International Hotels) was created by Pan American in 1946 and became the first international hotel brand. The first property opened in 1949 in Belem, Brazil. The airline, already flying throughout Latin America, was urged by President Franklin Roosevelt to build hotels in the area. The president wanted to develop trade with the Americas to the south, which

required hotels as well as transportation, as a way of improving intra-American relations. Early hotel development followed Pan Am's routes.

The Houshi Ryokan in Awazu, Japan, built in 718, is the world's oldest continuously operating hotel. In addition, its current owners are the 46th generation of the same family to own and operate the property.

According to the American Hotel & Lodging Association, average U.S. hotel room rates tracked as follows from 1930 on:

1930 – $5.60
1940 – $3.21
1950 – $5.91
1960 – $10.81
1970 – $19.83
1980 – $45.44
1990 – $58.70
2000 – $85.89

Some of the more exotic traditional hotel types are as follows:

* *Caravanserai.* Often associated with the Silk Road (which was really several routes stretching from the Mediterranean to China), the caravanserais, also called khans, were built with strong walls for safety and large enough to accommodate traders' goods and camels. They can be seen in Acre, Israel; at several sites in Turkey, as well as in Armenia and Georgia (the country). A few in Turkey are hotels now, and one in Ankara houses the Museum of Anatolian Civilizations. In Isfahan, Iran, the five-star Abbasi Hotel was a 17th-century caravanserai.

* *Funduk.* Also designed for traveling merchants, funduks typically had courtyards and space for storage; they have a smaller footprint but are taller than caravanserais. They are associated with the medieval Arab world and Turkey and can be seen as far west as Granada, Spain, as well as in Morocco. However, as functioning hotels, they are most often associated with Yemen and available to adventurous 21st-century tourists in Al-Hajjarah, Manakha, Thula, and other mountain villages.

Sleep on It

* *Ryokan.* These traditional Japanese inns can be old or new buildings but they have the uncluttered look, tatami mats, and paper walls associated with Japanese culture.

The Marriott hotel business, founded by J. Willard Marriott, Sr., got its start in Washington, D.C., in 1927 as an A&W root beer franchise and by the 1930s had morphed into the larger Hot Shoppes, a caterer to airlines. The first hotel opened in Arlington, Virginia, in 1957. Within minutes of cutting the ribbon for the new property, there came a call from someone offering to sell the new Disneyland Hotel in Anaheim, California. Was Marriott interested? "Heavens, no! We probably won't be able to make this one work," he said. Today, J.W. (Bill) Marriott, Jr., is chairman and CEO of Marriott International, with about 3,000 properties worldwide.

The 10-room Longfellow's Wayside Inn in Sudbury, Massachusetts, was immortalized by Henry Wadsworth Longfellow in his 1863 book of poems called "Tales of a Wayside Inn." At the time, the inn was called Howe's Tavern, and the fourth-generation innkeeper, Lyman Howe, was the featured character in the book's Landlord's Tale, in which Longfellow gave us the phrase, "Listen my children and you shall hear, of the midnight ride of Paul Revere."

A one-room hotel in the Dutch village of Eenrum calls itself the world's smallest hotel. In room No. 1 (yes, it has a number), the bed, which is a traditional box bed, is behind doors in what looks like a large cupboard. The name of this diminutive hotel? It is the Grand Hotel de Kromme Raake.

Travia

The Inn on Covered Bridge Green in Arlington, Vermont, was once the home of America's best-known illustrator/artist, Norman Rockwell.

There are several ways to sleep with or, more safely, near exotic "pets":

* The InterContinental Pyramids Park Resort in Cairo, Egypt, has a mini-zoo that houses deer, monkeys, peacocks, ostriches, and flamingos.

* Shangri-La's Rasa Ria Resort near Kota Kinabalu, East Malaysia, operates a 64-acre nature preserve and cares for a few of the area's rescued orphan orangutans. Guests can visit this troop of clowns but not touch.

* The Giraffe Manor outside Nairobi, Kenya, is adjacent to the Giraffe Centre, a sanctuary for once-endangered Rothschild giraffes. The long-necked residents are in the habit of popping their heads into the manor's windows and the front door for treats.

* At Vision Quest Ranch in Salinas, California, guests sleep on the sanctuary grounds. Breakfast in a basket is delivered by elephant, and the delivery "boy" will take his "tip" in fruit.

* Tourists can also overnight inside Australian zoos: the

Sleep on It

Werribee Open Range Zoo outside Melbourne; Sydney's Taronga Zoo, and the Western Plains Zoo in Dubbo.

———◆———

One founder of the Mount Kenya Safari Club at Nanyuki, Kenya, was actor William Holden, who also sought to protect area wildlife. One result of that is an animal orphanage on premises which includes a range of rescued critters. For one, Patricia the (friendly) ostrich was an abandoned egg. The site also includes the world's only zebroids, named Pete and Re-Pete. A cross between a zebra and a thoroughbred horse, they look like brown zebras.

———◆———

The creators of the Sheraton group of hotels bought their first property, the 200-room Stonehaven in Springfield, Massachusetts, in 1937. However, it was the 1939 purchase of a Boston hotel called Sheraton that gave the chain its name.

———◆———

When London's Langham Hotel debuted in 1865, a room cost one shilling sixpence to two shillings sixpence on the upper floors, but a room cost up to 10 shillings on the lower floors. The best choices were lower-floor combinations — drawing room, bed with dressing room, and (unlike other rooms) private bathroom facilities. All this started at 25 shillings (equal to £1.25) or about $10 based on the 1865 exchange rate of $8 to the pound. By 1879, in the "Dictionary of London" by Charles Dickens, son of the novelist, the Langham was described as "a special American resort," where a bed, full breakfast, and dinner could be had for 14 shillings sixpence.

———◆———

The Dutch have a thing for fairytale hotels. The rural Hotel de Tovenaarsberg, a converted farmhouse, is supposedly on the site where a wizard once lived. One guest room was designed as if for the reading of the "Tales From the Thousand and One Nights." Other rooms are called Magic Room, Troll Room, and Witch's Suite, and snacks carry names like flying carpets and troll balls.

The Efteling Hotel, at the entrance to the themed Efteling Enchanted Park, has the Sleeping Beauty Room, Circus Room, and Fata Morgana Suite. Then, there is the Fifties Room, where the bed is inside a 1952 Chevrolet Bel Air.

———◆———

Sample rooms, typical of hotels in the late 19th century and well into the 20th, were rented to salesmen along with their guest rooms. Or, in some cases, sample rooms were outfitted with in-room foldaway beds instead. Most sample rooms have long since disappeared, but London's Grosvenor House, even when overhauled and converted to a JW Marriott property, retained a sample room.

———◆———

In Japan, tourists can overnight at Buddhist temples. The lodgings, called "shukubo," may be basic, but the vegetarian cuisine (prepared by the monks) is said to be quite good. Other Japanese accommodations are not meant for tourists at all.

There are the so-called "love hotels," designed for romance and expected to be used for romantic trysts. Then, there are the "capsule hotels," which are stacked capsules small enough to be compared with large coffins. Used mostly by men, they include, besides the bed, a TV, radio, and alarm clock.

The Lighthouse Bed & Breakfast Inn in Two Harbors, Minnesota, is a working lighthouse. Guests are tapped as assistant lighthouse keepers and deemed "registered keepers of the light" while staying there.

The legendary Raffles Hotel Singapore was opened in 1887, and a short while later — around the turn of that century — waiter Ngiam Tong Boon created the famous Singapore Sling, a pink-hued drink originally intended for female guests. It is served to this day, and the recipe is 30 ml gin, 15 ml cherry brandy, 120 ml pineapple juice, 15 ml lime juice, 7.5 ml Cointreau, 7.5 ml Dom Benedictine, 10 ml Grenadine, a dash of Angostura Bitters, and a slice of pineapple and a cherry for garnishes.

After Jamshetji Tata was refused lodging in 1902 at an English-owned hotel in India because he was Indian, he decided to open his own hotel. That is how the Taj Hotels chain, a collection of often very upscale properties was born. The first project, the Taj Mahal Hotel in Bombay, describes itself as the oldest luxury hotel in India and the country's first five-star property. The Taj Hotels group also includes the Rambagh Palace in Jaipur, once a maharaja's hunting palace, and the unforgettable Lake Palace (set in a lake, of course) in Udaipur, once a maharana's summer palace.

———◆———

For really tasty service:

* The *Hotel de la Cite* in Carcassonne, France, doesn't put just any old chocolates on bed pillows. The chef creates hand-painted chocolates with images depicting the hotel and the countryside. In a town noted for its medieval citadel, the chef also is noted for recreating a medieval castle in chocolate.
* The spa at the *Hotel Hershey* in Hershey, Pennsylvania, offers the Whipped Cocoa Bath and the Chocolate Fondue Wrap. The local Hershey factory produces more than a billion pounds of chocolate products a year.
* The spa at the *Courthouse Hotel Kempinski* in London serves up Chocolate Facials, Chocolate Body Treatments, Chocolate Manicures, and Chocolate Pedicures.

———◆———

Speaking of sweet services: The spa at the George V in Paris uses honey plus roses and lotus flowers for one facial, whereas the Sugar Dream body treatment relies on a red sugar flower scrub followed by sugar and bitter orange oil.

———◆———

For a few more amenities you did not know you wanted:

* *Burj Al Arab*, Dubai, United Arab Emirates. Beds rotate in the two Royal Suites.
* *Ciragan Palace Kempinski*, Istanbul, Turkey. Poolside

Sleep on It

attendants' duties include cleaning sunbathers' sunglasses. (A similar service is offered on the SeaDream yachts.)

* *Four Seasons Resort Chiang Mai*, Thailand. The live-in housekeeper is accessible around the clock.

* All *Loews* properties. Loaner items for in-room use include putting greens, barbells, and reading glasses.

* *Hotel Monasterio*, Cuzco, Peru. Supplemental oxygen is piped into most rooms (Cuzco is 11,024 feet above sea level).

* *Nxabega Okavango Safari Camp*, Botswana. Brunch can be served to honeymooners in a bubbly bathtub.

* *Oriental Hotel*, Bangkok, Thailand. Personalized stationery is delivered to VIPs and guests in selected suites; similarly, guests in the Skyloft units, *MGM Grand*, Las Vegas, receive engraved personalized stationery and business cards.

* *The Pierre*, New York. The concierge will tie guests' bowties.

* *Las Ventanas al Paraiso*, Los Cabos, Mexico. Staff delivers a personalized sewing kit to the room on the second day with thread colors selected to match what guests have hung in their closets.

* *W Seoul*, South Korea. Guest rooms called Media Rooms have private projection LCD screens and home theater systems.

And for the amenity that has occurred to you: All *Four Seasons* hotels have the Gourmet to Go service which enables guests to head to the airport with their in-flight (or pre-flight) meals in hand.

Planning ahead: Several Four Seasons hotels allow regular guests to leave behind a full set of clothes and personal effects for their return visit. The clothes can be cleaned and pressed, too. Many Four Seasons properties also take room service orders from guests before they get to the hotel. At the MGM

Grand in Las Vegas, the concierge calls guests booked in the Skyloft units to determine (before they leave home) what they want in their private bar and to begin making their dinner and entertainment plans.

———◆———

The Hassler was General Dwight Eisenhower's headquarters in Rome during World War II, then converted back to a hotel in 1947.

———◆———

Turn the designers loose and the fun begins:
* The Ice Bar in the Hotel Hilton Cologne, in Germany, earned that name: The bar has a real-ice bar top. This lounge is a cool place in every sense.
* At the Hilton Auckland, in New Zealand, seating options in the White restaurant (painted to match its name) include a sleek long white table that is supported by only one leg. The entire hotel, which sits partly out to sea on Princes Wharf, looks like a large cruise ship — and yes, it is white.
* The Trocadero Dokhans, Sofitel Demeure Hotel in Paris has an elevator designed like a Louis Vuitton trunk and upholstered in Louis Vuitton's signature logo leather.
* The WooBar at the W Seoul in South Korea, is noted for

egg-shaped chairs suspended from the ceiling. In the property's central gathering space, called the Living Room, interactive digital artwork compels attention to the walls and tabletops.

* * *

Just think what we take for granted: Around 1830, when the spanking new Tremont House opened in Boston, it gained notoriety because it provided free soap and individual door locks for each room. Gas lighting in public spaces got attention, too. Author Charles Dickens, a guest, talked about the Tremont in his book, "American Notes." The hotel was torn down in the 1890s.

* * *

In Columbus, Ohio, during the 1890s, fire destroyed three hotels. To rebuild and reassure the traveling public, 400 men invested $100 each to form the Great Southern Fireproof Hotel Company which, in turn, built the Great Southern Fireproof Hotel and Opera House. It was a grand property that debuted in 1897 with 222 guest rooms, 56 private bathrooms, and eight public baths. Today, it is the Westin Great Southern Hotel with 186 guest rooms, including 23 suites, and a lot more bathrooms.

* * *

Travia

Doubletree Hotels is famous for giving out its Doubletree cookie to every hotel guest. Each day, across North America, the hotel company distributes approximately 29,000 chocolate chip cookies, totaling more than 10.5 million a year. The two-ounce cookie averages 20 chips and is baked daily at each Doubletree property.

------◆------

Hilton Hotels likes to put its purchasing numbers into perspective. The following are totals for all brands except Hilton International:

* In a year, the several Hilton brands place 4,608,000 chocolate mints in guest rooms. Laid end to end, they would stretch from Los Angeles to San Diego (145 miles).
* The hotels serve 8,719,693 pounds (about 4,360 tons or the weight of 528 elephants) of beef to guests each year.
* Annually, Hilton guests consume about 3.7 million eggs. That's enough eggs to make 740 renditions of the 5,000-egg giant omelette produced each year at the Giant Omelette Festival in Abbeville, Louisiana.
* The Hilton brands sold 58 million cups of coffee in 2004. That required an estimated 580 tons of coffee or nearly enough coffee for 13 Boston Tea Parties.

------◆------

The Mount Nelson Hotel in Cape Town, South Africa, is famous for its pink color. Paint is specially mixed for the hotel and formulated to fade to just the right shade for a lush Mediterranean look.

------◆------

In a Japanese inn, called a ryokan, guests are expected to shed their shoes, change to special slippers for the bathroom, and remove slippers to walk on the tatami. It is proper to bathe and rinse off the soap before stepping into hot bath water

Sleep on It

because the water is intended to be used by more
than one guest.

———◆◆———

There is a 14-room hotel inside a functioning Paris hospital.
It is atop the Hotel-Dieu Hospital, next to
Notre-Dame Cathedral.

———◆◆———

Here's how some buildings got a new lease on life:

* The *Courthouse Hotel Kempinski* in London was the scene
of playwright Oscar Wilde's trial. Formerly the Great
Marlborough Street Magistrate's Court, it also "hosted"
defendants Mick Jagger and Keith Richards — and Napoleon
III. Today, private tables in the bar are inside three original
prison cells, and iron bars separate the lobby from the bar. The
judge's bench, witness stand, and dock take center stage in
Silk, the hotel's fine-dining restaurant.

* The *Crowne Plaza Hotel Quaker Square* in Akron, Ohio, was
created from the 19th-century mills and silos that were the first
home to the Quaker Oats Company. The 36 silos are 120 feet
tall and once accommodated 1.5 million tons of grain. Today,
they house the Crowne Plaza's guest rooms, all round and all
24 feet in diameter.

* The five-star *De Koperen Hoogte* in Zwolle, Holland, was a
water tower. Each floor accommodates only one (a suite) or
two rooms, and the Top Suite is inside the top of the
water tower.

* *Le Meridien Turin Art + Tech* in Turin, Italy, is located in
a former Fiat factory. The factory's rooftop test track, with
its two steep parabolic bends, is now a jogging track. The
test track was made famous with its appearance in the 1969
version of the film, "The Italian Job."

* The *Ritz-Carlton Georgetown* in Washington, D.C., was

once an incinerator, and it is designed with fire as its theme. The smokestack is a small event space for up to 12, and the Fahrenheit restaurant retains the ceiling pulley that brought trash bins into the incinerator.

In 1945, it cost $5 a night to stay at the Waldorf-Astoria in New York; the rate was $6 a night at the Plaza a few blocks away.

The Athenee Palace Hotel, built in 1913 in Bucharest, Romania, was long known as a center for espionage in central Europe — and for good reason. From the beginning of World War I in 1914 through the communist era, which ended in December 1989, listening devices and specially trained "staff" were part of the "service." It is now the Athenee Palace Hilton.

It was an accident of history that Albert Steigenberger founded Germany's Steigenberger Hotel Group in 1930. He had lent large sums of money to a struggling hotel, the Europaischer Hof in Baden-Baden, Germany. When foreclosure put the property on the market at auction, Steigenberger bought it rather than be stuck with a stack of useless IOUs. He then upgraded the hotel and made the profits that allowed him to buy more hotels.

***

The Mandarin Oriental Hyde Park, London, is the only hotel with a private royal entrance to Hyde Park, access that dates to a time when the hotel was a private residence. From the days of Queen Victoria, the gate has been opened only with royal permission, which the hotel obtains occasionally for high-profile guests seeking privacy or for some wedding parties.

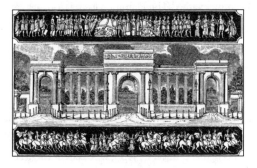

***

When not representing 6,000 bed-and-breakfast members worldwide in the usual ways, BedandBreakfast.com (an online directory and booking site) looks for the best in B&B ghostly experiences. For real goose bumps, the story at Prince Solms Inn Bed & Breakfast, New Braunfels, Texas, tops them all. Herewith, the short version: A bride was to wed in this inn, but the bridegroom did not appear. She vowed to stay at the inn until he came, so she worked there for two decades until her death in the late 1920s. In 1930, a man arrived on horseback seeking a woman. Staff saw a woman waiting in a wedding dress. The couple embraced and vanished. No one came to claim the man's horse. The bride has returned numerous times, it says here.

It's chocolate chip cookies at the Doubletree hotels, but at the Holiday Inn Express sites in the United States, the sweet du jour is cinnamon rolls. The hotel company tested a dozen recipes before settling on its exclusive iteration of the breakfast treat. In a year, the group makes 15 million cinnamon rolls.

The Flamingo hotel in Las Vegas, opened by mobster Bugsy Siegel in 1946, was named for his girlfriend Virginia Hill. She had been nicknamed The Flamingo for her long legs and red hair. Annette Benning played Virginia in the movie "Bugsy" opposite her future husband Warren Beatty.

When London's Grosvenor House opened for business in 1929, the banquet hall now known as the Great Room was an ice rink. It was the venue for hockey matches, ice galas, and recreational skating. It could be converted into an exhibition hall as needed and once, in 1933, was a circus ring. The rink was closed and the room converted for banqueting purposes in 1935, producing what is still Europe's largest banquet space, at 20,454 square feet. When planners renovated the property, making it the Grosvenor House JW Marriott, one thing did not change: The water pipes for the ice rink are still there.

The InterContinental Hotels Group manages the world's first and largest hotel loyalty program, Priority Club Rewards, with more than 25 million members.

A 1935 flyer promoting the Herald Square Hotel in New York bragged that it was quite close to the Pennsylvania

Sleep on It

Railway Station "in this metropolis of vast extent and tedious distances" and that "the wonder of the age, the Empire State Building, is on the next square [heading] east." Rates for double rooms with running water were $2.50 and, for a double room with private bath, $3. Meals in the Colonial Restaurant, "with foods cooked by women to please the most critical," cost 20 cents to 50 cents for breakfast, 45 cents to 85 cents for lunch, and 65 cents to $1 for dinner.

———◆◆◆———

When the Mount Washington Hotel (opened 1902 at Bretton Woods, New Hampshire) was under construction, its Italian construction crew varied the number of steps leading to the second floor by using 33 steps from the registration area but only 31 in the South Tower. The difference was intended to confuse ghosts.

———◆◆◆———

The Ritz-Carlton New York, Central Park in 2004 sold 597 bottles of Opus One from its in-room minibars at more than $100 a pop. Nevertheless, the hotel group reports that its overall top-selling honor bar items are (in this order) bottled water, Diet Coke, Coca-Cola, M&Ms candies, and Pringles potato chips.

———◆◆◆———

Rates in 1912 at the Chateau Frontenac in Quebec City, Quebec, ranged from $4 to $5.50 for a room without bath and $5.50 to $8 for a room with a bath. The price varied based on the location of the room — and no wonder. That extra $1.50 to $2.50 bought a heck of a view, given the hotel's superb position looking straight down the side of a cliff to a lower town at riverside and the St. Lawrence River itself.

———◆◆◆———

When the first Statler installed bathrooms in all sleeping rooms, it set a standard for the future. However, there is an earlier record of a property with baths in each room — in the Mount Vernon hotel in Cape May, New Jersey, which opened in 1853. It was big, too, able to accommodate more than 2,000 and considered the world's largest hotel. However, it burned in 1856.

There was a time when the hotel minibar was for snack foods and something to drink, but no more. These days, guests may find everything from makeup and lotions to playing cards and stuffed animals, golf balls to umbrellas and disposable cameras. Some of our favorites appear below:

* Harmonicas, a Chicago kind of thing, in the Windy City's House of Blues and Hotel Allegro (the Allegro also stocks the minibar with Chicago blues CDs).

* Red Bull, Red Hook, red Jelly Bellies, red pistachios, red licorice, and red wax lips (there is a theme here) at the Hotel Rouge, Washington, D.C.
* Soy candles by E'rgo in select guest rooms at the Ritz-Carlton Golf & Spa Resort, Rose Hall, Jamaica.
* Voodoo dolls, Mardi Gras masks, and jazz CDs at the Hotel Monaco, in New Orleans, naturally.
* Yo-yos that glow in the dark and foot-long Tootsie Rolls (for kids, right?) at the Pacific Palisades Hotel, Vancouver, British Columbia.

Sleep on It

Minibars in the W hotels are entertaining places to survey. For example, there are the Emergency Survival Kits, comprising lip glosses, mascara, and perfume from Diane von Furstenberg's cosmetics line, part of a broader partnership between DVF and the W properties to assist female guests with beauty and fashion emergencies. All Ws also include W Shorts, not something to wear but small books of short stories written by famous people, and the Intimacy Kits, another name for a condom kit. W calls its minibars "munchie boxes," but we presume the name refers to the other contents.

———◆———

Kimpton Hotel & Restaurant Group properties in the company's hometown San Francisco include the following in minibars: binoculars (Harbor Court Hotel); "good books" (Monticello Inn); Chris the Crab, a wind-up toy that walks sideways (Tuscan Inn); monogrammed telescopes (Argonaut Hotel); puzzles, yo-yos, and other games (Serrano Hotel); and a rubber duckie for the bath or a rubber-duck key chain (Hotel Triton).

———◆———

The Villa San Michele, originally a Franciscan monastery and today a top hotel in Fiesole, overlooking Florence, Italy, boasts a facade attributed to Michelangelo. The monastery's library is now the Michelangelo Suite.

———◆———

The Emirates Palace, a 346-room Kempinski hotel that debuted in Abu Dhabi in 2005, cost approximately $1.5 million per room to build, making it the world's most expensive hotel construction project. The property makes a number of other claims in the superlative category: It has more domes than any other hotel on the globe (114), and the largest, the Grand Atrium, is higher than the dome of St. Peter's

Basilica in Rome. The Emirates Palace Archway is bigger than l'Arc de Triomphe in Paris. Finally, the hotel has 22 three-bedroom suites that can host as many heads of state with their entourages without one ever bumping into the other.

The Chateau Frontenac in Quebec City, Quebec, was host during World War II to two Allied war conferences. For the first and longest, in mid-1943, the property was requisitioned by the Canadian government for more than three weeks. As a result, 849 guests and permanent residents were required to leave, and close to 3,000 reservations were canceled, all with no explanation. At these meetings, the Allies laid the groundwork for the Normandy invasion of June 1944. The hotel bill was $8,000 a day, paid by the Canadian government. The traditional 4 p.m. teatime was honored every day throughout.

During the same war, London's Grosvenor House was used briefly as an annex to the Immigration Section of the U.S. Embassy. Also, the property's staff provided a 38-person platoon to the Home Guard. The platoon often drilled on the hotel's roof.

Sleep on It

There are numerous programs to accommodate pets that accompany their humans to hotels (even massages for cats!), but for the petless, the Ritz-Carlton on Beaver Creek Mountain in Colorado lends its resident labrador retriever for hiking duty. Other properties have a fishier plan: The Kimpton Group offers to put goldfish in the room at its seven Monaco-branded hotels, all in the United States; similarly, the Observatory Hotel in Sydney, Australia, lends a pair of pet goldfish.

——◆——

The Round Robin Bar in the InterContinental The Willard Washington, D.C. is where Kentucky's Senator Henry Clay mixed the U.S. capital's first mint julep — now the bar's signature drink.

——◆——

The first hotel minibars in North America were installed in 1978 at the Four Seasons Hotel Washington, D.C. However, the world's first minibars were made by Germany's Siegas and installed on the European continent more than a decade earlier.

——◆——

The 15-room Hotel Ostfriesland in Norden, Germany, gives each guest a choice: Pay the list price for a room or get on the scales and pay based on body weight, which can mean a considerable savings for the lighter travelers among us. Some guests, usually men, strip down to save money. Owner Juergen Heckrodt meant to extend the offer for one month in 2006, but he gets so much publicity and has so much fun, the offer is indefinite.

——◆——

The Hilton Maldives Resort & Spa operates the world's only underwater restaurant, called the Ithaa. Set 16 feet below the

Indian Ocean's surface, it provides views of reefs and marine life in all cardinal directions and overhead.

———— •◆• ————

Four Seasons Hotels and Resorts processes more than 177 million pounds of laundry a year.

———— •◆• ————

The Parker House in Boston, opened in 1855, is the longest continuously operating hotel in the United States. Launched with an immediate focus on food, its first chef was paid an astonishing $5,000 a year. The hotel, named for founder Harvey Parker and now the Omni Parker House, has a widely varied collection of other claims to fame:

* The Parker House roll was invented here and is still served at the property.

* The hotel was the first property in America to separate charges for food from charges for a room, creating what became known as the European Plan. Previously, American inns and hotels set one rate which included meals and imposed rigid dining schedules.

* Kitchen employees included Ho Chi Minh from 1911 to 1913 and Malcolm Little (Malcolm X) in the early 1940s.

* The Parker House was home to the legendary 19th-century Saturday Club which counted as members Ralph Waldo Emerson, Nathaniel Hawthorne, Oliver Wendell Holmes, Henry Wadsworth Longfellow, James Russell Lowell, David Thoreau, and John Greenleaf Whittier. Charles Dickens gave his first American reading of "A Christmas Carol" at a club dinner here.

* John Wilkes Booth was registered at the Parker House April 5 and 6, 1865, and was seen to be practicing pistol firing in various odd positions. On April 14, he shot President Lincoln in Washington, D.C.

Chapter 11

Looking Back

For the traveler in the days of the Caesars, eating out meant either a kind of snack bar for stand-up eating or a sit-down establishment best characterized as a dive. The better (and that is only a relative term) choices could be called lie-down restaurants because patrons could recline on couches to eat. Sit-down/lie-down restaurants also doubled as gaming dens and brothels, and wall paintings were graphically clear on that point. More unsavory still, the Roman physician Galen reported that butchers and innkeepers had been caught passing off human flesh as pork. We have to ask: Where were they sourcing that?

———◆———

The world's longest recorded business trip started in 1271 and ended back in Venice in 1295. Marco Polo, his father, and his uncle were traders who spent at least 17 years in the court of Kublai Khan, the Mongolian emperor in Cathay. Marco dictated his trip report while in a Genoa prison, and judging by the introduction, he and his family were better connected than any Web surfer for getting the best deals: The Polos traveled much of the time compliments of the khan. And there is no evidence Marco brought any pasta to Italy — Italy already had it.

———◆———

In ancient Greece and Rome, there were numerous inns along most roadways, although amenities — if that word can even be used — were quite basic. In "Frogs," the playwright Aristophanes has his character Dionysus preparing to travel and asking for a list of "landladies with the fewest bedbugs." At some establishments, a single long chamber served as dining room by day and dormitory by night. Another layout in the Greek world was a square or oblong courtyard surrounded by a two-story structure accommodating guest rooms and public spaces. The courtyard was for feeding animals and offloading and loading goods. The layout is that of the later caravanserais, suggesting that the Greek model lived on.

For centuries, the pilgrimage was the biggest trip anyone would ever make. However, for Tangier-born Ibn Battuta, Mecca was just a start. The 14th-century "Muslim Marco Polo" traveled farther than any man on record by his day: 75,000 miles, from the Niger River to China. In 20 years, he braved bandits, pirates, the Black Death, and lethal despots — and came home to a family that could not immediately recognize him. Like Marco Polo, Ibn Battuta was not into travel writing. He dictated his tales.

The 19th-century Sir Richard Burton was another story: This scholar/explorer/government agent immersed himself in cultures from India to West Africa, from Arabia to Brazil, learning 29 languages along the way. He wrote more than 50 books, translated many others (including "Arabian Nights" and "Kama Sutra"), shocked Victorians in his homeland, and found time to coin the phrase "ESP."

Travia

The urge to leave messages behind when traveling is so pervasive it must be genetic. Examples date back as far as 4,000 years. Early scribblers were military men on expeditions, and some of those long-ago Kilroy-was-here messages appear in Egypt on the Abu Simbel temple far up the Nile. But in the first and second centuries, it was tourists — writing in Latin or Greek or both — who marked up the popular statue of Amenhotep III (mistakenly called Memnon) outside Luxor, the tombs in the Valley of the Kings, Giza's pyramids and sphinx, and just about any temple of interest. Some messages were long (even in verse) and carefully carved, most likely by professionals. Lionel Casson in "Travel in the Ancient World" tells us more than 100 missives cover Memnon's legs and base, and there are more than 2,100 graffiti in the tombs, nearly half of those in the Ramses VI tomb.

Because many messages were dated, archaeologists can determine that the high season for travel in Egypt was November to April, much as it is today.

———◆———

In the Age of Discovery, three achievements were big: rounding the tip of Africa, crossing the Atlantic, and circling the globe. If you think you have trouble getting around in new places, get a load of our heroes.

Explorer Bartholomeu Dias accidentally rounded the Cape of Good Hope in 1488 because a storm blew him thataway. After making landfall, he did figure out where he was, but it was someone else (Vasco da Gama) who went to India and got rich. As for Christopher Columbus, we defer to Newsweek's take: He "got a little lost on the way to India but discovered the Caribbean vacation." The world's first round-the-world sailing took three years and was led by Ferdinand Magellan, an excellent navigator who encountered a very big, atypically calm

ocean. So he named it the Pacific. He also joined a tribal fray
in the Philippines in 1521 and was killed.

———◆◆◆———

The first known female transatlantic traveler was Gudrid
Thorbjarnardottir, who traveled from Iceland to the New
World soon after 1000 and, with her husband, scouted
unsuccessfully for a settlement site. Her son was the first
European born in the New World, as well. A well-traveled lass,
she returned to Iceland and later made a pilgrimage to Rome
on foot.

———◆◆◆———

In 1783, a pair of French brothers, Joseph and Etienne
Montgolfier, were the first to demonstrate a hot-air balloon
successfully. Later the same year, France's King Louis XVI
and Queen Marie Antoinette were witnesses to the first
demonstration of a hot-air balloon carrying passengers. Fueled
by burning wood and straw, the balloon rose from a courtyard
at Versailles carrying a sheep, a duck, and a rooster. During
the U.S. Civil War in the 1860s, hot-air balloons were used to
provide vantage points for observing enemy activities.

———◆◆◆———

Beginning from well before and extending through Roman times, innkeepers were typically women. In the days of the Roman Empire, hotel staff were usually slaves (and sometimes the manager was, as well). In a typical inn for the not-so-rich, rooms were small and guests were expected to share with other travelers. Washing up meant a trip to a public bath. There was room service, meaning travelers could order food from the inn's kitchen. Room service could also mean sending for a maid, who doubled as a prostitute. Even respectable inns included prostitutes as part of their services.

So that travelers could choose their housing wisely, innkeepers indicated the kind of business they sought by posting notices (which could be in verse) outside the doors and decorating their establishments with murals of, say, wine jars or erotic scenes. Into this world strode Christian missionaries who, naturally, traveled and, like St. Paul, had to take public lodgings at times.

It wasn't merely the ancients who expected to share their room at the inn with others. Fast forward to medieval Europe, and things don't look any better: Travelers typically slept in flea-ridden, rat-infested public houses where they shared rooms and beds with strangers. Things were not much improved in 18th-century America, either, where travelers (usually men) overnighted at roadside taverns, sharing rustic bedrooms and sometimes their beds.

———◆———

The Vikings invented sleeping bags — they camped out a lot more than we do — and they carried these bags along when Leif Ericsson led the first exploratory journey by Europeans to North America in 999. (It's no wonder Leif wanted to get away from his Greenland home. His father, Eric the Red, had been outlawed several times for multiple murders. His sister Freydus was handy with an axe, as well.)

———◆———

The first person to circumnavigate the globe was Ferdinand Magellan's slave Enrique. When Magellan's ships reached the Visayan islands (part of the Philippines today) in 1521, Enrique had returned to the land of his birth and hence completed a trip around the globe east to west.

———◆———

Tourism to Egypt was good business in the first century, and even stronger in the second century. In those days, as in modern times, tourists were offered diversions to complement their visits to the pyramids and the pharaohs' tombs, but we are not talking about cultural dance programs here. One performance had locals climb the then-smooth sides of the pyramids all the way to the top. Farther up the Nile, visitors could bring food and wine to the sacred crocodiles and watch a priest hand-feed the animals. A better display, however, would have been this one: The crocs opened their jaws on command (well-trained, obviously) and allowed the priests to clean and dry their teeth (well-fed, too).

Chapter 12

Business Matters

Travia

American Express was founded in 1850 in New York as an express delivery business, carrying parcels and freight to the U.S. West that the postal service either could or would not. It created the world's first travelers checks in 1891, but its travel business came later, in 1915 when Europe was ablaze with World War I and two years before America's 1917 entry.

———◆◆◆———

The atomic bomb increased tourism to Las Vegas. After the first atmospheric nuclear detonation at the Nevada Test Site in 1951 (65 miles from Las Vegas), people came to town to see the blasts and, in a time when no one was aware of the dangers, hotels were set up to promote viewing areas and viewing parties. Souvenirs and menu items had "atomic" themes. It also was the practice to name atomic bomb tests after famous people. This is part of the tale told at the Atomic Testing Museum, which opened in Las Vegas in 2005. The museum also includes the Ground Zero Theater, designed so the audience can see, hear, and feel the effects of a nuclear blast.

———◆◆◆———

Seeing the importance of food in tourism, professionals in the food, beverage, and travel businesses in 2003 created the nonprofit International Culinary Tourism Association, based in Portland, Oregon. It has more than 600 members. A 2007 Travel Industry Association of America study found that 27 million Americans sought food and wine experiences while traveling. These travelers are educated and affluent.

———◆◆◆———

Herodotus, born in the fifth century B.C. in today's Turkey, was the world's first travel writer as the term is understood today. He earned this honor, as well as the sobriquet "father of history," for his book "History of the Persian Wars." To give that history perspective, he described in some detail the far-flung components of the Persian Empire, based on his experiences traveling through the ancient world.

———◆◆◆———

Thomas Cook, who founded a travel agency that is now known worldwide, was a former Baptist minister who, in 1841, asked British rail officials for a chartered train to take 500 like-minded colleagues 12 miles from Leicester to Loughborough to a temperance meeting. He charged one shilling — that would be five pence in current parlance — for each roundtrip ticket and still made a profit for the Temperance Society. That was the birth of conducted tours. In 1855, he led his first tour to the European continent. He sent his first group to the United States in 1866, led by his son John Mason Cook.

———◆◆◆———

Yap, part of the Western Caroline Islands southwest of Guam, has the world's largest money. The traditional tender looks like a large millstone with a hole in the middle and can be as big as 12 feet in diameter. The stones are generally displayed in an upright position, in front of homes or beside the road. Owners can use the holes, with a strong pole, for moving the stones. However, no one moves these "coins" anymore (although they do change hands, usually in ceremonial situations). For portable currency, Yapese still use smaller stones and shells, but tourists, who generally come for diving and snorkeling, can use American dollars, Japanese yen, travelers checks, and credit cards.

In the early 1920s, a young bank clerk named Arthur Taucknitz dropped a cigar box containing coins, and as he retrieved and counted them, he had an idea for an aluminum tray that would hold a specified number of coins and eliminate the need for counting. When he began traveling to sell his invention, he discovered most of his fellow travelers were also salesmen, and he figured other people were missing out.

He ran an ad in the Newark (New Jersey) Evening News asking people to join him on a one-time New England tour. For one price, he would provide the best hotels and best sightseeing, and while his companions were on their own, he would make sales calls. He said he wanted "a congenial party," and he did not want "grouches or pessimists." The effort was so successful that Taucknitz shortened his name to Tauck and launched Tauck Tours. That was 1925. For many years the business mainstay was escorted motorcoach tours in North America. In 2000, the company changed its name to Tauck World Discovery to reflect the fact the company operates tours to all seven continents now. Management includes one of the founding Tauck's grandchildren, Robin Tauck.

Travelpro Luggage was the originator of (and holds the patent for) the soft-sided, upright luggage that travelers can roll onto an aircraft. The creator of the rolling suitcases, and the founder of the Travelpro business in 1989, is a former Northwest pilot, Bob Plath, who started by devising a rolling bag for himself and then began making them for airline colleagues equally eager for an easier way to carry their things.

Business Matters

Numerous travel companies carry the name of a founder or the owner who built the business. In the case of Hyatt Hotels, the company's developer was not a guy named Hyatt. Chicago financier Jay Pritzker bought the Hyatt House at Los Angeles Airport in 1957 and kept the original name (for the seller, Hyatt R. von Dehn) saying no one would stay in a hotel named Pritzker's.

The International Society of Travel Medicine, an organization of professionals (doctors, nurses, and other travel-medicine specialists) dedicated to the advancement of the travel-medicine specialty, counts 2,000 members in 65 countries.

Travelers or their travel agents booked $85 billion worth of travel on the Web in 2006, for 30 percent of U.S. travel sales, according to JupiterResearch's "U.S. Travel Forecast, 2006 to 2011." The report projected those numbers will grow to $128 billion or 38 percent of all U.S. travel sales in 2011.

The Travel Industry Association of America's 2006-2007 Survey of U.S. State and Territory Tourism Office Budgets identified the following state tourism offices as the top 10 spenders:
Hawaii — $70.7 million
Pennsylvania — $64.7 million
Illinois — $49.0 million

Florida — $33.1 million
Texas — $29.1 million
California — $28.8 million
Colorado — $22.2 million
Arizona — $20.7 million
Virginia — $20.4 million
New York — $19.3 million

The total for all 50 states was $765.2 million. The U.S.
Department of Commerce in 2007 awarded $3.9 million to
the Travel Industry Association of America (TIA) to build
Web sites promoting the United States. However, Congress
does not fund a national tourism promotion board, so TIA (in
partnership with more than 2,000 travel industry organizations)
developed the SeeAmerica brand which, with private funding,
has assumed the role of a U.S. tourism agency overseas.

———————

Before its destruction by terrorists in 2001, New York's World
Trade Center was the world's largest commercial complex. The
twin towers were a major tourist attraction, and some 150,000
people visited them each year for business and pleasure.

Business Matters

The first automatic teller machine, which read magstripe cards, was installed in September 1969 in a Chemical Bank branch on New York's Long Island. It was the brainchild of Don Wetzel, who developed the machine for Docutel, where he worked at the time as vice president of product planning. He did not dream the devices would be used by travelers thousands of miles from their home branches.

The first cash dispensers, introduced by Barclays two years earlier, were simpler. The machines dispensed £10 notes against a special paper voucher that the customer inserted into the machine, but, even then, the customer used a personal code number to get his money.

Richard Bangs, founder of Mountain Travel/Sobek in Emeryville, California, gets the credit for originating the term "adventure travel."

American Express has served government in colorful ways: To curb swindling among independent money changers on Ellis Island, the U.S. Immigration Department awarded American Express a contract in 1905 to provide official currency exchange services for immigrants. Thus, for countless new arrivals, their first transaction in the United States was with American Express on Ellis Island. During World War I, American Express was the British government's official agent to deliver letters, relief parcels, and money to British prisoners of war. At its busiest, it was delivering 150 tons of packages daily to prisoners in Bulgaria, Germany, Holland, Norway, Switzerland, and Turkey. Staffers even entered POW camps to cash drafts for British and French prisoners and to arrange for the prisoners to receive money from home.

The Michelin guides, which had been useful for French troops during World War I, also went to the Normandy beaches on D-Day in June 1944. That spring, Allied commanders were concerned that progress at pushing the Nazis out of France

would be hampered because road signs had been destroyed or removed by the enemy. With permission from Michelin's Paris management, the Allies reproduced the most recent relevant edition (1939) because it contained hundreds of detailed town and city maps. It was produced in Washington, unabridged, and distributed to officers with the words "For official use only" stamped on the cover.

Diners Club created the first modern charge card in 1950 (the brainchild of Diners Club founder Frank McNamara), but those first cards were cardboard. Diners Club went to plastic in 1961. American Express launched its card in 1958, and it was made of paper with purple ink to match the color of the company's travelers checks. The banks did not want to be left out of this action. The Franklin National Bank in New York was the first to offer credit on a card in 1951. However, Bank of America claimed a first with the 1958 launch of a revolving-credit card, called BankAmericard, and, after other smaller banks signed on as additional sponsors, it eventually became Visa. The Interbank Card Association (ICA) was created in 1966 and eventually became MasterCard International. Barclaycard, set up in 1966, was Britain's first credit card. Carte Blanche, meanwhile, was born as the credit card of the Hilton hotel company; it was founded by Barron Hilton in 1959 and operated as a division of Hilton. It was sold to Citibank six years later.

The World Federation of Tourist Guides Associations, based in Vienna, Austria, represents an estimated 88,000-plus individual tour guides around the world.

The American Automobile Association employs 65 full-time tourism editors who cumulatively travel more than a million miles a year to inspect and rate (on a scale of one to five) 60,000 hotels and restaurants throughout North America and the Caribbean. In 2008, 100 lodgings and 60 restaurants topped the lists with five diamonds, which came to only 0.27 percent (essentially, one-half of one-half of 1 percent) of rated sites. The ratings are published in AAA's TourBook guides. AAA published its first hotel directory in 1917 and started inspecting hotels and restaurants 20 years later. The rating system known to many travelers today was inaugurated in 1963 and evolved into the one- to five-diamond designations for hotels with the 1977 editions of the TourBook guides and, for restaurants, in the 1989 guides.

The worldwide nude tourism business is now estimated to be worth about $400 million, according to the American Association for Nude Recreation in Kissimmee, Florida.

Travia

The Washington, D.C.-based International Ecotourism Society, with members in more than 70 countries, is the world's largest and oldest (from 1990) ecotourism organization. The Society undertakes projects meant to foster conservation, poverty alleviation, and protection of cultures and biodiversity. On a theoretical level anyway, the group has a lot of support in the United States. At least a third of adult American travelers have said in surveys they are interested in environmental and cultural preservation, and twice that many said it is important that their trips not damage the destinations visited.

The world's most expensive tourist trip costs between $20 million and $25 million. That buys transport, provided by Russia, to the International Space Station. The first customer was American businessman Dennis Tito, with an April 28-to-May 4 journey in 2001.

Las Vegas is the No. 1 host for major conventions in the United States. In 2006, it hosted 45 of the top 200

conventions, for a 22.5 percent share. The largest of them attracted more than 140,000 delegates to the city.

At the time Marcellus Berry, an American Express employee, invented the travelers check in 1891, currency exchange rates were so stable, the face of each check listed its value in seven foreign currencies. A $100 check bought 20 British pounds, seven shillings, 11 pence; 512.5 (Belgian, French, or Swiss) francs; 412.5 German marks; 512.5 lira; 370.35 (Danish, Norwegian, or Swedish) kronors, or 245.1 Dutch florins. The exchange rate with Canada's dollar was one to one. American Express dropped the practice soon after World War I because rates weren't all that stable anymore. Then, as World War II brought most travel to a halt, it seemed travelers checks were doomed. However, the U.S. government encouraged American military personnel to carry their accumulated pay in travelers checks, and many did.

The dead zone around the Chernobyl power plant that produced history's worst civilian nuclear disaster in 1986 opened for guided tours in 2002. By 2005, about 900 tourists came for a tour that included Pripyat, Ukraine, the deserted town that once was home to about 45,000.

In 2001, a Dutch travel agency announced a corporate team-building travel plan: Drop small groups of people, with a guide, on the streets of major European cities without money, to live like the homeless for three days. They would be given sleeping bags and musical instruments or sketchpads so they could try to earn money. The idea brought howls of protest from some officials who work to get vagrants off city streets.

Travia

"There will be travelers in outer space, and where there are travelers, there must be Hiltons," according to one Hilton executive, who described a projected Lunar Hilton. It would be below the moon's surface on three levels for consistent temperature control and more workable hotel space. Rooms would be large, with wall-to-wall television for programs from Earth and for views of the moon and space. And, "if you think we're not going to have a cocktail lounge, you don't know Hilton — or travelers." Those remarks were made by Barron Hilton, then president and CEO of Hilton Hotels, before a meeting of the American Astronautical Society in 1967.

———◆———

Dracula-themed tourism brought an estimated $70 million to Romania in 2007. The estimate is extrapolated from the numbers of visitors to the so-called Dracula Castle and tourists who visit Romania on Halloween tours.

———◆———

"Voluntourism" is a coined word to describe the way some people choose to spend their vacations — by doing volunteer work. A couple of U.S.-based sponsors of volunteer programs see a growing interest in this travel option. For Georgia-based Habitat for Humanity, participation in its Global Village trips (mostly to points outside the United States) rose from 4,000 in 2002 to more than 10,000 in 2007. Each year, Habitat sponsors an additional project, the Jimmy Carter work site, which can be in the United States or overseas. In 2007, that drew more than 5,000 people plus the ex-president. Another 13,700-plus students used a school break in 2006-2007 to travel to a home-construction site in the United States. That number is up from about 9,600 in 2000.

Business Matters

Minnesota-based Global Volunteers said its number of volunteers rose from 700 in 1994 to 2,700 for 2007. Its participants work in 19 countries including the United States, and volunteers are mostly Americans, although Canadian and European involvement is growing.

Barnes & Noble Booksellers, which operates 675 stores across the United States, maintains more than 5,000 active travel book titles in its database plus more than 5,000 active map titles.

The 1960-61 edition of "Europe on $5 a Day" lists 10 ship lines plus eight freighter companies as options for traveling from the United States to Europe. The author, Arthur Frommer, slammed the ship lines for duplicating services for three classes of passengers, which he said produced overpriced passage across the ocean (sample: $217 one way on the Queen Mary in summer's peak season). It would be better, he said, to skip the six-day crossing (or 10 to 14 days on a freighter), take the bus from New York to Idlewild Airport (now John

F. Kennedy International) for $1.35, and "settle down for the 12-hour trip to London."

Mobil Travel Guide gave 41 hotels and 17 restaurants a five-star rating for 2008; another 125 hotels and 149 restaurants received four-star ratings. Mobil, which started putting its stamp of approval on hotels and restaurants in 1958, each year rates about 7,500 hotels and 6,500 restaurants in the United States and Canada and publishes those recommendations in its guidebooks. Regular inspections touch more than 8,000 in each category but typically about 10 percent to 15 percent of the candidates don't make the cut. Mobil started rating spas in 2004, and in 2008, Mobil gave five stars to three spas and four stars to 84 spas.

Receipts from international tourism totaled $735 billion in 2006, according to the World Tourism Organization. That came to nearly $84 million per hour.

France welcomes more international visitors than any country in the world, with 79.1 million arrivals in 2006, more than nine percent of the total of 842 million international travelers that year. Others in the top 10 were Spain, 58.5 million; United States, 51.1 million; China, 49.6 million; Italy, 41.1 million; United Kingdom, 30.1 million; Germany, 23.6 million; Mexico, 21.4 million; Austria, 20.3 million, and Russia, 20.2 million. However, it is the United States that earns the most from international tourism. Its receipts in 2006 were $85.7 billion. Others in the top 10 were Spain, $51.1 billion; France, $46.3 billion; Italy, $38.1 billion; China, $33.9 billion; United Kingdom, $33.5 billion; Germany, $32.8 billion; Australia, $17.8 billion; Turkey, $16.9 billion, and Austria, $16.7 billion.

Note: Results for China, Hong Kong and Macau are calculated separately although all three are China. Old habits die hard, but there are real differences in the tourism arena, too. For example, visa rules are different for Hong Kong and Macau from those for the mainland.

U.S. tour guides are licensed in the following jurisdictions: Charleston, South Carolina; New York City; New Orleans, Louisiana; Savannah, Georgia; Washington, D.C., and two Civil War battlefields: Gettysburg, Pennsylvania, and Vicksburg, Mississippi. That's it.

Based on a snapshot of Web activity taken by Web monitor Hitwise in March 2007, Expedia.com is the most popular travel agency Web site in the United States. In that month, it received 16.3 percent of all visits to online agencies. Others on the list of top 10 online travel agencies were, in descending order, Orbitz, Travelocity.com, Cheap Tickets, Priceline.com, Yahoo! Travel, Hotwire, Kayak, CheapoAir.com, and

Travia

Vacations to Go. The most popular travel site of all, however, was not a travel seller — it was MapQuest. Nos. 3 and 4, for overall popularity, also were map sites: Yahoo! Maps and Google Maps.

Thomas Cook & Son published its first Cook's Continental Time Tables and Tourist's Handbook in 1873. The Thomas Cook European Timetable is still produced monthly, and the Thomas Cook Overseas Timetable is published six times a year.

Medical tourism, meaning travel to a foreign country for medical purposes, is worth untold millions of dollars to host countries. Host nations — attractive for the quality or price of their medical care, or both — range from Argentina and Brazil to Lithuania and Israel, Mexico to India, South Africa to Southeast Asia.

Singapore attracts more than 150,000 medical tourists a year. The bulk of the patients (60 percent) are accommodated by the Parkway Hospitals group and produce about $60 million in revenues for the group (based on in-patient care only). Malaysia reported more than 75,000 foreign patients in 2001, producing roughly $11.6 million in revenues for the country; the numbers climbed to nearly 175,000 patients in 2004, worth around $27.6 million to the country. Bangkok's Bumrungrad International hospital, which attracts the lion's share of Thailand's medical tourists, reports it treats 350,000 international patients yearly for about $58 million in hospital revenues. This does not count travel spending. The importance of this business is clear: The Raffles Hospital in Singapore promotes its rooms as five-star hotel quality. Bumrungrad in mid-2005 established a visa service center for medical tourists.

For their first 20 years (from 1900 to 1920), the Michelin guides were free and distributed to European drivers by the thousands. Andre and Edouard Michelin, French tire makers, had seen the value for them in encouraging travel. Between 1931 and 1933, an early rating system evolved into the well-known one-, two- and three-star system. Then, in 1933, the Michelin restaurant inspector was born, and the guidebooks no longer relied on outside contributors.

The paper currency in Australia is not paper; it is plastic and has been since the mid-1990s because plastic money, which pretty much looks and acts like paper, lasts four to five times longer than paper money. That more than makes up for the fact it costs about 50 percent more to produce. Actually made from a polymer substrate, the longer-lasting, cleaner bills are also (most importantly) harder to counterfeit because of a see-through window and a hologram effect. When they do wear out, the bills can be recycled into granules that are converted into plastic products for use outdoors. Australia was the pioneer on this one, creating the first plastic note in 1988. By 2002,

Mexico became the 20th country worldwide, and the first in North America, to begin a conversion to plastic. The bulk of converts are in the Asia/Pacific region; they are Bangladesh,

Brunei, China, Hong Kong (which still uses its dollar), Indonesia, Malaysia, Nepal, New Zealand, Papua New Guinea, Samoa, Singapore, Solomon Islands, Sri Lanka, Taiwan, Thailand, and Vietnam. Other adopters are Brazil, Chile, Kuwait, Nigeria, Northern Ireland, Romania, and Zambia, for a total of 25 entities that have issued at least some plastic money.

———————

Northern Ireland was able to have plastic money even while the rest of Great Britain does not because Northern Ireland is one of three places (including Hong Kong and Singapore) where private banks are still empowered to issue currency. The Northern Bank issued a limited edition of polymer £5 notes in late 1999 and early 2000 to commemorate the millennium.

———————

Thailand, like other countries in Asia, marketed medical services overseas to foster recovery after the Asian economic crisis of 1997, but Thailand had a unique expertise to offer. Beginning from the late 1980s, it had become the medical-tourism destination of choice for a small subculture — Western men seeking sex-change operations at a manageable price from doctors who were good at it.

———————

The five most-visited theme parks in the world are all Disney sites. Based on the most recent available estimates (for 2006) provided by the Themed Entertainment Association and Economics Research Associates, they are Magic Kingdom (with 16.6 million visitors); Disneyland (14.7 million); Tokyo Disneyland (12.9 million); Tokyo Disney Sea (12.1 million); and Disneyland Paris (10.6 million).

———————

In the 1960-61 edition of his "Europe on $5 a Day," Arthur Frommer offered advice for the budget-minded that covered the gamut:

* Stay away from the gondolas in Venice; they cost as much as $3 an hour in the summer.

* Attend London theater, any theater, where the top price is rarely more than a pound ($2.80 at the time, by the way).

* The best hotel find in Europe is the Berchielli in Florence, Italy, where prices "soar as high as $3 for a single (taxes and services included) and $5 for a double" during peak season. But the hotel on the Arno with Renaissance-style rooms was worth it, he said.

* Buying first class rail is "unwise" on major international expresses because of the "infinitesimal" difference between first and second class. (Obviously, this preceded Eurailpasses).

* Forget good food in Britain and eat on the dirt cheap: "Your meat-pie-with-cabbage will turn out to be just as tasteless for 40 cents ... as it will for $2 in a posh London hotel."

What a difference a few decades make!

———◆———

Aside from leading the first conducted tour in 1841, Thomas Cook and the company that survived him (Thomas Cook & Son) were industry innovators several times over, seen in these milestones:

Travia

1845: A 60-page handbook (forerunner to the brochure) for Cook's first commercial trip: a group trip to Liverpool from Derby, Leicester, and Nottingham.

1868: A system of hotel vouchers redeemable at select hotels in major cities.

1872-1873: The first world tour, led by Thomas Cook (this became practical in 1869 with the Suez Canal and U.S. transcontinental rail service in place).

1874: Cook's Circular Note, which could be exchanged for local currency, launched in New York (the precursor to modern travelers checks).

1919: The first travel agency to offer pleasure trips by air.

1927: The first agency to operate a conducted air tour (a New York-to-Chicago trip to attend the Dempsey-Tunney heavyweight boxing fight).

The oldest surviving guidebook, called "Guidebook of Greece," was written by one Pausanias in the late second century. There had been guides before his, but they covered single places or monuments, not a whole country. Tourists would not carry this guidebook around; the treasure (handwritten on leather or papyrus) would have been too bulky and too valuable for that.

How far can reward-point programs go? Into space, apparently. American Express cardholders enrolled in the Amex Membership Rewards program can redeem points for out-of-this-world experiences.

A zero-gravity flight costs 500,000 points; and, for the big one, it will be 20 million points for a suborbital space flight when it is available. (A cardholder with a million points on his balance sheet has charged roughly $1 million on his Amex card.) The points are redeemable with Space Adventures, an Arlington, Virginia, specialist in "space experiences" and organizer of the first private journeys to the International Space Station.

———◆◆◆———

The Baedeker guidebooks were born in 1827, the same year their creator, 26-year-old Karl Baedeker, founded his publishing house of the same name in Koblenz, Germany. Baedeker and members of his family traveled incognito around Europe to check out the facts that had been provided by on-site agents. The purpose of creating such well-researched and thorough written guides was to dispense with the need for paid tour guides. The first editions in French appeared in 1846, the first in English in 1861.

———◆◆◆———

In the days of the Roman Empire, the traveler whose baggage was stolen while he was a guest at an inn or while taking passage on a ship could hold the innkeeper or ship's captain liable. Also, those traveling in wheeled vehicles could not drive about in populated areas by day because many towns and cities (including Rome) forbade wheeled traffic between dawn and dusk.

———◆◆◆———

Travia

American Express, the best-known travel agency in the United States, in 1929 nearly ceased to exist as an independent company — and not because of the stock market crash. In that year, it came to light that Chase National Bank had quietly purchased 97 percent of the company's shares. After Congress in 1933 passed a law prohibiting banks from engaging in nonbanking businesses, Chase was forced to sell its stock.

———◆———

The British government called on a travel agency, Thomas Cook & Son, in 1884 to arrange for the transfer of 18,000 troops, close to 40,000 tons of supplies, and 40,000 tons of coal to Khartoum, Sudan, where General Charles Gordon needed relief during a revolt by Mahdi (nee Muhammad Ahmed). The agency and its subcontractors completed their assignment in November, but Khartoum fell in January of 1885 and Gordon was killed.

———◆———

Perhaps not surprisingly, France has more Michelin three-star restaurants than any country on Earth, by a long shot. In 2007, Michelin guidebooks listed 26. That left only 30 for the rest of the world.

———◆———

Jesse Shwayder founded the Shwayder Trunk Manufacturing Company in Denver, Colorado, in 1910, with the goal of creating trunks and hand luggage that could stand the roughest travel conditions. In 1941, he introduced the first line of coordinated luggage and called the new style Samsonite Streamlite. It was named Samsonite for the powerful Biblical giant to stress strength and durability and Streamlite because it was tapered in shape. It wasn't until 1965 that the company name was changed to Samsonite Corporation.

———◆———

Business Matters

Carlson Companies, co-owners of the Carlson Wagonlit travel agency business, was founded in 1938 by Curtis and Arleen Carlson — but it wasn't a travel business. The original operation was the Gold Bond Stamp Company, launched with $55 of borrowed capital after Curtis left his job at Proctor & Gamble as a soap salesman. Today, Carlson Companies brands include T.G.I. Friday's and Pick Up Stix restaurants, and a collection of hotel names: Country Inns & Suites by Carlson, Park Inn hotels, Park Plaza, Radisson Hotels & Resorts, and Regent International Hotels.

Windmills are a particularly popular attraction for tourists to the Netherlands, but some tourism promoters in the U.S. Southwest have aspirations for their windmills, too. They are promoting the Wind Power Trail in Texas and Oklahoma, highlighting 23 sites. Some are working windmills or windmill farms, generating energy every day, and two are windmill museums in Spearman, Texas, and Shattuck, Oklahoma.

Travia

Creators of the Wind Power Trail, Wildsteps.com, Inc., are in the business of bringing tourism to rural America, but their purposes are educational, as well. Consider these factoids: In 2003, wind farms generated enough electricity to serve 1.3 million households. The environmental benefits of a single wind turbine, on a yearly basis, are equivalent to planting one square mile of forest. And, U.S. wind resources are on a par with Saudi Arabia's oil resources.

———◆◆◆———

Aside from the United States itself, 13 countries and territories use the U.S. dollar as their currency. Eight are U.S. territories or affiliates as follows: American Samoa, Guam, Marshall Islands, the Federated States of Micronesia, the Northern Mariana Islands, Palau, Puerto Rico, and the U.S. Virgin Islands. The others are the British Virgin Islands, East Timor, Ecuador, El Salvador, and the Turks and Caicos Islands. In addition, the British Indian Ocean Territory, Guatemala, and Panama use the dollar as one of their accepted currencies.

Business Matters

The first travel agency in the United States was Ask Mr. Foster Travel, founded in 1888 in St. Augustine, Florida. After being purchased by entrepreneur Curtis Carlson, it became Carlson Travel Network, and still later (through mergers and acquisitions) it became today's Minneapolis- and Paris-based Carlson Wagonlit Travel.

The American Association for Nude Recreation (AANR), with nearly 50,000 members in North America, helps those members find resorts and other facilities for clothes-free or clothing-optional vacations. It also works with the fittingly named tour operator Bare Necessities Tour and Travel in Austin, Texas, to offer members specially priced cruises under the brand name AANR World Adventure. The AANR and the Naturist Society, which counts 20,000 or so mostly American members who also like to relax au naturel, jointly sponsor Nude Recreation Week each July.

New Zealand established the world's first national tourist office in 1901 and installed the first two airport baggage carousels at the Auckland Airport in December 1977.

Tourism has a dark underside, called sex tourism, which refers to travel undertaken by men from economically developed countries for the purpose of sexually exploiting women and girls in poorer countries. Sex tourism is estimated to be a $1 billion-a-year industry, and in the United States alone, there are approximately 25 companies dedicated to promoting sex tours. Additional promoters include similar tour businesses in other developed countries, at least a dozen Web sites, and some mail-order bride companies. On the good news side, more than 225 travel companies in at least 21 countries

Travia

have signed on to a code of conduct for the protection of children from exploitation by tourism. They agree to abide by ethical policies, to educate staff and raise awareness among travelers, and to require business partners to repudiate sexual exploitation of children as well. The code was created by the awkwardly named End Child Prostitution, Child Pornography, and Trafficking of Children for Sexual Purposes (ECPAT for short).

Reading about "big splurges" — as described in Arthur Frommer's 1960-61 "Europe on $5 a Day" — is a gas provided one overlooks how painfully changed the scene is today.

* *Brussels:* Four-course dinner at Aux Armes de Bruxelles, $2.50.

* *Copenhagen:* Smorrebrod (open sandwiches) at Oskar Davidsen's, 30 cents per sandwich.

* *London:* A "superb" meal at La Speranza, less than $2 (never mind statements in the same book about bad food in England).

* *Munich:* A meal at the Walterspiel in the city's most expensive hotel, Vier Jahreszeiten, less than $3 (for the meal, not a room).

* *Nice:* Prix fixe lunch menu at the seaside Restaurant la Girelle, with appetizer, wine, dessert, and tip, about $2.

* *Paris:* Three-course prix fixe meal at La Bouteille d'Or on the Left Bank, $1.80.

* *Rome:* A four-course dinner (start with spaghetti alla boscaiola) at Trattoria Romolo, not quite $1.75.

* *Venice:* Lunch at the Gran Caffe-Ristorante Quadri on the Piazza San Marco, for one course only to keep to a moderate $2.50.

Business Matters

* *Zurich*: Fondue Bourguignonne at the Restaurant Canova, $2.

The United Nations Educational, Scientific, and Cultural Organization (UNESCO), as of July 2007, had inscribed 851 properties or places as World Heritage Sites. Of the total, 660 are cultural sites, 166 are natural sites, and 25 a combination. The sites are in 141 nations.

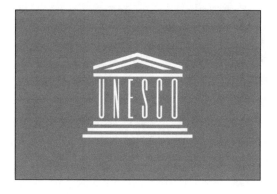

For years, American Express and Carlson Wagonlit operated the largest travel agencies in the United States. However, the top 10 largest agencies have come to include Web operations: Expedia.com, Orbitz, Priceline.com, and Travelocity.com.

The forerunner to modern soft luggage was a laundry bag called The Steamer Bag, created by Louis Vuitton luggage makers in 1901. The idea was that the traveler would carry it inside a wardrobe trunk. A half a century earlier, company founder Louis Vuitton invented the flat trunk (1854) and launched his business in France the same year.

Travia

Fischer Travel Enterprises, a New York travel agency that caters to the very rich and the very famous, created a business model to match: New customers pay a $50,000 initiation fee plus an annual $10,000 retainer. The agency's telephone number is unlisted.

Appendix

Travia

Look at what goes on in the New World in the way of odd excuses for coming to town:

* *Alabama's Coondog Graveyard Celebration*, for a chance to picnic in the world's only graveyard for coondogs, hunting man's best friend; all this in Helen Keller's hometown (Tuscumbia).

* *Alaska's Moose Dropping Festival*, where, in the world's most peculiar raffle "drawing," numbered and shellacked moose nuggets are dropped (their second dropping, as it were) from a balloon onto revelers below; also on offer, souvenirs like Moose Poop Earrings and Gourmet Poopon Mooseturd plus the Mountain Mother Contest (must be a mother, shoot a bow and arrow, diaper the baby and ... you get the idea).

* *Arkansas' BeanFest and Championship Outhouse Races*, with outhouses mounted on wheels; one of at least two dozen such events in the United States and Canada (outhouses are on skis up north), but the Arkansas event has a name that makes us snicker.

* *California's St. Stupid's Day Parade*, honoring the patron saint of the First Church of the Last Laugh on April Fools Day, including "sermons" and, to poke fun at capitalism, the Pacific Sock Exchange, which — no surprise — degenerates into a smelly sock fight.

* *California's TarantulaFest and Barbecue*, celebrating the tarantula with eats (no tarantulas on the menu) and a chance to pose for photos while holding one of the fuzzy eight-legged guests of honor.

* *Colorado's Great Fruitcake Toss*, promising rewards for most creative uses of past-their-season cakes, as well as the chance to heave those old things for prizes.

* *Delaware's World Championship Punkin' Chunkin'*, pumpkins shot like cannonballs from custom-built machines to achieve best distance and, no doubt, a very satisfying splat; the English team made it international for real in 2005; cooking contests, too.

* *Louisiana's Frog Festival*, draws 15,000 to Rayne, dubbed Frog Capital of the World, for froggie events worthy of Mark Twain, plus a frog-leg-eating contest.

* *Montana's Big Mountain Furniture Race*, end-of-ski-season competition to see which (helmet-protected) participant can stop his or her ski-mounted couch (or whatever) closest to target at the bottom of a beginner's trail.

* *New Hampshire's World Mud Bowl Championships*, a mud football competition, played in knee-deep slop, that kicks off in North Conway's Hog Coliseum; also, synchronized mud swimming.

* *New Jersey's Miss Crustacean Hermit Crab Beauty Contest*, in which humans exert creative powers to see who can put the best costume on a little ungrateful crab; crab races, too.

* *New Mexico's Great American Duck Race*, where humans dress as ducks but real duckies (rented) do the racing, by land and by sea; also Tournament of Ducks Parade and (for humans only) more contests: tortilla toss, green chili cook-off, and outhouse race.

* *North Carolina's National Hollerin' Contest*, with adult men in the competition, plus a separate Ladies Callin' Contest, meaning women do the calling.

* *Ohio's Circleville Pumpkin Show*, a big deal with up to half a million attendees, strives for biggest pumpkins ever (largest: 1,353 pounds) and world's largest pumpkin pie (400 pounds); entices with hog-calling, egg-tossing, pumpkin-tossing, and pie-eating contests.

* *Ohio's National Lawn Mower Racing Championships*, the big one among 100-plus mower races a year in the United States; "mow downs" a British import, undertaken for "the love of sport and a weed-free yard," says the racing association's self-described Mr. Mow It All, Bruce Kaufman, president.

* *Oklahoma's Mangum Rattlesnake Derby*, for snake-hunting competitions, the Rattlesnake Run (whatever that means) and a chance to sample rattler as food, attended by more than 40,000 people and an awful lot of snakes; one of several Oklahoma rattlesnake-hunt festivals.

* *Oklahoma's World Championship Cow Chip Throwing Contest*, tossing dung barehanded, a well-established local pastime, good for when there are no rattlesnakes to chase; one of several cowpie-hurling events in the United States.

* *Ontario's Rock Paper Scissors International World Championships*, called "a decision-making game of wits, speed, dexterity, and

strategy between players who are unable to reach a decision using other means," in other words, unfathomable, but the name is sufficiently nutty.

* *Pennsylvania's Bark Peeler's Convention*, celebrating the state's lumbering past, featuring greased-pole, frog-jumping, tobacco-spitting, birling, and fiddling contests.

* *South Carolina's Chitlin' Strut*, with a chitlin' strut dance contest plus hog-calling contest to go with a pig-out eating event whose central menu item is, naturally, pig guts (aka chitterlings) and lots of 'em; up to 40,000 come for the eats.

* *South Carolina's World Grits Festival*, including a rolling-in-the-grits contest; winner is the one who gains the most weight (from wearing the stuff not eating it); also, corn-shelling, corn-tossing, and grits-eating contests.

* *Texas' Fire Ant Festival*, celebrating the fire ant with events like ANTsmash dodgeball.

* *Texas' O. Henry Pun-Off World Championships*, included so this list won't be totally without intellectual content (see last two items).

* *Washington's Slug Festival*, celebrating slug species native to the state with live-slug displays (no slug races though, too darned slow), human-slug games, and things like "slug tentacle headbands" and "slug slime treats" on offer. It's a real slug fest.

* *Wisconsin's U.S. Watermelon Seed-Spitting & Speed-Eating Championship*, includes watermelon bowling; spitting record: 61 feet, 3 inches. Enough said.

Bibliography

BOOKS

Abbott, Patrick. "Airship: The Story of R.34 and the First East-West Crossing of the Atlantic by Air." New York: Charles Scribner's Sons, 1973.

Allan, Peter. "The 91 Before Lindbergh." Shrewsbury, England: Airlife Publishing, 1984.

Axtell, Roger E., editor. "Do's and Taboos Around the World." New York: A Benjamin Book, John Wiley & Sons, Inc., third edition, 1993.

Bryson, Bill. "In a Sunburned Country." New York: Broadway Books, a division of Random House, Inc., 2001.

Bryson, Bill. "Made in America." New York: William Morrow and Company, Inc., 1994.

Burnam, Tom. "The Dictionary of Misinformation." New York: Thomas Y. Crowell Company, 1975.

Casson, Lionel. "Travel in the Ancient World." Baltimore, Md.: The Johns Hopkins University Press, paperback edition, 1994.

Coleman, Alexander and Charles Simmons, editors. "All There Is to Know." New York: Simon & Schuster, 1994.

Connolly, Peter and Hazel Dodge. "The Ancient City, Life in Classical Athens & Rome." Oxford, England; Oxford University Press, 1998.

Dal Maso, Leonardo B., translated by Michael Hollingworth. "Rome of the Caesars." Florence, Italy: Officine Grafiche, 1978, c1974.

Davis, Fanny. "The Palace of Topkapi in Istanbul." New York: Charles Scribner's Sons, 1970.

Bibliography

Durant, Will. "Our Oriental Heritage." New York: Simon and Schuster, 1963.

Durant, Will. "The Life of Greece." New York: Simon and Schuster, 1966.

Durant, Will and Ariel. "The Age of Napoleon." New York: Simon and Schuster, 1975.

Fairservis, Walter A. Jr. "The Ancient Kingdoms of the Nile." New York: New American Library, 1962.

Freeman, Morton. "The Story Behind the Word." Philadelphia: iSi Press, 1985.

Frommer, Arthur. "Europe on $5 a Day." New York: Crown Publishers, 1960-61 edition.

Fysh, Sir Hudson. "Qantas Rising: The Autobiography of the Flying Fish." Sydney: A&R (Angus and Robertson publishers), 1965.

Garvey, William and David Fisher. "The Age of Flight, a History of America's Pioneering Airline." Greensboro, N.C.: Pace Communications, 2002.

Gascoigne, Bamber. "The Great Moghuls." New York: Harper & Row, Publishers, 1971.

Hancock, Graham, Richard Pankhurst and Duncan Willetts. "Under Ethiopian Skies." London: editions HL, division of H&L Communications, 1983.

Harrell, Mary Ann, managing editor. "Builders of the Ancient World." Washington, D.C.: National Geographic Society, 1986.

Hawkes, Jacquetta, editor. "Atlas of Ancient Archaeology." New York: McGraw-Hill Book Company, 1974.

Travia

James, Peter and Nick Thorpe. "Ancient Inventions." New York: Ballantine Books, 1994.

Kaplan, Robert D. "Eastward to Tartary." New York: Random House, Inc., 2000.

King, Ross. "Brunelleschi's Dome: How a Renaissance Genius Reinvented Architecture." New York: Walker Publishing Company, 2000.

Kraus, Naomi P., editor. "Frommer's Europe by Rail." Hoboken, N.J.: Wiley Publishing, Inc., 2004.

Kriwaczek, Paul. "In Search of Zarathustra." New York: Vintage Books, a division of Random House, Inc., 2004, c2002.

Kurlansky, Mark. "Salt, a World History." New York: Penguin Books, 2003, c2002.

Kuttner, Paul. "History's Trickiest Questions." New York: Henry Holt and Company, 1992.

Landphair, Ted and Carol M. Highsmith. "The Mount Washington: A Century of Grandeur." Bretton Woods, N.H.: (self published), 2003.

Mackay, Charles. "Extraordinary Popular Delusions and the Madness of Crowds." New York: Harmony Books, a division of Crown Publishers, Inc., 1980. (First published in London, 1841, by Richard Bentley)

Manchester, William. "A World Lit Only by Fire." Boston: Little, Brown and Company, 1993.

Markham, Beryl. "West With the Night." San Francisco: North Point Press, 1983. (First published in Boston, 1942, by Houghton Mifflin Company)

Marriott, J.W. Jr. and Kathi Ann Brown. "The Spirit to Serve." New York: HarperCollins, 1997.

McQuain, Jeffrey and Stanley Malless. "Coined by Shakespeare." Springfield, Mass.: Merriam -Webster, Inc., 1998.

Mills, A.D. "Dictionary of English Place Names." Oxford, England: Oxford University Press, 1997, c1991.

Milton, Joyce. "Loss of Eden: A Biography of Charles and Anne Morrow Lindbergh." New York: HarperCollins Publishers, 1993.

Mish, Frederick C., editor. "The Merriam -Webster New Book of Word Histories." Springfield, Mass.: Merriam-Webster Inc., 1991.

Munson, Kenneth. "Pictorial History of BOAC and Imperial Airways." London: Ian Allan, 1970.

Nelson, Derek. "Off the Map." New York: Kodansha America, Inc., 1999, c1997.

Panati, Charles. "Extraordinary Origins of Everyday Things." New York: Harper & Row, Publishers, 1987.

Perring, Stefania and Dominic. "Then and Now." Edison, N.J.: Chartwell Books, 1999, c1991.

Pratte, France Gagnon and Eric Etter, translated by Linda Blythe. "The Chateau Frontenac: One Hundred Years in the Life of a Legendary Hotel." Quebec City: Editions Continuite, 1998, c1993.

Radevsky, Anton. "Architecture (pop-up)." New York: Universe Publishing, 2004.

Rice, Edward. "Captain Sir Richard Francis Burton." New York: HarperPerennial, a division of Harper Collins Publishers, 1991, c1990.

Serling, Robert J. "A Century of Wings." Washington, D.C.: Air Transport Association of America, 2003.

Serling, Robert J. "Eagle: The History of American Airlines." New York: St. Martin's Press, 1985.

Soukhanov, Anne H., executive editor. "Word Mysteries & Histories." Boston: Houghton Mifflin Company, 1986.

Steel, Tom. "The Langham, A History." London: (self published), 1990.

Steindorff, George and Keith C. Seele, revised by Keith C. Seele. "When Egypt Ruled the East." Chicago: The University of Chicago Press, 1971, c1957.

Strong, Sir Roy. "The Story of Britain." London: Hutchinson in association with Julia Macrae, Random House, 1996.

Sturken, Barbara and James Glab. "Rapid Descent: The Shakeout in the Airlines." New York: Simon & Schuster, 1994.

Tournikiotis, Panayotis, editor. "The Parthenon and Its Impact in Modern Times." Athens: Melissa Publishing House, G. Rayas & Co., 1994.

Weatherford, Jack. "The History of Money." New York: Three Rivers Press, a trademark of Random House, Inc., 1997.

Wharton, Annabel Jane. "Building the Cold War: Hilton International Hotels and Modern Architecture." Chicago: University of Chicago Press, 2001.

Wilson, Kemmons, with Robert Kerr. "Half Luck and Half Brains The Kemmons Wilson Holiday Inn Story." Nashville, Tenn.: Hambleton-Hill Publishing, Inc., 1996.

Woodford, Susan. "The Parthenon." Cambridge, England: Cambridge University Press, 1981.

Bibliography

SPEECHES

Damon, Ralph Shepard. "TWA: Nearly Three Decades in the Air." Newcomen Address, New York, Dec. 4, 1952.

Maldutis, Julius. Wings Club speech, New York, May 18, 2005.

May, James C. Wings Club speech, New York, June 21, 2005.

ARTICLES

Crouch, Tom D. "First Flight? Says Who?" "The Meaning of Flight in the 20th Century: National Aerospace Conference Proceedings." Dayton, Ohio: Wright State University, 1999, Pages 114-121.

Dolan, Robert and H. Grant Goodell. "Sinking Cities." American Scientist, January-February 1986, Pages 38-47.

Lewis, W. David. "A Man Born Out of Season: Eddie Rickenbacker, Eastern Airlines, and the Civil Aeronautics Board." Business and Economic History, Volume 25, No. 1, Fall 1996, Pages 154-164.

OTHER

Columbia Gazettteer

Newsweek Magazine

The New York Times

Travel Weekly

Almanacs, dictionaries, and encyclopedias

Web sites maintained by travel companies, tourist offices, and governments.

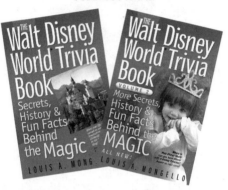